S0-ABD-832

r
Comprehensive catalog of
U. S. paper money.

DATE DUE			

The
Comprehensive Catalog
of

U.S.
PAPER
MONEY

Library of Congress Cataloging in Publication Data

Hessler, Gene, 1928-
    The comprehensive catalog of U.S. paper money.

    Bibliography: p.
    1. Paper money—United States. 2. Paper
money—Catalogs. I. Title.
HG591.H47   769.55973   73-6461

Published by Henry Regnery Company
180 North Michigan Avenue, Chicago, Illinois 60601
Manufactured in the United States of America
Library of Congress Catalog Card Number: 73-6461
International Standard Book Number: 0-8092-7994-0

Published simultaneously in Canada by
Beaverbooks
953 Dillingham Road
Pickering, Ontario L1W 1Z7
Canada

The
Comprehensive Catalog
of

U.S. PAPER MONEY

Gene Hessler

Completely Revised and Updated

Henry Regnery Company • Chicago

During the winter of 1861–62, S. M. Clark, then Chief of Construction and later Chief of the First Division of the National Currency Bureau, submitted a recommendation to Secretary of the Treasury Salmon P. Chase. Chase accepted this proposal which would have placed engravings of three subjects of historical significance on the $1, $2, and $5 United States notes. Engravings were prepared but the notes for which they were intended were never issued with these designs.

The three designs illustrated opposite in their unfinished state, and the other six subjects, all of which were later adapted for the backs of the first national bank notes, adorn the rotunda of the Capitol in Washington, D.C.

James Duthie, the first engraver to be employed by the National Currency Bureau, prepared John Vanderlyn's painting of The Landing of Columbus. *See Nos. 274–286.*

J. P. Ourdan* engraved Robert W. Wier's painting of the Embarkation of the Pilgrims *while employed by the National Bank Note Co. See Nos. 953–964 and 1493.*

W. H. Powell's Discovery of the Mississippi by DeSoto *was Clark's design choice for the $5 note. This recently discovered engraving, executed by Henry Gugler, may be the third engraving in Clark's original plan. See Nos. 497–508 and 1370–1371.*

---

*In the first edition of this catalog, James Duthie was incorrectly credited as the engraver.

Contents

Acknowledgments vii
Foreword by Bob Medlar
   President, Society of Paper Money Collectors xi
Foreword to First Edition by J. Roy Pennell, Jr.
   Former President, Society of Paper Money Collectors xiii
Preface xv
Syngraphics xvii
Paper Money Terms xviii
1. A History of Paper Money   1
2. Types of U.S. Paper Money   31
3. Catalog of U.S. Paper Money
   Using the Catalog   47
   Regular Issues
      One Dollar   51
      Two Dollars   73
      Five Dollars   88
      Ten Dollars   125
      Twenty Dollars   165
      Fifty Dollars   200
      One Hundred Dollars   234
      Five Hundred Dollars   269
      One Thousand Dollars   282
      Five Thousand Dollars   298
      Ten Thousand Dollars   306
      One Hundred Thousand Dollars   313
      Unissued and Rejected Designs   314

Fractional Currency   325
Encased Postage Stamps   362
Uncut Sheets   370
Notes of Special Interest   388
Error and Freak Notes   395
Counterfeit Notes   427
Souvenir Cards from the Bureau of Engraving and
   Printing   437
Paper Money Circulated Outside the Continental U.S.
   Alaska   443
   Hawaii   445
   Philippines   446
   Puerto Rico   454
   Virgin Islands   456
Allied Military Currency   459
Military Payment Certificates   469
Food Stamps and Coupons   493
4. Cleaning, Housing, and Care of Paper Money   497
   Bibliography   501

Acknowledgments

Below is a list of those people, departments, and societies who contributed to the making of this catalog. Some contributed as little as one important photograph; others spent hours of their time locating bits of information. It would have been impossible to compile this book without their assistance, for which I am most grateful.

W. Thomas Allen
William T. Anton, Jr.
Aubrey E. Bebee
Louis Van Belkum*
John Breen
Walter Breen
Major Sheldon S. Carroll,
   Curator Numismatic Collection,
   Bank of Canada
Amon Carter, Jr.
James Conlon, Director of the
   Bureau of Engraving and Printing
Mark Davison
Charles A. Dean
William P. Donlon
William Doovas
Dennis Forgue, Rarcoa
Martin Gengerke
James Grebinger
John Hickman
Robert Hield
Richard Hoenig
Peter Huntoon
Dr. Glenn E. Jackson
Harry E. Jones
Abe Kosoff
Chester L. Krause
H. T. Krisak
Phil Lampkin
Lester Merkin
Barbara Mueller

Ed Neuce
Dean Oakes
Chuck O'Donnell
Morey Perlmutter
W. A. Philpott, Jr. (deceased)
Michael L. Plant
Margo Russell
Bruno S. Rzepka
C. F. Schwan
Neil Shafer
Gary F. Snover
George Wait
M. O. Warns
L. Werner
The American Numismatic Society
The Bureau of Engraving and Printing
The Comptroller of the Currency
The Essay Proof Society
The Federal Reserve Bank of
   New York
The Higgins Foundation
The Society of Paper Money
   Collectors
The National Archives
The U.S. Secret Service
William Devine is responsible for
   photographing most of the
   illustrations; the author
   photographed a lesser number.
Larry Stevens, photographs of COPE

---

*"New Information on Seldom-Seen Notes," *Paper Money*, vol. 8, no. 1; 1969.

Special Acknowledgments

Those who have the first edition of this catalog will notice different, as well as additional, printed and/or issued figures in certain places in this edition. I have three researchers to thank for this information. Walter Breen has continued to make available to me the results of his scholarly research. His most noticeable contribution to this second edition are the figures for the 1918 Federal Reserve notes. In the fractional currency section, new as well as reinterpreted figures were compiled by a gentleman I have come to respect, Martin Gengerke. Chuck O'Donnell is responsible for most of the new figures listed next to notes issued after 1928. Mr. O'Donnell has labored tirelessly to compile these figures and has had them copyrighted. I am grateful to all contributors but I owe a special debt of gratitude to W. Breen, M. Gengerke, and C. O'Donnell.

Foreword

BOB MEDLAR
President, Society of Paper Money Collectors

It is with a great deal of pleasure that I am introducing this expanded and updated second edition of what is becoming a highly respected work on American paper money. Two years ago, Gene Hessler's first edition of this catalog appeared—the result of two years of hard, original research. This scholarly work was recognized by awards from two organizations in our collecting field. One award was from the Society of Paper Money Collectors in 1974. In 1975, I was privileged to present the award from the Professional Numismatists Guild to Mr. Hessler for his excellent new and comprehensive catalog.

We are happy to report that interest in the paper money of all countries is expanding. I feel that the increasing awareness of the collecting opportunities in the field of U.S. paper money was stimulated in a large measure by Mr. Hessler's first catalog. He did fundamental work in establishing the study of paper money by introducing the new word, *syngraphics*, in this book. This word establishes our fraternity as a separate but equal branch of scholarship with numismatics and philately. It has entered the language and is being used more and more in official circles. This new edition should be on the bookshelf of every person needing the newest and most complete reference work on U.S. paper money. One reviewer said, "Mr. Hessler shows that notes have a beauty and history of their own." Another said, "the catalog will be recognized as a standard work." Peter Huntoon, paper money specialist and columnist wrote, "the pictures alone are worth the price of the book."

The second edition has all that is contained in the old but has been expanded and updated in many areas. In this new book, Mr. Hessler has continued his research into the numbers of notes printed and issued. Before, there were many instances where the true scarcity of many notes was unknown. This new edition of Mr. Hessler's catalog has the most recent discoveries in this area, enhancing note values and collector interest. New historical information is also included. There are catalog listings of Allied Military Currency and U.S. Food Stamps and Coupons to acknowledge these new collecting fields.

As a dealer and as a collector, I have found Mr. Hessler's contributions to my life's principal interest to have been invaluable. I know I speak for many others, both novices and advanced specialists, who have been enchanted by the wonderful world of paper money in all its aspects. Gene is well known to almost all of us in his role as frequent speaker at our conventions and meetings and as curator of The Chase Manhattan Bank Numismatic and Syngraphic Collection.

Principally because of his research in bringing us his definitive cataloging of U.S. paper money, he is now being recognized in such publications as *Who's Who in the East* and *Men of Achievement*. We all share in these recognitions with Gene, since recognition of Gene and his work means that our beloved syngraphics is being recognized and established as a most distinguished branch of study and endeavor.

Foreword to First Edition

J. ROY PENNELL, JR.
Former President, Society of Paper Money Collectors

To introduce a new paper money catalog with a fresh, vibrant text such as this is truly an honor and a pleasure. Such is my pleasant task. We have had several catalogs issued in the past, and with these to build on, it is only natural that a culminating work would appear. This new perspective and approach of Mr. Hessler's catalog is most welcome. It is a work that will become a standard for collectors of United States paper money.

Mr. Gene Hessler is the curator of The Chase Manhattan Bank Money Museum in New York. He has held this position for the past seven years. His intimate association with one of the great (if not greatest) bank numismatic collections makes him eminently qualified to write on many phases of numismatics. That he has chosen United States paper money is good fortune for the paper money fraternity.

This book has many features that we have long wished would be incorporated into one catalog that would serve as the standard reference work. Its arrangement is the best we have seen. There is a very good narrative covering the history of paper money. The inclusion of notes that circulated in the United States districts, possessions, and territories outside the continental United States is an interesting and worthwhile survey. Military payment certificates are steadily gaining in interest and therefore belong in this catalog. I have often wondered about paper money designs that were never issued. Now for the first time we are able to see illustrations of these unpublished notes. The sections outlining the colonial and confederate issues should help this book find a place as a standard reference on library shelves for the student or librarian who needs an outline on these subjects as well as a guide to further reading.

From our own experience we know how much work must have gone into this catalog. Two years of searching out rare notes in private collections and files of the Bureau of Engraving and Printing have gone into this work. All previous catalogs had to be reviewed for faults or virtues to be excluded or included in this new work. Mr. Hessler has conferred with just about every expert in the field and has taken advice and recommendations with the objectivity of a true scholar. His objective is to make this catalog the finest.

One great innovation is the introduction of the new word for our hobby, *syngraphics*. Mr. Hessler and Reverend Richard E. Doyle, S.J., Ph.D., Chairman of the Department of Classical Languages at Fordham University, have provided us with this new word, based on the most proper philological base for the science of paper money collecting. Now we must see that the word takes hold and enters the language. Equal rights for *syngraphics*! We all should use this new word in all our writings and correspondence. We should see to it that it is used at conventions and that it be made familiar to our fellow collectors in other fields.

Just this one idea alone would make this catalog worthwhile. But now we must leave it to the reader to find the many other fine features of this book. We feel that Mr. Hessler may have introduced not one but two new words to the paper money collecting world. One is the new word *syngraphics*. The other may well be *Hessler*, as Hessler numbers from this catalog take hold in auction lists and collection records.

Preface

      Why do we need still another catalog of United States paper money? There are already about half a dozen such catalogs in print. All of these catalogs have good features, but none has the scope one would need from a definitive work.

Neil Shafer's *Modern U.S. Currency* includes two additional types of paper money: U.S. military payment certificates, and Philippine notes issued by our government in that country during our stewardship. If these latter two categories are part of the complete picture, then a truly complete catalog must include Allied Military Currency and all the notes that circulated under U.S. authority in the districts, territories, and possessions outside the continental United States. I have sought to bring these features together in one work.

In addition I have included a large section devoted to error notes, and I have listed the numbers of large-size notes that were issued. Many of these figures are printed here for the first time. In addition to the figures I have gathered, others have been added thanks to the research of Walter Breen and Louis Van Belkum.

It would be demeaning to our field of study to say that there has been no new research to increase our knowledge of United States paper money. New discoveries, new varieties, and new background information increase collecting interest. In the past ten years, for instance, the signature combinations on current Federal Reserve notes have changed nine times. Even non-collectors take interest in such developments, and so this catalog tries to keep the reader up to date on changes in our field.

Finally, the hobby of paper money collecting has grown enormously in recent years. It will continue to grow if good catalogs are available. Even now, coins no longer dominate major numismatic conventions and auctions. Paper money now fetches record prices, and all signs indicate that the new field of syngraphics will continue to challenge numismatics and philately.

I sincerely hope that the information within these pages will serve the syngraphist and make the collecting of paper money a more rewarding and a more exciting experience.

Mr. Hessler has received two awards for *The Comprehensive Catalog of U.S. Paper Money.* In 1974 he was awarded the Nathan Gold Memorial Award which is sponsored by Chester L. Krause and presented by the Society of Paper Money Collectors. In 1975 the author was the recipient of the Robert Friedberg Award presented by the Professional Numismatists Guild on behalf of the Louis Reagan Memorial Foundation.

Syngraphics

A new word was born with the publication of the first edition of this catalog. *Syngraphics* will be used in this book to denote the collecting and study of paper money. Now syngraphics will take its place beside numismatics, the study of coins, and philately, the study of stamps.

The Reverend Richard Doyle, Chairman of the Department of Classical Languages at Fordham University in New York, coined this long-needed word at the request of the present author. The word comes from the Greek *syn*, meaning *with* or *together*, and *graphe*, meaning writing. In Latin *syngrapha* meant a written agreement to pay, a promissory note, a bond. The *Oxford English Dictionary* defines *syngraph* as an obligation or bond between two or more people. The art of engraving, etching, and other methods by which copies of an original design are printed from a plate, block, or the like is referred to as *graphic* art. Modern bank notes are no longer handwritten but are made from engraved plates. *Syngraphics* thus means the study of bonds or written notes. Our science, so defined, will no longer be a department of numismatics with a branch in philately.

The new word was officially announced by the author and Father Doyle at The Chase Manhattan Bank Money Museum before members of the numismatic community and journalists from our trade and hobby publications.

Several editors of dictionaries, as well as several heads of English and classical language departments of universities, were invited to give their opinions on the word.

Soon after the first edition of this catalog was published in 1974 the word syngraphics was seen in journals printed for coin and currency enthusiasts. A few of the prominent authors who have used the term syngraphics in their writing are: Yasha Beresiner, Walter Breen, Chuck O'Donnell, N. Goldstein, M. Perlmutter, Barbara Mueller and Carlton F. Swan. A new column has been added to *Paper Money* magazine, the title, "Syngraphi-chat."

Paper money collectors deserve to have their branch of knowledge distinguished by a proper name. The new word *syngraphics* has been given to us by one of the finest scholars in the country. Now it is up to us to use the word. So, from one *syngraphist* to another, may the hobby and science of *syngraphics* flourish and advance as it should.

Paper Money Terms

Federal Reserve District Seal

Serial Number

Treasury Seal

District Number

Back Plate Number

Series

Check Letter and Face Plate Number

CHAPTER ONE

A
History
of
Paper Money

All money, whether paper, metal, stone, or shell, is a symbol of goods or services that can be swapped as needed. In the simplest economic arrangements it is easy enough to exchange my cow for your horse or my cabbage for your cantaloupe. But we would have trouble exchanging cows for cantaloupes if we did not have some common measure of value. Metals serve well as such a measure because of their durability and intrinsic value, and so in early Greece we find an iron spit (obol) or a handful of iron spits (drachma) serving as tokens of exchange. In early Rome blocks of bronze were used as exchange symbols.

The earliest metal money had a face value equal to its intrinsic value. The first coins were those ingots and nuggets that were stamped by a sovereign authority as being guaranteed full weight and quality. It wasn't long, though, before the coins themselves became lighter, less pure, and more like present-day paper money. The coin became a document inscribed that it was worth such and such. For example, there were the very degenerate coins minted by the Roman Empire during the inflation of the fourth century, coins made of the cheapest possible mixture of base metals.

Even the cheapest coins took much valuable metal from the economy, though. It was in China, in the Ming Dynasty of the fourteenth century, that a government first took the step of minting coins on material that was almost free—paper.

THE DEVELOPMENT OF PAPER MONEY

The manufacturing of paper money involves three elements: the ink, the technique of engraving, and the paper. Of these elements, ink was the first to be developed. Ink had been in use even before the invention of papyrus in ancient Egypt. Lampblack, a form of carbon, was dissolved in gum or glue as early as 2,500 B.C. in both Egypt and China. Today, inks for printing are vegetable or mineral materials suspended in a vehicle, usually a type of linseed oil. Modern chemistry has developed a wide variety of printing inks for different conditions. Paper monies need inks that resist fading in sunlight, resist humidity and rubbing, and lack odor.

The second element to be developed was paper. The history of paper begins with papyrus, made by laying strips of the stems of the papyrus plant criss-cross and pressing the strips together. Parchment is the dried skin of sheep. Both papyrus and parchment are too variable in shape and quality and too frail for use in currency. True paper was improved in China in A.D. 105 by Ts'ai Lun,* who made his paper from rags, bark, fish nets, and hemp. The Japanese took this marvelous invention and improved it in 610 by using the bark of the mulberry tree.

Paper is made by macerating any of a variety of cellulose fibers, cooking them in soda and lime, bleaching the result, and then pressing the mash into sheets for drying. In the fifteenth century rag pulp was bleached in sour milk and wood ash and then dried in the sun. On fine eighteenth century paper the pressing lines can be seen by holding the sheet to the light. Watermarks can be left in the paper during the pressing process, and many foreign governments use elaborate watermarks to further deter counterfeiting. One of the earliest watermarks can be traced to Fabriano, Italy, in the year 1293.

Fine paper came to Europe through the Arabs, who had learned the secret from Chinese artisans in 751. Flax and its derivatives, such as linen cloth and linen rags, were used for the best papers. Linen papers in eighteenth century books can be as fresh and clean as the day they were made. Today, papers made from wood pulp that brown and crumble in a year or two are used for ephemeral items such as newspapers or cheap novels. Governments, however, will use the best paper obtainable for paper money for obvious reasons. The first paper of quality made in the United States was produced by William

*In 1957 in Shensi province, a paper fragment was found in a tomb dating earlier than A.D. 105.

Rittenhouse and Son of Germantown, Pennsylvania, in the year 1690.

Engraving is the third element of a successful paper currency. Engraving differs from printing from wood cuts or stones in that an engraved imprint is made by incised lines rather than raised surfaces. The design is cut into the plate in intaglio. The surface of the plate is covered with ink and then wiped off carefully so as to leave the incisions filled with ink. The advantage of engraving is that the plates are practically immortal since the whole face of the plate wears down slowly and evenly. This effect cannot be reproduced photographically. If plates are chromed periodically, they are virtually indestructible. When printing with raised lines it's the design that wears and soon blurs or breaks. Of course some parts of modern notes are surface printed, such as seals, control symbols, and serial numbers that differ from one bill to another.

Printing was within the capabilities of the Romans, who used seal stamps and stencils extensively. Perhaps the lack of an abundant medium on which to print made printing impractical for the Romans. In any event, the advantages of printing were not explored until Gutenberg developed movable type in the fifteenth century.*

Engraving was invented between 1410 and 1430. The inventor's name is unknown, but he is called "The Master of the Playing Cards." Playing cards, as we shall see, played a large role in the history of paper money. The master engraver was probably a goldsmith in southern Germany or Switzerland who applied his training as a gold chaser by incising a design into plates and printing playing cards.

As governments began to use the techniques of printing and engraving to issue paper money, they employed fine artists in order to foil counterfeiters and to enhance the prestige of the issuing authority. Great printing offices in major capitals took on the job of printing other nations' money, with the engraving done by the best *etaliers*.

Of course, it's always the battle of the gun against armor, and as superior guns are invented, better armor is developed. The counterfeiters were clever, and as soon as paper notes were made more elaborate the efforts of the counterfeiters improved. The counterfeiters strived to duplicate the official printing process. Fine engravers made careful copies of the real note, and paper was used that was close to the original. Of course the governments

---

Movable type for characters made from individual molds was already in use in Korea at this time. Printing was in use in China as early as the 7th century B.C. Movable type was developed there in the 11th century, multi-colored printing followed in the 14th century.

kept up the race with better paper and with more sophisticated engravings.

Today, counterfeiters use photoengraving devices that eliminate the need for a dishonest master engraver. In order to get around the engraving problem some small-time counterfeiters will slice a high-denomination note across with a microcutter, paste half of the high-denomination note to half of a low one, and thus make two valuable bills out of one. And of course there is the story of the very small-time maker of the "queer" (a counterfeit note) in New York City who hand-drew only $1 bills for his daily needs and led the Secret Service on the longest case of its history.

In times of war enemy governments have been known to counterfeit each other's currencies to try to weaken the other's economy. Japan tried to add to the troubles of Chiang Kai-shek during World War II by duplicating Chinese money. The Chinese government tried to stop the endeavor by having their national currency printed in the United States by the American Bank Note Company and flown over the Hump to China.

EARLY PAPER MONEY IN EUROPE AND AMERICA

Marco Polo (1254-1324) was the first to bring news of Ming Dynasty paper money to Europe. Some of the European rulers believed his reports, but paper money was too big a step to take just then. Gold and silver were still the basis of monetary exchange, with bronze abundant enough to supply the token coinage of everyday small change.

Of course promissory notes, IOUs, contracts, and other promises to deliver goods or services had been imprinted on clay, papyrus, parchment, metal, or stone since the beginnings of writing. All these promissory notes were private, exchanged between individuals. In the case of a money note, however, the promisor is individual, either a bank or a government, but the promisee is unspecified and general. In 1661 the first European banknote under this definition was issued in Sweden by the Stockholm Banco. This bank tried the experiment of issuing notes that stated they stood in place of a given amount of metal, which was stored at the Bank and redeemable on demand by any note-holder.

This innovation didn't meet with much approval and lasted only one year. Merchants feared that foreigners would accumulate the paper and remove the national metal reserve from the country. Economists of the period worked under the mercantile theory that the only real wealth of a nation was its gold reserve, and that any exchange or drain would be fatal.

In 1685 a second attempt at issuing paper money was made in Canada. The paymaster for the French army had been delayed at sea, and since there is nothing more surly than an unpaid army, the Intendant of New France, Jacques de Muelles, staved off mutiny by issuing promissory notes redeemable when the ship came in. His desperate expedient was to gather up all the locally available paper, which happened to be playing cards, and to imprint it with values to be redeemed and with seals and signatures to dress up the promise. The notes were to be redeemed within three months.

The basic ills of paper currency policies soon appeared. The first problem was counterfeiting. The second was depreciation—discouraged soldiers sold off their notes at a reduced rate when the ship failed to appear. The third ill to appear was inflation, which was caused by the issuer and not the receiver. The authorities soon discovered how easy it was to solve financial problems by printing as much paper as was needed to cover expenses and worrying about redemption in metal tomorrow. The authorities tried to refrain from this practice, but the playing card money was revived periodically as wars and ship delays caused more pay problems. As for the three problems of counterfeiting, devaluation, and overissuance, they are still with us today.

However, the usefulness of paper currency outshone its drawbacks. Thus the Massachusetts General Court decided to imitate its northern neighbor and authorize the first notes on what was to be United States soil. These "Old Charter" bills were engraved in denominations of 5, 10, and 20 shillings and 5 pounds. With the outbreak of hostilities with Canada in King William's War in 1689, large numbers of these "Old Charter" bills were issued to meet the provincial payrolls. These bills were not the modern paper currency that is legal tender for all private debts and transactions. The bills were valid for paying taxes, a clever way for the government to issue excessive paper and then recall it at will.

The real troubles with paper currencies that were not backed sufficiently by metal had not yet begun, however. In 1694, the Bank of England issued notes to cover war expenses. In November 1696 the world's first bank run collapsed the true value of the notes by 20 percent, making it apparent that what counted was not the value stated on the note but what the holder believed the note to be worth.

Paper money became well established across Europe in the following century, although France almost went bankrupt under Louis XVI because of experiments by Finance Minister John Law, who tried to overprint notes with

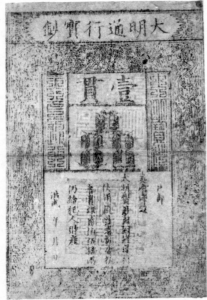

(Actual size 8" x 13".)

(Left) A Ming Dynasty note for one kwan, similar to the type reported by Marco Polo. (Below) An early bank note from Sweden.

Canadian playing card money. There are only about fifty acceptable examples of this type of money; the Bank of Canada has half of them.

(Above) A $40 *continental currency note dated September 26, 1778.* (Below) A *Pennsylvania colonial note printed by Benjamin Franklin.*

One of the early privately issued bank notes from New London, Connecticut, dated September 26, 1794.

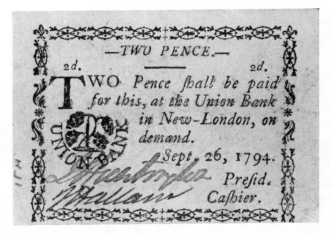

(Above) *A United States Treasury note dated 1815.* (Below) *The vignette in the center is adapted from the painting* Indian Camp *by Felix O.C. Darley.*

reinforced royal promises to pay. The assignats issued during the French Revolution were equally disastrous. Paper money was obviously a good invention, but without controls of some sort it had a poor future in any stable society.

PRIVATE BANK NOTES IN AMERICA

In 1732 the first private bank notes were issued in New London, Connecticut. Later in the century, during the Revolution, the Continental Congress tried to finance the war with voluminous issues of continental currency. By the end of the war the new government was in a state of financial chaos. Alexander Hamilton came to the rescue and proposed that the central government assume all war debts incurred by the individual states. He also proposed a tariff on imports to raise revenues. Thus began a financial struggle between private and central banks that was to last more than eighty years.

The Bank of the United States

In 1781 the Continental Congress authorized the Bank of North America as the first incorporated bank, giving it a perpetual charter. Three years later the Bank of New York and the Massachusetts Bank were formed. The Bank of New York, under the leadership of Alexander Hamilton, was granted a charter in 1791.

Soon after his appointment as Secretary of the Treasury, Hamilton proposed the establishment of a national bank. He would have favored the Bank of North America as a national bank, but the state charters that the bank had accepted disqualified it. Although both Jefferson and Madison opposed him, Hamilton succeeded in establishing the Bank of the United States as the first national bank.

The Bank of the United States received the first of two charters in 1791, being preceded only by the Bank of North America, the Bank of New York, and the Massachusetts Bank. (The latter three banks are still operating; the Massachusetts Bank is now the First National Bank of Boston.) The Bank of the United States could have continued to serve the needs of the new nation if it had not been for the problem of whether the Bank was constitutional. The effect of the Bank was obviously beneficial. Not only did it render valuable financial assistance to the government, but it exerted a profitable influence on the general economy. In a period of tremendous and sometimes precarious expansion and speculation, the Bank of the United States acted as a moderating force. For example it refrained from calling in its loans from state banks when such a move would have led to a financial panic.

The first charter of the Bank was not renewed, and when the War of 1812 forced the United States to borrow money the state banks proved inadequate. Treasury notes were issued in denominations of $5 to $100 amounting to $37 million, although up to $60.5 million had been authorized, receivable in public dues and debts only. These notes were not meant to circulate and were retired soon after the war. The Bank of the United States was rechartered in 1816, and it again opened for business on January 17, 1817.

In 1832, five years before the Bank's second charter was to expire, Andrew Jackson vetoed its recharter. Samuel D. Ingham, former Secretary of the Treasury, said, "The United States Bank has given us the best currency known among nations. It supplies a medium equal in value to gold and silver in every part of the Union. . . . [The Bank] enables the government to transmit its funds from one extremity of the Union to another . . . with a dispatch which is more like magic than reality."*

Despite Ingham's protests, the Bank's second charter was not renewed. The Bank of the United States continued to operate, however, even though it was now maintained by a charter from the state of Pennsylvania.

With the demise of the Bank of the United States, state banks began to flourish, but they soon caused a severe inflation. There was no uniformity in the laws under which the state banks operated. The banking system was up for grabs. When the Civil War was imminent, Salmon P. Chase, then Secretary of the Treasury, devised a plan to stabilize the currency. His plan "included non-interest-bearing notes payable on demand, interest-bearing notes for short terms, and bonds for long terms; the first to be convertible into the second and the second into the third form of obligation." **Thus he expected to avert the evil that many of his predecessors had experienced of being compelled to receive as payments to the Treasury the notes of state banks, most of which were fluctuating in value and might even become valueless. On July 17, 1861, Congress adopted Chase's plan and authorized the borrowing of $250 million. The demand notes, or "greenbacks," that soon followed saved the Union and were the beginnings of our national paper money.

Varieties of U.S. Paper Money

United States paper money falls into five major categories: continental,

---

*A History of Currency in the United States, p. 120.
**A History of Currency in the United States, p. 181.

Bank of the United States, state bank (broken bank), confederate, and national. Only the national currency has survived into the twentieth century.

Of these five categories we already have discussed the continental and Bank of the United States notes. The history of state bank and confederate notes will be surveyed later in this chapter. The primary subject of the present work will be the national currency, which will take up the bulk of this book. Before we proceed, however, it might be appropriate to mention some of the literature on the five categories of United States paper money since the problem of cataloging relates directly to the study of the state bank notes.

The continental and colonial issues have been learnedly cataloged by Eric Newman in his *Early Paper Money of America,* as have the confederate issues by Grover Criswell. No book has been printed that catalogs the Bank of the United States notes, and in the absence of such a work the reader is referred to *A History of Currency in the United States,* by A. Barton Hepburn. What may be the largest series of all, the broken bank note series, is still being cataloged. Over 30,000 varieties of these notes were issued by 1,600 different banks in 34 different states between 1790 and 1865.

The gigantic task of cataloging the broken bank notes is being tackled by the Society of Paper Money Collectors on a state-by-state basis, and we hope to see the completion of this very important work in the near future. The Society has completed and published catalogs for the following states: Florida, Illinois, Maine, Minnesota, Mississippi, New Jersey, Texas, and Vermont. Catalogs for additional states are now in preparation. Information on the notes of California, Oklahoma and the Indian Territories, and Kansas has been listed in the Society's publication, *Paper Money.*

Three additional states have been cataloged privately. For Michigan we have *State Bank Notes of Michigan* by Harold L. Bowen. For Nebraska there is *The Bank Notes, Scrip, and Currency of Nebraska Prior to 1900* by J. L. McKee. A handsome two-volume work by Charles Affleck, *The Obsolete Paper Money of Virginia,* has been published by the Virginia Numismatic Society.

We are including a survey of this large and interesting series in this book because we want to call it to the attention of those note collectors who may have neglected the field because of the complexities involved. With adequate catalogs for all the states here or on the way, however, broken bank note collecting soon will be a major part of the hobby. Collectors like to have a series cataloged so that they can have the satisfaction of knowing when a group is completed. They also need to know values and rarities so that they can buy and sell intelligently. We have seen collectors' items rise in price as collecting increases, and this is one reason for taking an interest in broken bank notes now.

One collecting pattern for broken bank notes is a set of odd denomination bills. Just about every amount up to $13 was printed. A collection of $4 or $7 bills should prove interesting; or how about a collection of $1.75 notes? Bills such as these are related to the pieces of 8 that were accepted in the United States as legal tender until 1857. The 8 real, or piece of 8, was divided—at times physically—into bits equalling 12½¢. As you may already know, our term *two bits* is derived from one quarter of one piece of 8.

As for the cost of broken bank note collecting, numerous privately issued notes may be purchased for $8 or less, an inexpensive way to collect a tangible bit of history.

Very often works of art were chosen to be reproduced as vignettes on these obsolete notes. The famous American painter Gilbert Stuart is frequently represented; so is Felix O. C. Darley, who illustrated *Scenes of Indian Life* in 1843, *Rip Van Winkle* in 1848, and *The Legend of Sleepy Hollow* in 1849. Darley is also responsible for more than five hundred drawings illustrating the novels of James Fenimore Cooper. James B. Longacre, U. S. Mint engraver from 1844-1869, undoubtedly prepared many of the vignettes for Draper, Toppan, Longacre and Company, one of the major printers of obsolete currency. More than one painting by Queen Victoria's favorite artist, Edwin Landseer, adorns state bank notes.

A History of Broken Bank Notes

As the name implies, a broken bank note is a note issued privately by a bank (or sometimes a mercantile establishment) that went broke. The confusion in the strange episode of our history represented by these notes can be laid to our long distrust of a central government and of a central economic authority. Some of this distrust can be traced to the Continental Congress. The volumes of continental currency poured out to finance the Revolution originally were backed by Spanish milled dollars, but soon that backing was removed. The continental currency depreciated to a point where a $40 continental note was worth only $1 and then nothing at all. In accordance with Gresham's Law that bad money drives out good money, gold and silver went out of circulation and into hoards. These hoards of coins that have survived till today may be a boon to the modern coin collector, but they helped engender a deep distrust of any national currency that lasted until the Civil War.

In 1789 the new Constitution of the United States tried to prevent a repetition of the continental currency fiasco by forbidding any state or federal authority to issue "bills of credit." However, an enormous loophole was included since the Constitution did not ban bills of credit issued by private or municipal authorities. Paper money is too great a convenience to be omitted altogether from any nation's economic life.

The first privately issued paper notes in the area to become the United States were issued in New London, Connecticut, in 1732, the year George Washington was born. The experiment failed then but began its great run when Washington was on his way to the Presidency in 1790. State bank notes became a flood in the 1800s.

The history of broken bank notes ranges from the hilarious to the tragic. Crooks and sharpies at once perceived that what governments could do with paper money, they could do as well. A printing press, an impressive design, and a con-man's talent could bring riches overnight. An example from the earliest days of state bank notes might be instructive. In 1806 Judge Augustus B. Woodward of the village of Detroit, Michigan (population 600), organized the Bank of Detroit. He announced its capital at $1 million, ordered from the printer at least $3 million in notes of $1 to $10, signed them all, and shipped them East. Smart Easterners can always take advantage of country folk, so they bought up the issue at discounts of 10 to 25 percent. When they tried to redeem the notes at face value in 1808, however, they found that the Bank of Detroit had closed its doors. Judge Woodward, a cheshire cat smile on his face, had in the meantime put quite a bit of money in the form of hard coin in another, honest bank. As late as 1824 outraged citizens were still trying to prevent Judge Woodward's continuing reappointments by the U.S. Senate to the local bench. Woodward's Bank of Detroit notes are today among the commonest of broken bank notes.

Bank swindles do not always seem that light-hearted. The Michigan General Banking Law of 1837 really opened the gates of the paper flood. Immediately 55 banks were organized, most of them for the sole purpose of issuing paper money. A year later, after the disaster had almost wrecked the state, the law was suspended. All the 55 new banks and many previously established banks, honest or not, had broken, adding notes for the modern collector and subtracting wealth from the Michigan citizenry of the period.

A little caution might well have averted such a disaster. Supervision of bank operations seems obvious to our modern minds, and the bank inspector is a well-known contemporary official. But we underestimate how deep the *laissez faire* philosophy lay in the American character. What little inspection was done then was satisfied with false books, uncollectable collateral and mortgages, or cash borrowed for the day of the inspection.

Many banks had their "main offices" far out in the woods to discourage inspectors or note holders from paying a visit. Some notes were postdated or had false bank addresses to hamper any attempts at redemption. The Bank of Battle Creek, Michigan (1838-1840), used the ruse of having its cashier, Tolman W. Hall, run out the back door whenever a note holder came in the front. The "pigeon" found the bank deserted except for a singing janitor, who eventually drove the note holder away by singing out of tune and answering all questions with gibberish. In Barry, Michigan, the Farmers' Bank of Sandstone tried to be honest in that it offered to redeem its notes in merchandise of the locality. Since the principal natural resource of the area named *Sandstone* was exactly that, the Bank would redeem a $10 note with one millstone, a $5 note with one grindstone, and a $1 note with one whetstone. As can be imagined, few note holders bent on redemption took advantage of the offer, especially if they had come by buggy from New York or Chicago.

One more example of such fraud is the story of the three principal officers of the Bank of Coldwater, Michigan, who absconded as soon as they received from the printer some $25,000 worth of notes. They said they were going to "create specie," which means to get together gold and silver coin to back the notes. They did this by peddling the notes at increasing discounts in other states until the news of their broken bank caught up with them.

Bowen's book *State Bank Notes of Michigan* has many such stories, some comic and some tragic. Many of these stories represent not only broken banks but broken homes, hopes, farms, and families. The ultimate victims of these frauds were the working people, the immigrants, the settlers.

If that wasn't enough, the broken bank problem was compounded with counterfeiting. Notes that were almost worthless were nevertheless altered or counterfeited by other crooks trying to get in on the orgy. In order to combat these privately issued notes, dozens of *Counterfeit Detectors* were published to assist bankers and merchants in the detection of bogus bills. An Iowa banker, H. Price, said, "The two most important books that every businessman needed were a Bible and a *Counterfeit Detector*. And of these

Thomas F. Buchanan Read's painting of Alice, Allegra, and Edith Longfellow was adapted for this note.

Henry Clay is portrayed on the right of this note printed by the National Bank Note Co.

The portrait on the left is from a vignette entitled Mary Lamar. *The printer was the American Bank Note Co.*

State bank notes often pictured silver dollars in numbers equal to the denomination of the bill. Rawdon, Wright and Edson and the New England Bank Note Co. jointly printed these notes.

This note, printed by Rawdon, Wright and Edson, bears a portrait of Peter Stuyvesant originally painted by Hendrick Courturier.

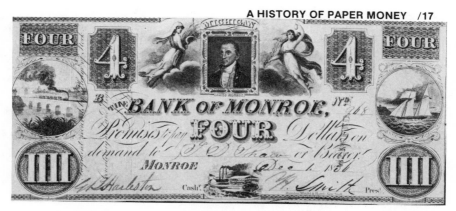

James Monroe is in the center of this odd-denomination note printed by Rawdon, Wright and Edson.

This is one of the many notes prepared by the American Bank Note Co.

This attractive proof $12 bill was printed by Rawdon, Wright and Edson.

This sheet was prepared by Casilear, Durand, Burton and Edmonds of New York.

This $13 bill was printed by Rawdon, Wright and Hatch of New York.

two, the *Detector* seemed to be the more important for at least six days out of the seven."

The private banks retaliated against the counterfeiters and made the process of manufacture more and more complex by using fancier paper, more complicated designs, more watermarks, secret printing marks, indentures, marbling, laminated papers, polychrome printing, "mice" and/or fiber inclusions, composite plates, elaborately engraved ornaments, and portraits engraved by the finest artists of the period. All these countermeasures helped to create some exceptionally beautiful notes, some surpassing in many respects our present-day currency with its more limited designs and subject matter.

Even during the worst period of the broken bank note era there were honest and far-seeing bankers who issued reliable money to the best of their abilities. These men realized that the convenience of paper money was necessary if the nation was to develop and expand. These bankers were the ones who took the countermeasure of superb production to its limit. Several of the top engraving companies that served these bankers merged to form the American Bank Note Company, which to this day continues to produce quality currency for other nations.

The history of the broken bank notes ended with the Civil War. When the Confederacy was formed, paper money issued by the Richmond government and by the "sovereign states" supplanted private bank issues very quickly. In the beginning the Confederacy tried to back its paper issues with cotton bales stored in Southern ports, but the confederate notes went the way of the continental currency and ended as worthless paper.

In 1863 a new law levied a 10 percent face value tax on all private bank notes. The law also forbade the issue of scrip below $1 denominations. With the $10 compound interest Treasury notes and the $10 interest-bearing notes authorized by Act of Congress on March 3, 1863, with signatures to be engraved in the plates and bills to be printed by the First Division of the National Currency Bureau, the era of broken bank notes ended and the era of our national paper money began.

U.S. PAPER MONEY SINCE THE CIVIL WAR

When Congress authorized a national paper currency on July 17, 1861, it was up to the executive branch of the government to see that the new notes were printed and distributed in a proper manner. The Secretary of the Treasury and the Office of the Treasurer of the United States thus became the means for all financial and monetary functions of the federal government.

Office of the Secretary of the Treasury

As a major policy advisor to the President, the Secretary and his office have primary responsibility for formulating and recommending domestic and international financial policy; formulating and recommending tax policy; participating in formulating broad fiscal policies that have general significance for the economy; managing the public debt; and formulating policies for and generally overseeing all operations of the Department, which are carried out by its ninety thousand employees located in Washington, D.C., and some eighteen hundred field offices in this country and abroad.

Office of the Treasurer of the United States

With fewer than one thousand employees, this office receives, holds, and pays out the public moneys for the federal government by maintaining accounts of the source, location, and disposition of these funds; paying government checks and reconciling the payments with records of issuing officers; processing claims for lost or forged checks; publishing daily reports of the federal government's receipts and expenditures; and overseeing the destruction and replacement of unfit currency.

Thus the people of the United States authorize their representatives in Congress to issue paper money. Acting on congressional legislation, the Chief Executive delegates the task to the Secretary of the Treasury, who in turn delegates the details of the manufacture of the notes to the Treasurer of the United States. The Treasurer needs a factory for the job, and this plant is the Bureau of Engraving and Printing.

The Bureau of Engraving and Printing

On August 29, 1862, four women and two men began to separate and trim $1 and $2 United States (legal tender) notes that had been printed by private bank note companies. In 1863 seventy additional women were employed to perform this operation.* This manual chore was done practically in a state of siege in beleagured Civil War Washington, with sandbags filling the windows of the old Treasury Building, still at Fifteenth Street and Pennsylvania, N.W. Thus began the Bureau of Engraving and Printing.

As the Civil War continued, the need for a truly national currency became

*Late in life Francis E. Spinner, Treasurer of the United States, said, "I don't claim that I have done much good in the world; but my success in introducing women into government employment makes me feel that I have not lived in vain."

Bureau of Engraving and Printing.

more and more apparent. The small cutting operation described above, designated as the First Division of the National Currency Bureau, was the first step toward such a national currency. By the fall of 1863 the Bureau had printed its first currency notes. In 1864 the Secretary of the Treasury, Salmon P. Chase, established a distinct entity in the Treasury Department to be called "The Engraving and Printing Bureau of the Treasury Deparment." With more important matters at hand, such as Gettysburg and Appomatox, it wasn't until March 3, 1869, that an appropriation act was signed by President Johnson to give recognition to this agency.

In succeeding years the Bureau became increasingly important. In 1877 an appropriation act authorized the Bureau to print all internal revenue stamps. On October 1, 1887, the printing of all United States paper money was entrusted to the Bureau. Seven years later, postage stamps were added to the list of items to be produced. In addition, Treasury bonds, certificates, food coupons, certificates of award, and permits now emanate from the Bureau of Engraving and Printing.

From a basement room with six employees, the Bureau has grown to a modern industrial plant housed in two buildings and employing more than thirty-five hundred people.

The First Machinery. As mentioned earlier private bank note companies printed the first greenbacks for the Treasury Department in 1861. In 1862 Secretary Chase introduced a proposal in Congress that would authorize the Treasury Department to print and engrave notes. Approval of the proposal was granted in July of the same year, and work commenced one month later.

The first notes produced at the Treasury were the second issue of fractional currency, the compound interest notes of 1863, and the 5 percent Treasury notes of 1863. These notes were printed on presses operated by hand. The paper had to be dampened before it could receive the imprint of the engraved plate since it was necessary to force the paper under pressure into the engraved lines of the plate. This method of wet printing continued until 1957, with the exception of the period between 1864 and 1869.

On June 3, 1864, Secretary Chase wrote that hydrostatic presses were in daily use, producing "impressions of unexcelled perfection and beauty." Along with 72 hydraulic presses, the following equipment was in use at this time: 15 transfer machines, 96 hand presses, 14 sealing presses, 6 ink mills, and 22 numbering machines. There were 237 men and 288 women employed. Then for some unknown reason these hydrostatic presses were discontinued, in 1869, and wet printing was resumed with the return of hand presses.

In 1878 a steam press was introduced at the Bureau. Additional machines of improved design were operating by January 1887. The Bureau's annual report for 1888 stated that "The steam presses are now printing much more than one-third of the work of the Bureau with a great economy of room, labor, and expense. The cost of the printing done by them is less than $80,000. To print the same work by hand would cost $180,000." Although the number of subjects per sheet increased from 4 to 8, 12, 18, and presently 32, the method of printing remained basically the same until 1957.

In 1957 nine high-speed, sheet-fed rotary intaglio presses were installed. Each accommodated one plate, which produced 32 subjects. The Bureau of Engraving and Printing was now running in high gear, but more improvements were yet to come.

Currency Overprinting and Process Equipment (COPE). The Bureau of Engraving and Printing now has seven machines called COPE—Currency Overprinting and Process Equipment. Before the European-manufactured machine was installed, all processing procedures following printing operations were essentially manual. COPE feeds sheets and cuts and packs notes into packages of 100.

Thirty-two numbering machines and an equal number of seals are contained in one cylinder. Another cylinder contains 32 forms, enough to overprint two sheets of 16 subjects each. 100 overprinted sheets are then cut into two-note subjects and finally into single notes. A carousel unit then wraps notes into packages of 100. In one hour $200,000 in $1 notes is produced. If a

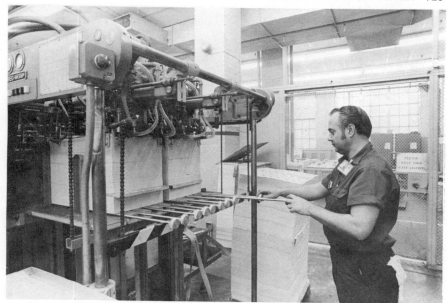

(Above) *Pressman inserts rods under one of two piles of 16-subject sheets to facilitate the addition of more plate-printed piles.* (Below) *Blocks 100 deep of $1 notes move to the right, where each sheet is cut into 8 pairs of 2 notes and then into single notes.*

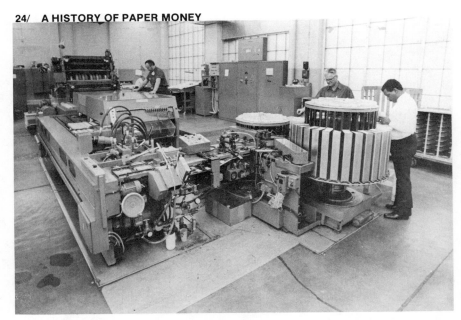

(Above) COPE *bands the single notes into packages of 100 and sorts them into 32 bricks of 4,000 notes, which are sent to Federal Reserve Banks.* (Below) *The carousel's 32 containers each hold 40 packages of 100 notes. Code letters atop the carousel match those printed on the notes.*

sheet of currency is accidentally folded or creased, COPE will stop and a light on an indicator panel will indicate the precise point of the malfunction. No final manual inspection is performed; if an undetected error is made during the overprinting process, it will automatically enter circulation.

COPE will save the Bureau of Engraving and Printing 281 man-years and more than $2 million in production costs on an annual basis. During the spring of 1972 the Director of the Bureau of Engraving and Printing, James A. Conlon, reported to a Senate Appropriations subcommittee, "With regards to our currency presses, for example, which are a critically important item, by virtue of our having developed . . . an ink formulation which differs from any others, we are able to produce currency without interleaving between sheets in stacks of 10,000 sheets to a skid.

"As a consequence our design of press equipment differs from that ordinarily used in other security printing plants in the world."

During the 1976 fiscal year, 2.8 billion notes were delivered.

During 1976, the Bureau of Engraving and Printing installed four, two-plate monocolor intaglio presses which are modified versions of the American Bank Note Company's Magna press. Each press is capable of printing over 8,000, 32-subject sheets per hour, and handling a stack of 10,000 sheets with a second 10,000 sheets in reserve position. After 20,000 sheets are printed, the press is stopped to verify the count.

Three types of presses are now in use at the Bureau: The one-plate De La Rue, the four-plate Giori and the Modified American Bank Note Company Magna.

Treasury Department Signatures

Paper notes are essentially promissory notes, and we just wouldn't feel right if the note didn't bear a signature or two to make the note seem official. Handwritten signatures or facsimile signatures lend authority to a note, especially if the prospects of repayment are shaky. During the time of the Confederacy, numerous young women spent much of the war carefully signing confederate bills in what are now spidery brown letters, faded into historical obscurity.

Handwritten signatures were also thought necessary on the Union side in those bleak days of 1861, when the Confederate campfires could be seen across the Potomac from the Treasury Building. Nineteen days after the first paper money was issued, President Lincoln signed a bill allowing the Sec-

Register of the Treasury	Treasurer of the U.S.	Terms of Office Began	Ended
Lucius E. Chittenden	F. E. Spinner	4-17-1861	8-10-1864
S. B. Colby	F. E. Spinner	8-11-1864	9-21-1867
Noah L. Jeffries	F. E. Spinner	10- 5-1867	3-15-1869
John Allison	F. E. Spinner	4- 3-1869	6-30-1875
John Allison	John C. New	6-30-1875	7- 1-1876
John Allison	A. U. Wyman	7- 1-1876	6-30-1877
John Allison	James Gilfillan	7- 1-1877	3-23-1878
Glenni W. Scofield	James Gilfillan	4- 1-1878	5-20-1881
Blanche K. Bruce	James Gilfillan	5-21-1881	3-31-1883
Blanche K. Bruce	A. U. Wyman	4- 1-1883	4-30-1885
Blanche K. Bruce	Conrad N. Jordan	5- 1-1885	6- 5-1885
William S. Rosecrans	Conrad N. Jordan	6- 8-1885	5-23-1887
William S. Rosecrans	James W. Hyatt	5-24-1887	5-10-1889
William S. Rosecrans	J. N. Huston	5-11-1889	4-21-1891
William S. Rosecrans	Enos H. Nebeker	4-25-1891	5-31-1893
William S. Rosecrans	Daniel N. Morgan	6- 1-1893	6-19-1893
James F. Tillman	Daniel N. Morgan	7- 1-1893	6-30-1897
James F. Tillman	Ellis H. Roberts	7- 1-1897	12- 2-1897
Blanche K. Bruce	Ellis H. Roberts	12- 3-1897	3-17-1898
Judson W. Lyons	Ellis H. Roberts	4- 7-1898	6-30-1905
Judson W. Lyons	Charles H. Treat	7- 1-1905	4- 1-1906
William T. Vernon	Charles H. Treat	6-12-1906	10-30-1909
William T. Vernon	Lee McClung	11- 1-1909	3-14-1911
James C. Napier	Lee McClung	3-15-1911	11-21-1912
James C. Napier	Carmi A. Thompson	11-22-1912	3-31-1913
James C. Napier	John Burke	4- 1-1913	9-30-1913
Gabe E. Parker	John Burke	10- 1-1913	12-31-1914
Houston B. Teehee	John Burke	3-24-1915	11-20-1919
William S. Elliott	John Burke	11-21-1919	1- 5-1921
William S. Elliott	Frank White	5- 2-1921	1-24-1922
Harley V. Speelman	Frank White	1-25-1922	9-30-1927
Walter O. Woods	Frank White	10- 1-1927	5- 1-1928
Walter O. Woods	H. T. Tate	5-31-1928	1-17-1929
Edward E. Jones	Walter O. Woods	1-22-1929	5-31-1933

Secretary of the Treasury

William G. McAdoo	John Burke	4- 1-1913	12-15-1918
Carter Glass	John Burke	12-16-1918	2- 1-1920
D. F. Houston	John Burke	2- 2-1920	1- 5-1921
A. W. Mellon	Frank White	5- 2-1921	5- 1-1928
A. W. Mellon	H. T. Tate	4-30-1928	1-17-1929
A. W. Mellon	Walter O. Woods	1-18-1929	2-12-1932
Ogden L. Mills	Walter O. Woods	2-13-1932	3- 3-1933
W. H. Woodin	Walter O. Woods	3- 4-1933	5-31-1933
W. H. Woodin	W. A. Julian	6- 1-1933	12-31-1933
Henry Morgenthau, Jr.	W. A. Julian	1- 1-1934	7-22-1945
Fred M. Vinson	W. A. Julian	7-23-1945	7-23-1946
John W. Snyder	W. A. Julian	7-25-1946	5-29-1949
John W. Snyder	Georgia Neese Clark	6-21-1949	1-20-1953
George M. Humphrey	Ivy Baker Priest	1-28-1953	7-28-1957
Robert B. Anderson	Ivy Baker Priest	7-29-1957	1-20-1961
C. Douglas Dillon	Elizabeth Rudel Smith	1-30-1961	4-13-1962
C. Douglas Dillon	Kathryn O'Hay Granahan	1- 3-1963	3-31-1965
Henry H. Fowler	Kathryn O'Hay Granahan	4- 1-1965	10-13-1966
Joseph W. Barr	Kathryn O'Hay Granahan	12-21-1968	1-20-1969
David M. Kennedy	Dorothy Andrews Elston*	5- 8-1869	9-16-1970
David M. Kennedy	Dorothy Andrews Kabis	9-17-1970	2- 1-1971
James B. Connally	Dorothy Andrews Kabis	2-11-1971	7- 3-1971
James B. Connally	Romana Banuelos	12-17-1971	5-16-1972
George P. Shultz	Romana Banuelos	6-12-1972	5- 8-1974
William E. Simon	Francine I. Neff	6-21-1974	1-13-1977 **
W. Michael Blumenthal		1-23-1977	

*During her term of office, Mrs. Elston married Mr. Walter L. Kabis. This was the first time the signature of a United States Treasurer had been changed during the term of office.

** Mrs. Neff resigned 1-19-77.

retary of the Treasury to delegate personnel to sign the first demand notes for the Treasury officials. Seventy employees were assigned the task of signing their own names, with a handwritten *For the* before the appropriate title. Almost immediately the words *For the* were engraved into the printing plates. These signers received an annual salary of $1,200 in the greenbacks they had signed.

Starting in 1863 facsimile signatures were printed directly on the bills. Most United States paper money bears two signatures. National bank notes include two additional signatures, those of the bank president and the cashier. Federal Reserve bank notes bear the signatures of the governor and the cashier or the deputy governor of the issuing bank. A complete list of Treasury Officials' signatures is given on page 26.

The signature of the Register of the Treasury appeared from 1862 to 1925. The Register of the Treasury is an official appointed by the President. Seventeen Registers held office during the period during which they were required to sign notes.

The Treasury Seal

Following the first issues of United States paper money in 1861, Spencer Clark, the Chief Engineer of the small National Note Bureau, was requested by the Secretary of the Treasury to design a new seal for the Department.

The Department of the Treasury had had a variety of seals, with the first in 1778 supposedly designed by Gouverneur Morris. It was adopted by the Continental Congress and was used with many changes from 1782 onward.

The Treasury Seal appears on all notes emanating from the Bureau with the exception of the demand notes of 1861 and the first three issues of fractional currency.

Clark had these words to say about his design: ".... its interior a facsimile of the seal adopted by the Treasury Department for its documents on a ground of geometric lathe work, the exterior being composed of thirty-four points, similarly executed. The points were designed to be typical of the thirty-four states, and to simulate the appearance of the seals ordinarily affixed to public documents." Clark preferred not to recognize the secession of eleven states the year before.

Until January 1968 the legend of the Seal appeared in Latin, reading, *THESAUR[I] AMER[ICAE] SEPTENT [RIONALIS] SIGIL [LUM]* Translated, this would read, "The Seal of the Treasury of North America." The new version of the Seal in English made its first appearance on the $100 United States note, series 1966. This new Seal bears the legend, "The Department of the Treasury 1789."

The Great Seal of the United States

With the printing of the 1935 $1 silver certificates, the face and back design of the Great Seal was used for the first time on United States paper money. The Latin motto above the design, *Annuit Coeptis*, means "He [God] has smiled on our undertakings." Below the pyramid is a second motto, *Novus Ordo Seclorum*, or "A New Order of the Ages," signifying a new American Age. The pyramid is a symbol of strength and permanence. The eye in the triangle suggests the all-seeing Deity. The date 1776 on the base of the pyramid refers to the signing of the Declaration of Independence.

The National Motto

In 1957 our national motto, *"In God We Trust,"* was added to the backs of those $1 silver certificates that were printed on the Bureau of Engraving and Printing's new flatbed presses. The changeover to high-speed presses was completed in April 1968, and so the 1935G series of silver certificates printed in 1962 comes both with and without the motto.

The suggestion to include "In God We Trust" on our currency was presented to the Secretary of the Treasury, George M. Humphrey, in November

1953 by Matthew H. Rothert of Camden, Arkansas. Secretary Humphrey favored the idea but felt that Congressional sanction was desirable. In March 1955, through Mr. Rothert's efforts, bills to this effect were introduced into the Senate by Senator Fullbright of Arkansas and into the House of Representatives by Congressmen Bennett of Florida and Harris of Arkansas. The bill, which was approved by President Eisenhower on July 11, 1955, specified ". . . that at such time as new dies for the printing of currency are adopted . . . by the Bureau of Engraving and Printing, the dies shall bear . . . the inscription 'In God We Trust' and thereafter this inscription shall appear on all United States Currency and coins."

In 1864 the motto was first placed on a U.S. coin, the 2¢ piece. It took 93 years and an Act of Congress before the same motto was placed on our paper money.

SUMMARY

United States paper money, first issued in 1861, went through many variations as new economic necessities arose in the century after its initiation. Since our book is not an economic or a financial history of the United States, we will merely list in chapter 2 the types of notes issued, in the order in which they are usually arranged by collectors. We might mention that the variations were mostly due to changes in the backing of our notes. During the Civil War the notes were little more than promissory notes dependent on the outcome of the hostilities.

Paper money was backed by silver or gold coin as designated on the note itself. Definitions of the range and use of the notes varied from restricted uses to general legal tender for all debts, public and private. National bank notes and then Federal Reserve notes are recent attempts to back the paper with actual goods and services owed to banks so that the paper note could serve its original purpose as an integral part of the economic process.

CHAPTER TWO

Types of U.S. Paper Money

This chapter will deal with some of the mechanical aspects of U.S. paper money. Syngraphics begins with a knowledge of the various categories by which paper money can be classified, and we shall now survey some of these categories. First we shall examine the numbering systems used on U.S. currency. Then we shall present the various types of U.S. notes, along with the Acts of Congress that authorized them and some remarks about their rarity. Finally, this chapter will offer brief biographical sketches of those people whose portraits most frequently appear on U.S. paper money.

NUMBERING SYSTEMS ON U.S. PAPER MONEY

One of the chief functions of the numbering systems used on U.S. currency has been to foil counterfeiters. At first the Treasury Department kept the details of the numbering systems secret so that forgers could not find the correct combinations of serial numbers and plate-position numbers. More recently, the Treasury's *Know Your Money* campaign has stressed maximum publicity of all details of the currency so that the general public can be well prepared to detect counterfeits. Thus the details of the number systems have become better known, though, as we shall see, gaps still exist.

Repeat Numbering

The earliest numbering system used on U.S. paper money was repeat numbering. All notes from a given sheet would bear the same serial number, including prefix and suffix letters and ornaments, if any. These notes are differentiated only by plate-position letters, usually A, B, C, and D or E, F, G, and H on a 4-subject plate. A national bank note plate of $1-1-1-2 would have plate letters A-B-C-A. Sheets of other mixed denominations would usee etters similarily. Repeat numbering is found on all classes of interest-bearing notes except the refunding certificates of 1879, and on national bank notes of all charter periods. Repeat numbering was originally a device to avoid impossibly large serial numbers.

Consecutive Numbering

In consecutive numbering all notes on a sheet bear consecutive numbers. The bottom note of a 4-subject sheet has a serial number divisible by 4 and a plate letter D, or occasionally an H. Consecutive numbering is found on all large-size notes except compound interest Treasury notes, interest-bearing notes, and national bank notes. This numbering system was continued on all 12-subject small-size notes (1929-1953) except for the special uncut sheets issued for use in Hawaii and North Africa during World War II. The relation on these small notes between a serial number divisible by 12 and a plate position letter is an anticounterfeiting device.

Consecutive numbering enabled many early sheets to be reconstructed for display, affording an idea of the original appearance of plates even though no uncut sheets survived. This is in general not possible with skip numbering.

Our earliest bills—demand notes, United States notes, and gold certificates—bear serial numbers 1 to 100000. The numbering system was then repeated with the addition of "series 1," "series 2," and so forth. United States notes of 1862 and 1863 are known with series as high as 284. Interest-bearing notes were not issued in large enough quantities to require this method; repeat numbering to 6 digits was sufficient.

Skip Numbering

Beginning in November 1952, 18-subject sheets show skip numbering, the first sheet bearing numbers 1, 8001, 16001, and so forth to 136001. The next sheet would commence with 2, 8002, 16002, through a run of 8,000 sheets. A similar system is in use now for 32-subject sheets.

Block Numbering

With the 1869 United States notes, a new system began known as block numbering. Serial numbers were prefixed with A (1 to 10000000), then B,K, V, and Z advancing to the same figure. Other letters were used with a star suffix* on higher denominations. On the United States notes of 1880 prefix letters and ornament suffixes continue, but a complete block is 100000000; many blocks are incomplete because prefix letters were changed when different seals were introduced. United States notes of 1917 introduce letter suffixes as well—blocks A-A, B-A, D-A, E-A, H-A, K-A, M-A, N-A, R-A and T-A are found on $1 notes.

Silver certificates of 1878 are from block A-X, those of 1880 are from block B with ornament, those of 1886 are from block B with a different ornament, those of 1891 are from block E with yet another ornament, and the issues of 1896 (and the 1899 issue bearing signatures of Lyons and Roberts) have two pheons. Subsequent blocks are B,D,E,H,K,M, and so forth with an ornament as a suffix. In 1912 identical prefix and suffix letters were introduced, producing A-A, B-B, D-D, E-E, H-H.

From about 1917 we find the A suffix constant: B-A, D-A, E-A, H-A, through X-A. In small-size currency the block system is continued with the entire alphabet used except for O; after 100000000 (today a star note) in block Z-A, the numbering starts again with A-B. The exception to this is Federal Reserve notes, on which the prefix letter is always that of the Federal Reserve district, A through L.

Numbering of Small-Size National Bank Notes

Before August 22, 1925, all national bank notes bore both a Treasury serial number and a bank sheet number; after 1925 the bank sheet number was printed twice. The bank sheet number—generally not prefixed and never suffixed—is the cumulative total of notes of that denomination and type issued for that bank. Prefix A is rarely found on national bank notes issued between 1925 and 1929. Apparently, A signifies the second million sheets of that denomination and type. The Treasury number—up to six digits, at first plain, then with parenthesis, suffix, and letter prefix—was cumulative for sheets of the denomination and type over all the banks for which they were issued. Later, blocks in Treasury numbers were in general similar to those in other classes of notes. Double letters (A-A, B-B, D-D)

These are not replacement notes.

were in use between 1899 and 1908; letters *B-A*, *D-A*, *E-A* began on May 5, 1911. Information enabling one to date a national bank note accurately from the Treasury number is not available since certain archival records of 1916-1922 are incomplete.

Small-size national bank notes of Type I issued between 1929 and 1933 used repeat numbering with six subjects prefixed *A* to *F* and suffixed *A*. The millionth sheet was then numbered *A* to *F* with suffix *B*. The *B* suffix is known on $5 notes issued by the Chase National Bank of New York. Type II notes, issued from May 1933 through May 1935, were consecutively numbered with the bank's charter number in brown beside the bank serial number. The complete *A* block comprised 999,996 notes from 166,666 sheets; the next sheet was numbered *B*1 to 6. Five dollar notes of block *B* are known on the Bank of America, San Francisco, California.

Star or Replacement Notes

The use of a star on replacement notes that substitute for defective notes discovered at the Bureau during inspection began in 1910 with (☆) *B* on United States notes and silver certificates. Later on suffix *D* was used, and the system continued with the printing of small-size notes. However, Federal Reserve bank notes and Federal Reserve notes employ the star as the suffix. No stars appear on national bank notes.

The star is also used to complete a numbered series of each 100,000,000 notes. The highest number the eight-digit numbering cylinder can print is 99,999,999, and so the last note of the series becomes a star note. Throughout this catalog small-size star or replacement notes are indicated by a (☆) below the regular issue.

(☆) after a catalog number will also indicate large size notes which have been observed to bear stars. I wish to express my thanks to Walter Breen and Dr. Bernard Schaff who were kind enough to submit their observations to me.

A DESCRIPTION OF NOTE TYPES

On the following pages you will find a listing and description of each type of note issued by the United States since 1861. All notes issued since this date remain legal tender, although the collectors' value in most instances exceeds the face value many times over.

Demand Notes

Congressional Acts of July 17 and August 5, 1861, authorized $60 million in demand notes, or "greenbacks," as they were soon called by the populace. Notes of $5, $10, and $20 payable at New York, Philadelphia, Boston, Cincinnati, and St. Louis bore the obligation, "THE UNITED STATES PROMISE TO PAY TO THE BEARER... DOLLARS ON DEMAND... Payable by the Assistant Treasurer of the United States at. . . ."

Interest-Bearing Treasury Notes

Treasury notes were issued periodically between 1812 and 1861, and during this period the constitutionality of these notes was an omnipresent topic in Congress. Most interest-bearing treasury notes bore interest at 5 or 6 percent and were payable after two years. Examples of varying terms and lower interest rates have been found by Knox, whose work is the best source for those who wish to investigate these fascinating notes.

The $50 interest-bearing treasury note of the last issue is the only one included in this catalog; space does not permit additional listings. We can assume that with few exceptions all these notes have been redeemed and are therefore unavailable. Notwithstanding, the last issue does form an interesting transition into the greenback period.

Legal Tender or United States Notes

The first of five large-size issues in denominations of $5 to $1,000 bears the date March 10, 1862. These are two different obligations that appear on the reverse of the first issue.

First obligation: "This note is a legal tender for all debts, public and private, except duties on imports and interest on the public debt, and is exchangeable for U.S. six-percent, twenty-year bonds, redeemable at the pleasure of the United States after five years."

Second obligation: "This note is a legal tender for all debts, public and private, except duties on imports and interest on the public debt, and is receivable in payment of all loans made to the United States."

The second issue, dated August 1, 1862, included notes of $1 and $2 only. The third issue, dated March 10, 1863, once again included all denominations of $5 to $1,000. The Congressional Act of March 3, 1863, authorized the fourth issue in denominations of $1 to $10,000. Seven series are included in this issue: 1869 (labelled as a Treasury note), 1874, 1878, 1880, 1907, 1917, and 1923. A $10 note was the only denomination included in the fifth issue, series 1901.

Small-size legal tender notes of $1 (1928), $2 and $5 (1928, 1953, and

1963), and $100 (1966) have been printed; the $100 note is the only denomination still being printed.

Compound Interest Treasury Notes

Notes of $10, $20, $50, $100, $500, and $1,000 authorized by Congressional Acts of March 3, 1863, and June 30, 1864, bear the following obligation: "Three years after date the United States will pay the bearer . . . dollars with interest at the rate of six percent compounded semi-annually . . . . By Act of Congress, this note is a legal tender for . . . dollars but bears interest at six percent only at maturity as follows . . . . This sum . . . will be paid the holder for principal and interest at maturity of note three years from date."

These notes were issued in order to ease the scarcity of money during the Civil War.

Interest-Bearing Notes

Interest-bearing notes were the successors to the Treasury notes issued between 1812 and 1861, and they were issued for the same purpose as the compound interest Treasury notes. One-and two-year notes bearing interest of 5 percent were authorized by the Act of March 3, 1863. The three-year notes bearing 7.3 percent interest were issued at three different times, authorized by the Acts of July 17, 1861, June 30, 1864, and March 3, 1865. The three-year notes had five coupons attached, which were to be detached and redeemed at six-month intervals.

The one-year notes ($10–$5,000), two-year notes ($50–$1,000), and three-year notes ($50–$5,000) are all extremely rare, undoubtedly due to their immediate redemption on the expiration date.

Currency Certificates of Deposit

By the Act of June 8, 1872, the Secretary of the Treasury was authorized to issue certificates in denominations of $5,000 and to receive certificates of $10,000. The $10,000 notes were receivable on deposit without interest from national banking houses but were not to be included in the legal reserve. The $5,000 notes were payable on demand (in U.S. notes) at the place of deposit but were accepted in settlement of clearing house balances at the locations where such deposits were made. On March 14, 1900, the act authorizing these large denomination certificates was repealed.

Refunding Certificates

The government wanted to create more faith in paper currency, so on

February 26, 1879, they authorized refunding certificates of $10. The four percent annual interest was to accumulate indefinitely. In 1907 Congress passed a law that allowed the government to stop payment on July 1 of that year. By this time the notes were worth $21.30. The first of the two types is extremely rare; only two examples are known.

Silver Certificates

All silver certificates were authorized by the Acts of February 28, 1878, and August 4, 1886. The first of five large-size issues had "Certificate of Deposit" printed on the obverse of $10–$1,000 notes. The notes of 1878 all bear countersignatures of Assistant Treasurers. Notes of $1–$1,000 made up the second issue of 1886, 1891, and 1908. The $1, $2, and $5 notes account for the third issue (educational series) of 1896 and the fourth issue, series 1899. The fifth issue, series 1923, included only $1 and $5 notes.

Small-size silver certificates in denominations of $1 (1928, 1934, 1935, and 1957), $5 (1934 and 1953), and $10 (1933, 1934, and 1953) are no longer printed.

Treasury or Coin Notes

The Legal Tender Act of July 14, 1890, authorized coin notes of $1–$1,000, series 1890 and 1891. These notes were used to purchase silver bullion by the Treasury Department. The Secretary of the Treasury was left to decide if gold or silver would be paid out when these notes were redeemed. The redemption of Treasury or coin notes practically bankrupted the Treasury by 1893 and caused a major panic.

Federal Reserve Notes

The Federal Reserve Act of 1913 authorized all Federal Reserve notes. The series of 1914 included only notes of $5 to $100; the 1918 series included the higher denominations of $500 to $10,000. The obligation on the Federal Reserve notes was borne by the U.S. Government and not by the individual banks.

Small-size Federal Reserve notes have been printed in denominations of $1–$10,000; the $100 note is the largest note now being printed. These small-size notes were first printed in 1929 bearing a series date of 1928. Until 1934 the obligation of all Federal Reserve notes made a reference to redemption in gold. Following the passing of the Gold Reserve Act in 1933, our paper money was no longer redeemable in gold and the obligation was changed to read "redeemable in lawful money."

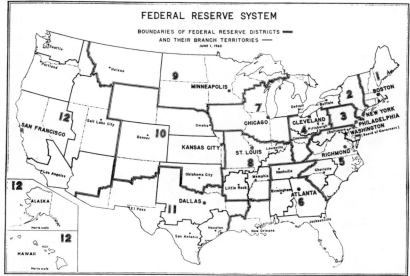

COMPLIMENTS OF COIN WORLD

Federal Reserve Bank Notes

There were two issues of large-size Federal Reserve bank notes—1915 ($5, $10, and $20) and 1918($1–$50)—authorized by the Federal Reserve Acts of December 23, 1913, and April 23, 1918. Not all banks within the Federal Reserve system issued notes of the first series, but all banks did issue notes bearing the series date 1918. The obligation to pay is made by the individual bank and not the U.S. Government.

The small-size Federal Reserve bank notes were authorized by the Act of March 9, 1933, and were issued to alleviate the shortage of paper money in early 1933 due to the massive withdrawal of Federal Reserve notes. National bank note plates bearing the date 1929 were adapted for this new issue, which is similar to the earlier national bank notes with the exception of the overprinting and a larger brown seal.

National Gold Bank Notes

These gold-tinted notes are extremely beautiful and extremely rare as well. To assuage the burden of handling the gold produced by the California gold rush, Congress authorized ten banks, nine in California and one in Boston,* to issue paper money in the denominations of $5–$500, redeem-

*It is not generally believed that the Kidder National Gold Bank of Boston issued notes although denominations of $50, $100, $500, and $1000 were printed. At least one proof impression is known to exist.

able in gold. These gold banks were also national banks, and therefore it was necessary for them to deposit U.S. Bonds as security with the U.S. Treasurer. The obligation on these notes is similar to that on national bank notes except that the gold bank notes are payable in "gold coin."

These beautiful gold notes must have circulated heavily, for the few that survive are in the lower grades of condition.

Gold Certificates

There were nine issues of large-size gold certificates, but only four issues saw any real circulation. The first three (issued between 1865 and 1875), the fifth (1888), and the sixth (1900) were used primarily within banks and clearing houses. The 1882 series, or fourth issue, in denominations of $20–$10,000, was the first to circulate widely. The seventh issue, series 1905, 1906, and 1907, included two denominations only, $10 and $20. The 1907 series, or eighth issue, was limited to the $1,000 note. The ninth and final issue consisted of two series, 1913 ($50) and 1922 ($10–$1,000).

Small-size gold certificates dated 1928 were recalled immediately following the Gold Reserve Act of 1933. Secretary of the Treasury Dillon's order of April 24, 1964, allowed gold certificates to be held legally.

National Bank Notes

Between 1863 and 1929 thousands of banks were granted charters whereby they could issue notes up to 90 percent of the value of government bonds. Such bonds were deposited with the federal government as security under rules established by the National Banking Act of 1863. Each bank was granted an individual charter number for a renewable 20-year period.

National bank notes were printed by the Bureau of Engraving and Printing and overprinted with the bank name and charter numbers as orders were placed by the individual banks.*

Large-size notes were issued during three charter periods. The first was divided into two issues, and notes of $1–$1,000 were produced. All of these notes were extremely attractive and rare in choice condition. The obligation reads, "This note is secured by bonds of the United States deposited with the U.S. Treasurer at Washington. . . . The . . . bank [city] will pay the bearer on demand . . . Dollars. . . . This note is receivable at par in all parts of the United States, in payment of all taxes and excises and all other dues to the United States, except duties on imports, and also for all salaries and other debts and demands owing by the United States to individuals, corporations

---

Prior to July, 1875 national bank notes were prepared by private bank note companies.

and associations within the United States, except interest on public debt."

Beginning with the second charter period and continuing during the remaining issues, the $1 and $2 notes were deleted, as were the $500 and $1,000 notes. During the second charter period there were three issues; only the backs of the notes were different in design.

The third charter period introduced a change in design for all denominations. Notes of this period and those of the second issue of the preceding were issued to alleviate a semi-crisis situation. Many banks did not have sufficient U.S. Government bonds to deposit and therefore other securities were accepted. This change is noted in the obligation on these two issues.

Small-size national bank notes were issued from 1929 to 1935 in two types. Type II has the charter number printed a second time near the serial number.

National Bank Note Rarity. Degrees of rarity ranging from R(arity) 1, the most common, to R(arity) 9, the most rare, have been arranged by William P. Donlon and Neil Shafer. I see no way of improving on this arrangement, so I have adopted a similar system.

For the most part the rarity of a national bank note is based on the number of such banks recorded for the state in question. However, there are other criteria that will affect the availability of particular notes. Such criteria are the size of the community or city, the length of time the bank operated (some banks were forced to close during the depression years), and the desirability created by odd or interesting names.

One example of desirability would be a note bearing the name of an historic locale, such as the Alamo. Another example would be notes issued by banks in small communities, such as the Gap National Bank and Trust Company in Gap, Pennsylvania. The earliest census figures I could find for this three-letter community were for 1948, when the total population was only 738. The number of notes issued by this bank in 1929 could not have been very great. Neither of the two notes mentioned (and illustrated on pp. 390–91) would conform to the general rarity for Texas (R2) and Pennsylvania (R1).

Rarity Table

State	Large-Size	Small-Size	State	Large-Size	Small-Size
ALABAMA	R4	R3 (126)	MONTANA	R7	R4 (69)
ALASKA	R9	R9 (6)	NEBRASKA	R4	R2 (218)
ARIZONA	R8	R5 (16)	NEVADA	R8	R6 (23)
ARKANSAS	R6	R3 (69)	NEW HAMPSHIRE	R5	R4 (70)
CALIFORNIA	R1	R1 (206)	NEW JERSEY	R2	R2 (311)
COLORADO	R5	R2 (113)	NEW MEXICO	R8	R5 (31)
CONNECTICUT	R4	R2 (77)	NEW YORK	R1	R1 (480)
DELAWARE	R7	R4 (23)	NORTH CAROLINA	R4	R2 (96)
DISTRICT of COLUMBIA	R5	R2 (21)	NORTH DAKOTA	R6	R3 (112)
FLORIDA	R6	R3 (109)	OHIO	R1	R1 (362)
GEORGIA	R6	R5 (70)	OKLAHOMA	R6	R2 (263)
HAWAII	R8	R5 (4)	OREGON	R6	R4 (78)
IDAHO	R8	R5 (38)	PENNSYLVANIA	R1	R1(1094)
ILLINOIS	R1	R1 (454)	PUERTO RICO	R9	
INDIANA	R1	R1 (228)	RHODE ISLAND	R7	R4 (22)
IOWA	R2	R1 (284)	SOUTH CAROLINA	R5	R2 (50)
KANSAS	R3	R2 (265)	SOUTH DAKOTA	R7	R3 (81)
KENTUCKY	R3	R2 (127)	TENNESSEE	R4	R2 (96)
LOUISIANA	R5	R3 (69)	TEXAS	R2	R1 (542)
MAINE	R6	R2 (89)	UTAH	R7	R4 (30)
MARYLAND	R4	R2 (124)	VERMONT	R6	R3 (56)
MASSACHUSETTS	R2	R2 (145)	VIRGINIA	R4	R2 (154)
MICHIGAN	R2	R2 (224)	WASHINGTON	R5	R3 (92)
MINNESOTA	R3	R2 (328)	WEST VIRGINIA	R5	R2 (124)
MISSISSIPPI	R7	R4 (57)	WISCONSIN	R3	R1 (254)
MISSOURI	R3	R4 (153)	WYOMING	R7	R4 (35)
			TERRITORIES	R9	

Near the charter number on some large-size national bank notes you sometimes find a letter. The letter simplified the sorting process when these notes were redeemed.

N — New England states   M — Middle states

E — Eastern states   W — Western states

S — Southern states   P — Pacific states

These geographical letters were used from January 11, 1902, until February 26, 1924.

The numbers in parenthesis adjacent to the small-size rarity listings indicate the number of different notes reported thus far.

National Bank Note Charter Numbers. Below is a listing of national bank charter numbers and the years in which the charters were granted. The First National Bank of Philadelphia received charter number 1 in 1863. The Roodhouse National Bank of Roodhouse, Illinois, received number 14,348 in 1935 and was the last bank to be chartered. In *The National Bank Note Is-*

sues of 1929-1935, published by the Society of Paper Money Collectors, one will discover that charter number 14,320 was granted to the National Bank and Trust Company of Louisville, Kentucky. This was the highest charter number to appear on notes delivered to the Comptroller of the Currency by the Bureau of Engraving and Printing. National banks with higher charter numbers were granted the privilege of issuing notes, but for one reason or another they did not.

Charter Numbers	Year Granted	Charter Numbers	Year Granted	Charter Numbers	Year Granted
1–179	1863	3833–3954	1888	10306–10472	1913
180–682	1864	3955–4190	1889	10473–19672	1914
683–1626	1865	4191–4494	1890	10673–10810	1915
1627–1665	1866	4495–4673	1891	10811–10932	1916
1666–1675	1867	4674–4832	1892	10933–11126	1917
1676–1688	1868	4833–4934	1893	11127-11282	1918
1689–1696	1869	4935–4983	1894	11283–11570	1919
1697–1759	1870	4984–5029	1895	11571–11903	1920
1760–1912	1871	5030–5054	1896	11904–12082	1921
1913–2073	1872	5055–5108	1897	12083–12287	1922
2074–2131	1873	5109–5165	1898	12288–12481	1923
2132–2214	1874	5166–5240	1899	12482–12615	1924
2215–2315	1875	5241–5662	1900	12616–12866	1925
2316–2344	1876	5663–6074	1901	12867–13022	1926
2345–2375	1877	6075–6566	1902	13023–13159	1927
2376–2405	1878	6567–7081	1903	13160–13269	1928
2406–2445	1879	7082–7541	1904	13270–13412	1929
2446–2498	1880	7542–8027	1905	13413–13516	1930
2499–2606	1881	8028–8489	1906	13517–13586	1931
2607–2849	1882	8490–8979	1907	13587–13654	1932
2850–3101	1883	8980–9302	1908	13655–13920	1933
3102–3281	1884	9303–9622	1909	13921–14217	1934
3282–3427	1885	9623–9913	1910	14318–14348	1935
3428–3612	1886	9914–10119	1911		
3613–3832	1887	10120–10305	1912		

PORTRAITS FREQUENTLY USED ON UNITED STATES PAPER MONEY

The portraits of 13 famous Americans have appeared frequently on United States paper money since 1861. I have arranged an alphabetical listing of these statesmen along with a brief biographical sketch and the catalog numbers of the notes on which their portraits appear. Information pertaining to individual portraits will be found near the illustration in the catalog.

Salmon P. Chase

Salmon P. Chase, the statesman who served as President Lincoln's Secretary of the Treasury and who practically established the National Banking System single-handed, was born in Cornish Township, New Hampshire, in 1808. After moving to Ohio as a boy, he later attended Dartmouth and began his law practice in Cincinnati. In 1864 Chase was appointed to the Supreme Court and remained in that position until his death on May 7, 1873.
Numbers 1–4, 493–496, 1396–1398, and 1493–1497

Steven Grover Cleveland

Steven Grover Cleveland was born in Caldwell, New Jersey, on March 18, 1837. He practiced law in New York, served there as governor, and was twice elected to the Presidency, in 1884 and 1892. Cleveland died in his native New Jersey on June 24, 1908.
Numbers 848–850 and all small-size $1,000 notes

Benjamin Franklin

Benjamin Franklin (1706–1790) is recognized by philatelists for his contributions to early postal service. In 1727 Franklin was appointed Postmaster in Philadelphia. In 1753, along with William Hunter, he was placed in charge of the Colonial Postal Service.
Numbers 603 and 604, 929–941, 1244–1245, 1499 all small-size $100 notes, 1¢ and 30¢ encased postage

Ulysses S. Grant

Ulysses S. Grant was born in Point Pleasant, Ohio, on April 27, 1822. Grant died at 63 after serving his country as a military officer and its eighteenth President.
Numbers 349–360, 1040–1042, 1044–1046, and all small-size $50 notes

Alexander Hamilton

It was through the genius of Alexander Hamilton that the financial chaos resulting from the Revolution was resolved. As the first Secretary of the Treasury (1789-1795), Hamilton established the Bank of the United States and a sensible federal monetary system. In 1799, along with Aaron Burr (the man who would mortally wound him in a duel), Hamilton founded the Manhattan Company in New York City. This company, which gave birth to the

Bank of the Manhattan Company, survived wars and epidemics and through a series of mergers became The Chase Manhattan Bank, one of the largest banks in the country.
Numbers 242–244, 703–723, 926–927, 942–945a, 1346–1347, 1413–1424, 1429, and all small-size $10 notes

Andrew Jackson

Andrew Jackson, born in 1767 in South Carolina, studied law in North Carolina and began his practice in Nashville, Tennessee. After serving in the House and the Senate, Jackson was elected to the Tennessee Supreme Court. Following his military career, Jackson served two terms as President of the United States.
Numbers 245–273, 492, 618–620, 1465–1492, all small-size $20 notes, and 2¢ encased postage

Thomas Jefferson

Thomas Jefferson, our third President, was knowledgeable in the fields of music, architecture, astronomy, and farming. At age 20 Jefferson began building his home, Monticello, on Carter's Mountain; this edifice was completed in Jefferson's sixtieth year. He died on the fiftieth anniversary of the signing of the Declaration of Independence, July 4, 1826.
Numbers 154–170, 203–207, 1502–1505, 1548–1551, and 5¢ encased postage

Abraham Lincoln

In 1861, during the first administration of our sixteenth President, the first demand notes (greenbacks) were issued. After George Washington and Alexander Hamilton, Abraham Lincoln is the most frequently portrayed person on our paper money.
Numbers 372, 380–382, 463–465, 1122–1136, 1359–1369, 1624–1625, and all small-size $5 notes

William McKinley

Our twenty-fifth President was born in Niles, Ohio, on January 29, 1843. McKinley was shot at the Pan-American Exposition in Buffalo and died soon thereafter on September 14, 1901.
Numbers 540–566 and 1372–1375

James Madison

James Madison was a member of the Continental Congress (1780–1783, 1787–1788) and later was elected as our fourth President. Madison did not favor government-issued paper money and voted against the establishment of the Bank of the United States. His portrait appears on $5,000 notes.
Numbers 1435, 1446–1464

James Monroe

Our fifth President, James Monroe, was born in Westmoreland, Virginia, on April 28, 1758. He studied law under Thomas Jefferson, became Governor of Virginia, and was appointed Secretary of State by President Madison.
Numbers 1212–1221

Robert Morris

Robert Morris, U.S. Senator 1789–1795, was one of the signers of the Declaration of Independence. As Superintendent of Finance 1781–1784, he was instrumental in founding the Bank of North America.
Numbers 578–589 and 1376–1378

George Washington

It is not generally known that the half-dimes of 1792 prepared by Robert Birch were struck from table silver that belonged to President Washington. At this time many people thought our first coins should bear the image of the first President. However, the House of Representatives and Washington himself felt that such a design seemed too indicative of monarchy.
Numbers 5–28, 45–46, 59–61, all small-size $1 notes, 187–196, 300–315, 834–842, 953–986, 1013–1014, 1137–1140, 1403–1404, 1461, 1499–1501, 1506–1509, 1514–1529, 1552–1558, and 1568–1572; 3¢, 9¢, 10¢, 12¢, 24¢, and 90¢ encased postage stamps

ANNOUNCEMENT OF SMALL SIZE CURRENCY

A few months before small-size currency entered circulation in 1929, circulars the same size as the new notes were distributed by banks and businesses. The backs of these handbills provided a splendid opportunity for advertisement.

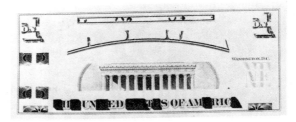

TEST PIECES

In January 1972 it was revealed that the Bureau of Engraving and Printing had sent experimental plates to Germany for a test run on the new Giori presses which were later acquired by the Bureau. The result of this test were pieces bearing two color combinations: one has black printing on the face with a reddish brown back, the other has green face printing with black print on the back. A very small number of these test pieces surfaced in the syngraphic marketplace. Although all of these pieces should have been destroyed, it is legal to hold them.

CHAPTER THREE

Catalog
of
U.S.
Paper
Money

Despite my best efforts to make this catalog as straightforward and clear as possible, the extraordinary variety of the subject makes the following pages more elaborate than I might have wished. It's the nature of the beast, and in the interest of taming some of its more snarling complexities, I offer a brief course of instruction in the use of this catalog.

USING THE CATALOG

The reader will need to understand the details of this book's system of numbering, grading, and valuation for the catalog to be useful. The numbering was perhaps the trickiest problem I encountered in organizing the catalog, so I will deal with that area first.

The system of numbering in this catalog is the simplest possible: I have used consecutive numbers in progression. Occasionally a letter follows the number, and this usually coincides with a series change.

In listing Federal Reserve notes I have added the letters of the various districts to the numbers.* In the case of Federal Reserve bank notes an additional number sometimes follows the district letter in order to differentiate the maximum five-signature combinations. If a catalog number is italicized, this indicates that the note is illustrated and represents the issue or series. A star after a catalog number indicates a replacement note.

---

*See map of the Federal Reserve system, page 38.

I hope that anyone with a minimum of collecting experience will be able to find the proper section in this catalog in order to identify any note he might have. This catalog is set up by denomination rather than by type, so identifying any note shouldn't take more than a minute or so.

At the end of each listing for Federal Reserve note denominations still being issued ($1–$100), additional numbers have been left open for future signature changes.

Written permission will be required for the use of the numbering system in this catalog if used in any book, pamphlet, or catalog. Publishers of magazines, newspapers, periodicals, journals, and auction catalogs are free to use this numbering system. Dealers in stamps, coins, and currency who send price lists to customers are also permitted to use this system providing reference is made to the present work and author.

Other Numbering Systems

I carefully examined all other comparable catalog numbering systems before deciding on the method for this book. Robert Friedberg has used a consecutive numbering system, but he does not indicate illustrated examples or star notes. I felt that this led to some difficulty in cross references.

The William P. Donlon and the Hewitt-Donlon catalogs, which cover small-size notes only, have a multiple cataloging system. Donlon uses a three-part numbering system: the first number indicates the note type, the middle two numbers show the denomination, and the last number gives the order of release for that particular series. In a separate catalog on large-size notes, Donlon uses a preliminary X to indicate a large-size note and adds additional numbers to identify numerous signature combinations.

The Hewitt-Donlon catalog shows an improvement on the Donlon small-size note numbering system but applied the same principle. A letter identified the note type, and a following number indicated the denomination. Two more numbers and a letter identified the series when necessary. The improved system had a great deal of merit for a catalog that dealt with small-size notes only.

Any numbering system is only a type of shorthand reference, and unwieldly cataloging systems that try to include as much information in the catalog number as in the description itself sometimes become redundant and difficult. So a simple consecutive numbering system is used throughout this catalog, and it should afford no difficulty for anyone.

A Note about Grading

Few syngraphists agree completely when it comes to the grading of paper money. Notwithstanding, a grading scale must be included in any syngraphic catalog. The following descriptions of grades or conditions are meant to act as a guide, and I hope not too many readers disagree with them.

New—Notes can be described as new only when they are in the same condition as when issued. There must be no folds, creases, or signs of handling. Any blemish that was the result of handling by a bank teller must be mentioned when a note is described as new.

Extra Fine—A note in this condition will still be crisp, although there probably will be evidence of handling, such as minor creases or folds. Any other blemish, such as tears or stains, would disqualify a note from the Extra Fine category.

Very Fine—Once a note has circulated to any extent it will be considered to be in Very Fine condition. The note will now have folds and creases, but it still might retain some of the original crispness.

Fine—A note in Fine condition has seen extensive circulation. Creases are more pronounced, the paper feels soft to the touch, and there may be signs of fading and stains.

Very Good and *Good*—Notes in these two conditions are unworthy of collecting unless the notes are rare or extremely scarce. Notes in these categories might have edge tears and stains, and corners could be missing.

A Note about Valuations

The values listed throughout this catalog are suggested or average prices. These figures reflect numerous price lists consulted as well as prices realized from recent auctions. Supply and demand and varying degrees of interest will affect the price of any note. All prices listed for national bank notes are for the most common prices in the R1 category.

Generally, notes above $100 will not be priced; few of us can afford to collect $100 notes. Many higher denominations are unobtainable at any price. Nevertheless, all known notes issued since 1861 must be included in a catalog of this type. Many pieces of currency that are rare or unique may not change hands often, and valuations are therefore difficult to ascertain. In many instances notes in these categories are priceless.

These heretofore unpublished back designs came to my attention too late to be placed within the body of this catalog. These brilliant yellow proof designs answer to the description of, and most certainly are those designs used for the first gold certificate issue under the Act of March 3, 1863.

No. 1358

No. 1442

No. 1466

United States Notes/1862/Red Seal

Face Design: The portrait of Salmon P. Chase was engraved by Joseph P. Ourdan. This illustrated note with serial number 1 and plate letter A was presented to Secretary of the Treasury Chase.

Back Design

The following notes bear the signatures of Chittenden-Spinner.

No.		Notes Issued	Very Good	Very Fine	New
1	National Bank Note Company— American Bank Note Company near lower border of face		45.00	80.00	265.00
2	Same as above with ABN Co. at upper right		45.00	80.00	265.00
3	National Bank Note Company printed twice near lower border	28,351,348	35.00	65.00	200.00
4	Same as above with ABN Co. at upper right		35.00	65.00	200.00

United States Notes/1869/Red Seal

Face Design: The
Washington portrait
was engraved by
Alfred Sealey.
*Columbus, Discovery
of Land*, a painting by
Charles Schussle was
engraved by Joseph
Ourdan.

Back Design

No.	Signatures	Notes Issued	Very Good	Very Fine	New
5	Allison-Spinner	42,456,812	20.00	50.00	385.00

United States Notes

Face Design:
Similar to No. 5
with the exception
of the changes
indicated below.

Back Design:
Legal tender
obligation and
counterfeiting
warning are printed
on the right.

The following have a red ornament circling ONE DOLLAR on the right.

No.	Date	Signatures	Seal	Notes Issued	Very Good	Very Fine	New
6	1874	Allison-Spinner	Red-r	18,988,000	25.00	80.00	325.00
7	1875A	Allison-New	Red-r		65.00	185.00	600.00
8	1875B	Allison-New	Red-r		75.00	185.00	625.00
9	1875C	Allison-New	Red-r		75.00	185.00	650.00
10	1875D	Allison-New	Red-r	26,212,000	75.00	185.00	800.00
11	1875E	Allison-New	Red-r		100.00	245.00	1,000.00
12	1875	Allison-New	Red-r		12.50	50.00	135.00
13	1875	Allison-Wyman	Red-r		12.50	50.00	135.00
14	1878	Allison-Gilfillan	Red-r	12,512,000	20.00	57.50	150.00

The following have a large seal on the right; serial numbers are red.

No.	Date	Signatures	Seal	Notes Issued	Very Good	Very Fine	New
15	1880	Scofield-Gilfillan	Brown		10.00	25.00	80.00
16	1880	Bruce-Gilfillan	Brown	57,600,000	10.00	25.00	80.00
17	1880	Bruce-Wyman	Brown		10.00	25.00	150.00

The following have blue serial numbers.

No.	Date	Signatures	Seal	Notes Issued	Very Good	Very Fine	New
18	1880	Rosecrans-Huston	Red (Large)		40.00	135.00	675.00
19	1880	Rosecrans-Huston	Brown		75.00	175.00	675.00
20	1880	Rosecrans-Nebeker	Brown	6,400,000	75.00	175.00	725.00

The following have a smaller seal on the left side.

No.	Date	Signatures	Seal	Notes Issued	Very Good	Very Fine	New
21	1880	Rosecrans-Nebeker	Red-sc		10.00	35.00	175.00
22	1880	Tillman-Morgan	Red-sc		10.00	35.00	175.00

The following have red serial numbers.

No.	Date	Signatures	Seal	Notes Issued	Very Good	Very Fine	New
23(☆)	1917	Teehee-Burke	Red-sc		10.00	20.00	50.00
24(☆)	1917	Elliott-Burke	Red-sc		10.00	20.00	60.00
25	1917	Burke-Elliott*	Red-sc	1,000,000,000	35.00	85.00	325.00
26(☆)	1917	Elliott-White	Red-sc		10.00	20.00	50.00
27(☆)	1917	Speelman-White	Red-sc		10.00	20.00	50.00

*The signatures were reversed in error.
r: with rays   sc: with scallops

United States Notes/Red Seal

Face Design:
Portrait of
George Washington

Back Design

No.	Date	Signatures	Notes Printed	Very Good	Very Fine	New
28(☆)	1923	Speelman-White	81,872,000	10.00	40.00	135.00

National Bank Notes/First Charter Period

Face Design:
The vignette of
Concordia was
designed by T. A.
Liebler and
engraved by
Charles Burt.

Back Design:
*The Landing of the
Pilgrims* by F. O. C.
Darley was engraved
by Charles Burt.

No.	Date	Signatures	Seal	Notes Issued	Very Good	Very Fine	New
29	Orig*	Colby-Spinner	Red-r		35.00	200.00	500.00
30	Orig*	Jeffries-Spinner	Red-r		650.00	1,375.00	3,850.00
31	Orig*	Allison-Spinner	Red-r		65.00	200.00	500.00
32	1875	Allison-New	Red-sc	23,167,677**	65.00	200.00	500.00
33	1875	Allison-Wyman	Red-sc		65.00	200.00	500.00
34	1875	Allison-Gilfillan	Red-sc		65.00	200.00	500.00
35	1875	Scofield-Gilfillan	Red-sc		65.00	200.00	500.00

*These original notes did not have a date printed on the face.
**339,723 notes are outstanding.
  r: with rays   sc: with scallops

Silver Certificates/1886

Face Design:
The wife of our first President was born in Williamsburg, Virginia, in May 1732 as Martha Davidside She married George Washington on January 6, 1759, and is the only woman to appear on United States paper money. The engraving, by Charles Burt, is based on a painting by Jalabert.

Back Design

No.	Signatures	Seal	Notes Printed	Very Good	Very Fine	New
36	Rosecrans-Jordan	Sm Red		25.00	75.00	285.00
37	Rosecrans-Hyatt	Sm Red		25.00	75.00	285.00
38	Rosecrans-Hyatt	Lg Red		25.00	75.00	285.00
39	Rosecrans-Huston	Lg Red	72,484,000	25.00	75.00	285.00
40	Rosecrans-Huston	Lg Brown		30.00	100.00	325.00
41	Rosecrans-Nebeker	Lg Brown		30.00	100.00	325.00
42	Rosecrans-Nebeker	Sm Red		35.00	200.00	525.00

The face design now dated 1891 is similar to the preceding note, but the back has been redesigned as illustrated here.

43	Rosecrans-Nebeker	Sm Red	65,408,000	25.00	90.00	235.00
44	Tillman-Morgan	Sm Red		25.00	90.00	235.00

Silver Certificates/1896/Red Seal

This is a preliminary sketch of *History* by W.H. Low, prepared on May 24, 1894.

W.H. Low's original design in the form of a painting hangs in the Bureau of Engraving and Printing.

Face Design: *History Instructing Youth* and most of Mr. Low's original design were retained. Thomas F. Morris was called upon to redesign the accepted version. Charles Schlecht engraved both the face and the back of this note.

Back Design: Thomas F. Morris was the designer of the back, which bears the portraits of Martha and George Washington. Charles Burt engraved the portrait of Martha Washington and Alfred Sealey executed the portrait of George Washington.

No.	Signatures	Notes Printed	Very Good	Very Fine	New
45	Tillman-Morgan		30.00	75.00	325.00
46	Bruce-Roberts	57,344,000	30.00	75.00	325.00

Silver Certificates/1899/Blue Seal

Face Design: G.F.C. Smillie's engraving, *The Eagle of the Capitol,* spreads its wings over portraits of Lincoln and Grant, also engraved by Smillie. The Lincoln portrait was based on a photograph by Mathew Brady.

Back Design

No.	Signatures	Very Good	Very Fine	New
	Series above serial number on right			
47	Lyons-Roberts	12.00	20.00	95.00
	Series below serial number on right			
48	Lyons-Roberts	12.00	20.00	85.00
49	Lyons-Treat	12.00	20.00	80.00
50	Vernon-Treat	7.50	15.00	60.00
51(☆)	Vernon-McClung	7.50	16.50	65.00
	Series to right of seal			
52(☆)	Napier-McClung	7.50	15.00	60.00
53	Napier-Thompson	60.00	225.00	575.00
54(☆)	Parker-Burke	7.50	15.00	65.00
55(☆)	Teehee-Burke	7.50	15.00	60.00
56(☆)	Elliott-Burke	7.50	15.00	60.00
57(☆)	Elliott-White	7.50	15.00	60.00
58(☆)	Speelman-White	7.50	15.00	60.00

A total of 3,604,239,600 notes were printed for Nos. 47–58.

Silver Certificates/Blue Seal

Face Design:
Portrait of George
Washington; the
serial numbers
are blue.

Back Design:
Similar to No. 28.

No.	Date	Signatures	Notes Issued*	Very Good	Very Fine	New
59(☆)	1923	Speelman-White	2,431,837,347	10.00	17.50	37.50
60(☆)	1923	Woods-White	223,472,467	10.00	17.50	37.50
61(☆)	1923	Woods-Tate	4,686,186	17.50	55.00	100.00

*The number of notes issued was deduced by F.A. Nowak, see *Paper Money* 1971, Vol. 10 No. 1.
The official total number of notes issued is 2,659,996,000.

Treasury or Coin Notes

Face Design:
Edwin M. Stanton
held the office of
Secretary of War
under Abraham
Lincoln and An-
drew Johnson. The
portrait was designed
by G.W. Casilear and
engraved by
Charles Burt.

Back Design:
Engraved by
D.M. Cooper,
W.A. Copenhaver,
W.H. Dougal,
E.M. Hall,
E.E. Myers, and
G.U. Rose, Jr.

No.	Date	Signatures	Seal	Very Good	Very Fine	New
62	1890	Rosecrans-Huston	Brown	75.00	300.00	750.00
63	1890	Rosecrans-Nebeker	Brown	75.00	325.00	800.00
64	1890	Rosecrans-Nebeker	Red	75.00	300.00	750.00

A total of 7,160,000 notes were printed for Nos. 62-64.

Treasury or Coin Notes/Red Seal

Face Design:
Similar to No. 62;
the seal is now
smaller.

Back Design:
Engraved by
H.L. Chorlton,
E.M. Hall, J.
Kennedy,
and S.B. Many

No.	Date	Signatures	Very Good	Very Fine	New
65	1891	Rosecrans-Nebeker	35.00	75.00	225.00
66	1891	Tillman-Morgan	35.00	75.00	225.00
67	1891	Bruce-Roberts	35.00	75.00	225.00

A total of 57,544,000 notes were printed for Nos. 65-67.

Federal Reserve Bank Notes/1918

Face Design:
Portrait of George
Washington.

Back Design:
The eagle with flag
was engraved by
R. Ponickau.

No.	Bank	Government Signatures	Bank Signatures	Notes Issued	Very Good	Very Fine	New
68A1(☆)	Boston	T-B	Bullen-Morss		10.00	17.50	42.50
68A2(☆)	Boston	T-B	Willet-Morss	39,600,000	20.00	45.00	175.00
68A3(☆)	Boston	E-B	Willet-Morss		10.00	17.50	42.50
68B1(☆)	New York	T-B	Sailer-Strong		10.00	17.50	35.00
68B2(☆)	New York	T-B	Hendricks-Strong	106,724,000	10.00	17.50	35.00
68B3(☆)	New York	E-B	Hendricks-Strong		10.00	17.50	35.00
68C1	Philadelphia	T-B	Hardt-Passmore		10.00	17.50	30.00
68C2	Philadelphia	T-B	Dyer-Passmore	51,056,000	15.00	30.00	45.00
68C3	Philadelphia	E-B	Dyer-Passmore		15.00	32.50	60.00
68C4(☆)	Philadelphia	E-B	Dyer-Norris		10.00	17.50	30.00
68D1(☆)	Cleveland	T-B	Baxter-Fancher		8.00	15.00	30.00
68D2(☆)	Cleveland	T-B	Davis-Fancher		10.00	20.00	40.00
68D3	Cleveland	E-B	Davis-Fancher		8.00	15.00	32.50
68E1(☆)	Richmond	T-B	Keesee-Seay	23,384,000	12.50	30.00	65.00
68E2	Richmond	E-B	Keesee-Seay		12.50	30.00	65.00
68F1	Atlanta	T-B	Pike-McCord		12.00	25.00	45.00
68F2	Atlanta	T-B	Bell-McCord		15.00	35.00	75.00
68F3	Atlanta	T-B	Bell-Wellborn		12.00	25.00	45.00
68F4(☆)	Atlanta	E-B	Bell-Wellborn		12.00	22.50	47.50

Federal Reserve Bank Notes/1918

No.	Bank	Government Signatures	Bank Signatures	Notes Issued	Very Good	Very Fine	New
68G1(☆)	Chicago	T-B	McCloud-McDougal		8.00	17.50	35.00
68G2	Chicago	T-B	Cramer-McDougal	64,432,000	12.00	20.00	40.00
68G3(☆)	Chicago	E-B	Cramer-McDougal		8.00	15.00	32.50
68H1	St. Louis	T-B	Attebery-Wells		15.00	35.00	62.50
68H2	St. Louis	T-B	Attebery-Biggs	27,908,000	12.00	27.50	55.00
68H3	St. Louis	E-B	Attebery-Biggs		12.00	27.50	55.00
68H4(☆)	St. Louis	E-B	White-Biggs		15.00	30.00	60.00
68I1	Minneapolis	T-B	Cook-Wold		20.00	55.00	140.00
68I2	Minneapolis	T-B	Cook-Young		200.00	625.00	1,500.00
68I3(☆)	Minneapolis	E-B	Cook-Young		20.00	55.00	150.00
68J1(☆)	Kansas City	T-B	Anderson-Miller		12.00	20.00	40.00
68J2(☆)	Kansas City	E-B	Anderson-Miller	24,820,000	12.00	20.00	40.00
68J3	Kansas City	E-B	Helm-Miller		12.00	20.00	40.00
68K1(☆)	Dallas	T-B	Talley-VanZandt		12.00	25.00	50.00
68K2(☆)	Dallas	E-B	Talley-VanZandt	17,864,000	45.00	135.00	350.00
68K3	Dallas	E-B	Lawder-VanZandt		12.00	25.00	50.00
68L1(☆)	San Francisco	T-B	Clerk-Lynch		12.00	20.00	45.00
68L2	San Francisco	T-B	Clerk-Calkins	23,784,000	12.00	20.00	45.00
68L3	San Francisco	E-B	Clerk-Calkins		12.00	22.50	50.00
68L4	San Francisco	E-B	Ambrose-Calkins		12.00	22.50	50.00

T-B: Teehee-Burke
E-B: Elliot-Burke

United States Note/Red Seal

Face Design:
The portrait of
George Washington
as seen on all
small-size notes of
this denomination
was engraved by
G.F.C. Smillie in
1918.

Back Design

No.	Date	Signatures	Notes Printed	Very Fine	Extra Fine	New
69	1928	Woods-Woodin	1,872,012	15.00	22.50	35.00
69(☆)	1928(☆)	Woods-Woodin		250.00	625.00	1,000.00

Silver Certificates/Blue Seal

Face Design:
Standard portrait of
George Washington.

Back Design:
Same as No. 69.

No.	Date	Signatures	Notes Printed	Very Fine	Extra Fine	New
70	1928	Tate-Mellon	638,296,908	—	8.50	15.00
70(☆)	1928(☆)	Tate-Mellon			25.00	60.00
71	1928A	Woods-Mellon	2,267,809,500	—	7.00	12.00
71(☆)	1928A(☆)	Woods-Mellon			16.50	32.00
72	1928B	Woods-Mills	674,597,808	—	8.50	15.00
72(☆)	1928B(☆)	Woods-Mills			30.00	72.50
73	1928C	Woods-Woodin	5,364,348	50.00	165.00	365.00
73(☆)	1928C(☆)	Woods-Woodin		185.00	385.00	750.00
74	1928D	Julian-Woodin	14,451,372	65.00	110.00	265.00
74(☆)	1928D(☆)	Julian-Woodin		135.00	265.00	625.00
75	1928E	Julian-Morgenthau	3,519,324	265.00	450.00	850.00
75(☆)	1928E(☆)	Julian-Morgenthau			Extremely Rare	

Silver Certificates/Blue Seal

Face Design:
A blue *1* is seen on the left above blue serial numbers.

Back Design:
Same as No. 69.

No.	Date	Signatures	Notes Printed	Very Fine	Extra Fine	New
76	1934	Julian-Morgenthau	682,176,000	—	5.00	12.00
76(☆)	1934(☆)	Julian-Morgenthau	7,680,000	30.00	60.00	125.00

The proposed back design for the 1935 $1 silver certificate shows initials expressing approval below the signature of Franklin D. Roosevelt. The President must have had second thoughts, crossed out his signature, and then penned a few changes he thought would improve the design.

The revised design carries the signatures of the President and Julian Morgenthau, Secretary of the Treasury. This was the first time both the face and back design of The Great Seal of the United States appeared on United States paper money.

Silver Certificates/Blue Seal

No.	Date	Signatures	Notes Printed	Very Fine	Extra Fine	New
77	1935	Julian-Morgenthau	1,681,552,000	—	5.00	12.00
77(☆)	1935(☆)	Julian-Morgenthau		25.00	40.00	100.00
78	1935A	Julian-Morgenthau	6,111,832,000	—	3.00	6.00
78(☆)	1935A(☆)	Julian-Morgenthau		5.00	8.00	17.50
79	1935A*	Julian-Morgenthau	35,052,000	5.00	8.00	17.50
79(☆)	1935A(☆)	Julian-Morgenthau		60.00	75.00	165.00
80	1935A**	Julian-Morgenthau	26,916,000	4.00	8.00	22.50
80(☆)	1935A(☆)	Julian-Morgenthau		45.00	75.00	175.00

*These notes bearing a brown seal and serial numbers with Hawaii overprinted twice on the face and once across the back were issued for use in the Pacific during World War II.
**These notes with yellow seals were issed for use in North Africa during World War II.

EXPERIMENTAL NOTES
Series of 1928A & 1928B
To test the durability of another type of paper, an experimental run of $1 silver certificates Series 1928A and 1928B was issued during the early 1930's. These extremely scarce notes bear blocks X-B*, Y-B**, and Z-B**.

Series of 1935
The *Numismatic Scrapbook* (October 1964, p. 2664 and February 1968, p. 196) published the following letter from A. W. Hall, Director of the Bureau, answering an inquiry by Mr. R. H. Lloyd.

December 23, 1938

Dear Sir:
Receipt is acknowledged of your letter of December 16, 1938, enclosing silver certificate No. CO1,263,845B, and inquiring as to the reason for the suffix letter 'B.'
Your certificate is one of the 3,300,000 $1 silver certificates, series 1935, delivered in the latter part of the calendar year 1937, numbered from C00,000,001B to C03,300,000B, which was regular work. At the same time there was delivered an equal number of $1 silver certificates, series 1935, numbered from B00,000,001B to B03,300,000B. This was platered by a new method. These two deliveries were made for the purpose of determining any objectionable condition due to the new method of platering. The silver certificate is returned herewith.

Very truly yours,
A. W. Hall, Director.

The above letter fails to mention notes bearing A-B serial numbers, however 6,180,000 notes were printed.

*10,728.000 printed.   **10,248,000 printed.

Silver Certificates/Blue Seal

No.	Date	Signatures	Notes Printed	Very Fine	Extra Fine	New
81	1935A(R)	Julian-Morgenthau	1,184,000	30.00	50.00	95.00
81(☆)	1935A(R)(☆)	Julian-Morgenthau	12,000	285.00	385.00	525.00
82	1935A(S)	Julian-Morgenthau	1,184,000	20.00	40.00	75.00
82(☆)	1935A(S)	Julian-Morgenthau	12,000	285.00	325.00	525.00

The above notes were issued as part of an experiment by the Bureau in order to test a
new type of paper. The R signified the regular issue and the S identified the special paper.

No.	Date	Signatures	Notes Printed	Very Fine	Extra Fine	New
83	1935B	Julian-Vinson	806,612,000	3.00	5.00	12.50
83(☆)	1935(☆)	Julian-Vinson		12.50	25.00	50.00
84	1935C	Julian-Snyder	3,088,108,000	—	3.00	6.00
84(☆)	1935C(☆)	Julian-Snyder		4.00	7.50	17.50
85	1935D	Clark-Snyder ⎤		—	2.50	6.00
85(☆)	1935D(☆)	Clark-Snyder ⎟		—	3.50	10.00
			4,656,968,000			
86	1935D(ND)	Clark-Snyder ⎟		—	2.00	5.00
86(☆)	1935D(ND)(☆)	Clark-Snyder ⎦		—	4.00	7.50

During the printing of the 1935D series the back design was narrowed by about 1/16 of an inch. All
subsequent $1 issues were printed with the narrow back design.

No.	Date	Signatures	Notes Printed	Very Fine	Extra Fine	New
87	1935E	Priest-Humphrey	5,134,056,000	—	2.00	5.00
87(☆)	1935E(☆)	Priest-Humphrey		—	3.00	6.00
88	1935F	Priest-Anderson	1,173,360,000	—	—	3.00
88(☆)	1935F(☆)	Priest-Anderson	53,200,000	—	—	6.00
89	1935G	Smith-Dillon	194,600,000	—	—	3.00
89(☆)	1935G(☆)	Smith-Dillon	8,640,000	—	2.00	6.00

Silver Certificates/Blue Seal

During the printing of the 1935G series the motto "IN GOD WE TRUST " was added.
The 1935G listings that follow include the motto, as do all the $1 notes that follow.

No.	Date	Signatures	Notes Printed	Very Fine	Extra Fine	New
90	1935G	Smith-Dillon	31,320,000	—	2.50	5.00
90(☆)	1935G(☆)	Smith-Dillon	1,080,000	3.00	6.00	12.00
91	1935H	Granahan-Dillon	30,520,000	—	—	3.00
91(☆)	1935H(☆)	Granahan-Dillon	1,436,000	—	3.00	10.00
92	1957	Priest-Anderson	2,609,600,000	—	—	3.00
92(☆)	1957(☆)	Priest-Anderson	307,640,000	—	2.00	4.00
93	1957A	Smith-Dillon	1,594,080,000	—	—	3.00
93(☆)	1957A(☆)	Smith-Dillon	94,720,000	—	2.00	4.00
94	1957B	Granahan-Dillon	718,400,000	—	—	3.00
94(☆)	1957B(☆)	Granahan-Dillon	49,280,000	—	2.00	4.00

Federal Reserve Notes

Face Design

1963 Series. Signatures of Granahan-Dillon				1963A Series, signatures of Granahan-Fowler			
No.	**Bank**	**Notes Printed**	**New**	**No.**	**Bank**	**Notes Printed**	**New**
95A	Boston	87,680,000	3.00	96A	Boston	319,840,000	2.50
95A(☆)	Boston	6,400,000	3.50	96A(☆)	Boston	19,840,000	3.00
95B	New York	219,200,000	3.00	96B	New York	657,600,000	2.50
95B(☆)	New York	15,360,000	3.50	96B(☆)	New York	48,800,000	3.00
95C	Philadelphia	123,680,000	3.00	96C	Philadelphia	375,520,000	2.50
95C(☆)	Philadelphia	10,880,000	3.50	96C(☆)	Philadelphia	26,240,000	3.00
95D	Cleveland	108,320,000	3.00	96D	Cleveland	337,120,000	2.50
95D(☆)	Cleveland	8,320,000	3.50	96D(☆)	Cleveland	21.120,000	3.00
95E	Richmond	159,520,000	3.00	96E	Richmond	532,000,000	2.50
95E(☆)	Richmond	12,160,000	3.50	96E(☆)	Richmond	41,600,000	3.00
95F	Atlanta	221,120,000	3.00	96F	Atlanta	636,480,000	2.50
95F(☆)	Atlanta	19,200,000	3.50	96F(☆)	Atlanta	40,960,000	3.00
95G	Chicago	279,360,000	3.00	96G	Chicago	784,480,000	2.50
95G(☆)	Chicago	19,840,000	3.50	96G(☆)	Chicago	52,640,000	3.00
95H	St. Louis	99,840,000	3.00	96H	St. Louis	264,000,000	2.50
95H(☆)	St. Louis	9,600,000	3.50	96H(☆)	St. Louis	17,920,000	3.00
95I	Minneapolis	44,800,000	3.00	96I	Minneapolis	112,160,000	2.50
95I(☆)	Minneapolis	5,120,000	3.50	96I(☆)	Minneapolis	7,040,000	3.00
95J	Kansas City	88,960,000	3.00	96J	Kansas City	219,200,000	2.50
95J(☆)	Kansas City	8,960,000	3.50	96J(☆)	Kansas City	14,720,000	3.00
95K	Dallas	85,760,000	3.00	96K	Dallas	288,960,000	2.50
95K(☆)	Dallas	8,960,000	3.50	96K(☆)	Dallas	19,184,000	3.00
95L	San Francisco	199,999,999	3.00	96L	San Francisco	576,800,000	2.50
95L(☆)	San Francisco	14,720,000	3.50	96L(☆)	San Francisco	43,040,000	3.00

Federal Reserve Notes

1963B Series, signatures of Granahan-Barr

No.	Bank	Notes Printed	New
97B	New York	123,040,000	2.00
97B(☆)	New York	3,680,000	2.50
97E	Richmond	93,600,000	2.00
97E(☆)	Richmond	3,200,000	2.50
97G	Chicago	91,040,000	2.00
97G(☆)	Chicago	2,400,000	2.50
97J	Kansas City	44,800,000	2.00
97J(☆)	Kansas City	None printed	—
97L	San Francisco	106,400,000	2.00
97L(☆)	San Francisco	3,040,000	2.50

1969A Series, signatures of Kabis-Kennedy

No.	Bank	Notes Printed	New
99A	Boston	40,480,000	1.75
99A(☆)	Boston	1,120,000	2.00
99B	New York	122,400,000	1.75
99B(☆)	New York	6,240,000	2.00
99C	Philadelphia	44,960,000	1.75
99C(☆)	Philadelphia	1,760,000	2.00
99D	Cleveland	30,080,000	1.75
99D(☆)	Cleveland	1,280,000	2.00
99E	Richmond	66,080,000	1.75
99E(☆)	Richmond	3,200,000	2.00
99F	Atlanta	70,560,000	1.75
99F(☆)	Atlanta	2,400,000	2.00
99G	Chicago	75,680,000	1.75
99G(☆)	Chicago	4,480,000	2.00
99H	St. Louis	41,420,000	1.75
99H(☆)	St. Louis	1,280,000	2.00
99I	Minneapolis	21,760,000	1.75
99I(☆)	Minneapolis	640,000	2.50
99J	Kansas City	40,480,000	1.75
99J(☆)	Kansas City	1,120,000	2.50
99K	Dallas	27,520,000	1.75
99K(☆)	Dallas	None printed	—
99L	San Francisco	51,840,000	1.75
99L(☆)	San Francisco	3,840,000	2.00

1969 Series, Signatures of Elston-Kennedy

No.	Bank	Notes Printed	New
98A	Boston	99,200,000	1.75
98A(☆)	Boston	5,120,000	2.00
98B	New York	269,120,000	1.75
98B(☆)	New York	14,080,000	2.00
98C	Philadelphia	68,480,000	1.75
98C(☆)	Philadelphia	3,616,000	2.00
98D	Cleveland	120,480,000	1.75
98D(☆)	Cleveland	5,760,000	2.00
98E	Richmond	250,560,000	1.75
98E(☆)	Richmond	10,880,000	2.00
98F	Atlanta	85,120,000	1.75
98F(☆)	Atlanta	7,680,000	2.00
98G	Chicago	359,520,000	1.75
98G(☆)	Chicago	12,160,000	2.00
98H	St. Louis	74,880,000	1.75
98H(☆)	St. Louis	3,840,000	2.00
98I	Minneapolis	48,000,000	1.75
98I(☆)	Minneapolis	1,920,000	2.00
98J	Kansas City	95,360,000	1.75
98J(☆)	Kansas City	5,760,000	2.00
98K	Dallas	113,440,000	1.75
98K(☆)	Dallas	5,120,000	2.00
98L	San Francisco	226,240,000	1.75
98L(☆)	San Francisco	9,600,000	2.00

Federal Reserve Notes

1969B Series, Signatures of Kabis-Connally   1969C Series, Signatures of Banuelos-Connally

No.	Bank	Notes Printed	New	No.	Bank	Notes Printed	New
100A	Boston	94,720,000	1.50	101A	Boston	None	—
100A(☆)	Boston	1,920,000	2.00	101A(☆)	Boston	None	—
100B	New York	329,440,000	1.50	101B	New York	49,920,000	1.50
100B(☆)	New York	7,040,000	2.00	101B(☆)	New York	None	—
100C	Philadelphia	133,280,000	1.50	101C	Philadelphia	None	—
100C(☆)	Philadelphia	3,200,000	2.00	101C(☆)	Philadelphia	None	—
100D	Cleveland	91,520,000	1.50	101D	Cleveland	8,480,000	1.50
100D(☆)	Cleveland	4,480,000	2.00	101D(☆)	Cleveland	480,000	3.00
100E	Richmond	180,000,000	1.50	101E	Richmond	61,600,000	1.50
100E(☆)	Richmond	3,840,000	2.00	101E(☆)	Richmond	480,000	2.00
100F	Atlanta	200,000,000	1.50	101F	Atlanta	61,360,000	1.50
100F(☆)	Atlanta	3,840,000	2.00	101F(☆)	Atlanta	3,680,000	2.00
100G	Chicago	204,480,000	1.50	101G	Chicago	137,120,000	1.50
100G(☆)	Chicago	4,480,000	2.00	101G(☆)	Chicago	1,748,000	2.00
100H	St. Louis	59,520,000	1.50	101H	St. Louis	23,680,000	1.50
100H(☆)	St. Louis	1,920,000	2.00	101H(☆)	St. Louis	640,000	3.00
100I	Minneapolis	33,920,000	1.50	101I	Minneapolis	25,600,000	1.50
100I(☆)	Minneapolis	3,200,000	2.00	101I(☆)	Minneapolis	640,000	3.00
100J	Kansas City	67,200,000	1.50	101J	Kansas City	98,560,000	1.50
100J(☆)	Kansas City	2,560,000	2.00	101J(☆)	Kansas City	1,120,000	2.00
100K	Dallas	116,640,000	1.50	101K	Dallas	29,440,000	1.50
100K(☆)	Dallas	5,120,000	2.00	101K(☆)	Dallas	640,000	3.00
100L	San Francisco	208,960,000	1.50	101L	San Francisco	101,280,000	1.50
100L(☆)	San Francisco	5,760,000	2.00	101L(☆)	San Francisco	2,560,000	2.00

1969D Series, signatures of Banuelos-Shultz.

No.	Bank	Notes Printed	No.	Bank	Notes Printed
102A	Boston	187,040,000	102G	Chicago	378,080,000
102A(☆)	Boston	1,120,000	102G(☆)	Chicago	5,280,000
102B	New York	468,480,000	102H	St. Louis	168,480,000
102B(☆)	New York	4,480,000	102H(☆)	St. Louis	1,760,000
102C	Philadelphia	218,560,000	102I	Minneapolis	83,200,000
102C(☆)	Philadelphia	4,320,000	102I(☆)	Minneapolis	None Printed
102D	Cleveland	161,440,000	102J	Kansas City	185,760,000
102D(☆)	Cleveland	2,400,000	102J(☆)	Kansas City	3,040,000
102E	Richmond	374,240,000	102K	Dallas	158,240,000
102E(☆)	Richmond	8,480,000	102K(☆)	Dallas	6,240,000
102F	Atlanta	377,440,000	102L	San Francisco	400,640,000
102F(☆)	Atlanta	5,280,000	102L(☆)	San Francisco	6,400,000

1974 Series, signatures of Neff-Simon. These notes are still being issued.

United States Notes/1862/Red Seal

Face Design: The portrait of Alexander Hamilton was originally engraved by Joseph P. Ourdan.

Back Design

No.	Signatures	Notes Issued	Very Good	Very Fine	New
153	Chittenden-Spinner Type I: American Bank Note Company in left border		75.00	200.00	575.00
		17,035,514			
153a	Chittenden-Spinner Type II: National Bank Note Company in left border		50.00	200.00	525.00

United States Notes/1869/Red Seal

Face Design: Thomas Jefferson. The portrait was engraved by James Smilie.

Back Design

No.	Signatures	Notes Issued	Very Good	Very Fine	New
154	Allison-Spinner	25,255,960	75.00	250.00	800.00

United States Notes

Face Design:
Similar to No. 154
with the exception
of the changes
indicated below.

Back Design

(The following have a red ornament behind Washington, D.C.; the seal is on the left)

No.	Date	Signatures	Seal	Notes Issued	Very Good	Very Fine	New
155	1874	Allison-Spinner	Red-r	11,632,000	60.00	225.00	600.00
155A	1875A	Allison-New	Red-r		100.00	265.00	675.00
155B	1875B	Allison-New	Red-r	11,518,000	100.00	265.00	725.00
156	1875	Allison-New	Red-r		30.00	75.00	225.00
157	1875	Allison-Wyman	Red-r		30.00	75.00	200.00
158	1878	Allison-Gilfillan	Red-r	4,676,000	35.00	85.00	250.00
159	1878*	Scofield-Gilfillan	Red-r		300.00	1,250.00	5,500.00

(The following have a large seal on the right)

160	1880	Scofield-Gilfillan	Brown		30.00	60.00	160.00
161	1880	Bruce-Gilfillan	Brown	24,000,000**	30.00	60.00	200.00
162	1880	Bruce-Wyman	Brown		30.00	60.00	200.00

(The following have blue serial numbers)

163	1880	Rosecrans-Huston	Red		85.00	265.00	725.00
164	1880	Rosecrans-Huston	Brown	4,000,000**	60.00	225.00	575.00
165	1880	Rosecrans-Nebeker	Red-sc		40.00	75.00	275.00
166	1880	Tillman-Morgan	Red-sc		30.00	60.00	200.00

(The serial numbers on the following are red once again)

167(☆)	1917	Teehee-Burke	Red-sc		10.00	20.00	75.00
168(☆)	1917	Elliott-Burke	Red-sc	331,800,000**	10.00	20.00	60.00
169(☆)	1917	Elliott-White	Red-sc		10.00	20.00	60.00
170(☆)	1917	Speelman-White	Red-sc		10.00	20.00	70.00

*Five are known, two in new condition.
**Estimated figures based on observed serial numbers.
 r: with rays   sc: with scallops

National Bank Notes/First Charter Period/Red Seals

Face Design:
This note is generally referred to as "The Lazy Two." The vignette of *Stars and Stripes* was engraved by James M. Duthie. Jerome B. Chaffee, whose signature appears on this note, was the first president of the First National Bank of Denver, founded in 1865.

Back Design:
Louis Delnoce engraved the vignette of Sir Walter Raleigh exhibiting corn and tobacco to the English.

No.	Date	Signatures	Notes Issued	Very Good	Very Fine	New
171	Orig*	Colby-Spinner		250.00	600.00	1,500.00
172	Orig*	Jeffries-Spinner		1,500.00	2,500.00	4,500.00
173	Orig*	Allison-Spinner		250.00	600.00	1,500.00
174	1875	Allison-New	7,747,519**	200.00	550.00	1,500.00
175	1875	Allison-Wyman		200.00	550.00	1,500.00
176	1875	Allison-Gilfillan		200.00	550.00	1,600.00
177	1875	Scofield-Gilfillan		265.00	650.00	1,625.00

*These original notes did not have a date printed on the face.
**80,844 notes are outstanding.

Silver Certificates/1886

Face Design:
General Winfield
Scott Hancock rose
from Captain to
Commanding
General of the Army,
the rank he held for
20 years until his
death in 1886. The
portrait was engraved
by C. Burt.

Back Design:
Engraved by E.M.
Hall, S.S. Hurlbut,
D.M. Cooper, and L.
Delnoce.

No.	Signatures	Seal	Notes Printed	Very Good	Very Fine	New
178	Rosecrans-Jordan	Sm Red ⎤		50.00	100.00	365.00
179	Rosecrans-Hyatt	Sm Red		50.00	100.00	365.00
180	Rosecrans-Hyatt	Lg Red	21,000,000	60.00	100.00	385.00
181	Rosecrans-Huston	Lg Red		60.00	125.00	425.00
182	Rosecrans-Huston	Lg Brown ⎦		60.00	125.00	475.00

Silver Certificates/1891/Red Seal

Face Design: William Windom was born in Belmont, Ohio, on May 10, 1827. He moved to Minnesota and served as United States Senator. In 1881 Windom resigned to become Secretary of the Treasury, and he died in 1891 holding this office. His portrait was engraved by W.G. Phillips.

Back Design

No.	Signatures	Notes Printed	Very Good	Very Fine	New
183	Rosecrans-Nebeker	20,988.000	65.00	250.00	850.00
184	Tillman-Morgan		65.00	225.00	800.00

Silver Certificates/1896/Red Seal

Face Design: The five female figures, representing Science presenting Steam and Electricity to Industry and Commerce, were designed by Edwin H. Blashfield and engraved by Charles Schlecht and G.F.C. Smillie. The remainder of the face and back was designed by Thomas F. Morris. This design originally was intended for the unissued $50 note.

Back Design: The portraits of Robert Fulton and Samuel F.B. Morse probably were engraved by Lorenzo Hatch.

This note is the second of the educational series.

No.	Signatures	Notes Printed	Very Good	Very Fine	New
185	Tillman-Morgan		65.00	300.00	850.00
186	Bruce-Roberts	20,652,000*	65.00	300.00	825.00

*Serial numbers observed exceed this official number.

Silver Certificates/1899/Blue Seal

Face Design: Our first President is seen here between the figures of Mechanics and Agriculture. This note is of special interest since it bears the personal autograph of "Houston B. Teehee, Register of the Treasury." The engraver was G.F.C. Smillie.

Back Design

No.	Signatures	Notes Printed	Very Good	Very Fine	New
187	Lyons-Roberts		15.00	35.00	215.00
188	Lyons-Treat		20.00	47.50	225.00
189	Vernon-Treat		15.00	37.50	200.00
190(☆)	Vernon-McClung		15.00	37.50	200.00
191(☆)	Napier-McClung		15.00	37.50	200.00
192	Napier-Thompson	509,249.000	85.00	275.00	725.00
193(☆)	Parker-Burke		15.00	37.50	200.00
194(☆)	Teehee-Burke		15.00	37.50	200.00
195	Elliott-Burke		15.00	37.50	175.00
196(☆)	Speelman-White		15.00	37.50	175.00

Treasury or Coin Notes/1890

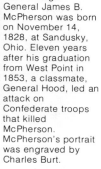

Face Design:
General James B.
McPherson was born
on November 14,
1828, at Sandusky,
Ohio. Eleven years
after his graduation
from West Point in
1853, a classmate,
General Hood, led an
attack on
Confederate troops
that killed
McPherson.
McPherson's portrait
was engraved by
Charles Burt.

Back Design:
Engraved by W.H.
Dougal, E.M. Hall,
A.L. Helm, and G.U.
Rose, Jr.

No.	Signatures	Seal	Notes Printed	Very Good	Very Fine	New
197	Rosecrans-Huston	Brown ⎤		135.00	375.00	1,075.00
198	Rosecrans-Nebeker	Brown	4,932,000	135.00	375.00	1,200.00
199	Rosecrans-Nebeker	Red ⎦		135.00	375.00	1,075.00

Treasury or Coin Notes/1891/Red Seal

Face Design: Similar to preceding note except seal is now smaller.

Back Design

No.	Signatures	Notes Printed	Very Good	Very Fine	New
200	Rosecrans-Nebeker		60.00	150.00	450.00
201	Tillman-Morgan	19,972,000	60.00	150.00	450.00
202	Bruce-Roberts		60.00	150.00	450.00

Federal Reserve Bank Notes/1918/Blue Seal

Face Design: The portrait of Thomas Jefferson is seen on the left. The letter and number in all four corners indicate the Federal Reserve district.

Back Design: World War I battleship.

No.	Bank	Government Signatures	Bank Signatures	Notes Issued	Very Good	Very Fine	New
203A1	Boston	T-B	Bullen-Morss		15.00	40.00	75.00
203A2	Boston	T-B	Willet-Morss	12,468,000	20.00	60.00	150.00
203A3(☆)	Boston	E-B	Willet-Morss		10.00	30.00	65.00
203B1(☆)	New York	T-B	Sailer-Strong		10.00	30.00	65.00
203B2(☆)	New York	T-B	Hendricks-Strong	15,216,000	10.00	30.00	65.00
203B3	New York	E-B	Hendricks-Strong		10.00	35.00	75.00
203C1	Philadelphia	T-B	Hardt-Passmore		15.00	40.00	85.00
203C2	Philadelphia	T-B	Dyer-Passmore		10.00	30.00	75.00
203C3	Philadelphia	E-B	Dyer-Passmore	8,004,000	30.00	125.00	300.00
203C4	Philadelphia	E-B	Dyer-Norris		10.00	35.00	75.00
203D1(☆)	Cleveland	T-B	Baxter-Fancher		20.00	50.00	100.00
203D2	Cleveland	T-B	Davis-Fancher		20.00	50.00	100.00
203D3(☆)	Cleveland	E-B	Davis-Fancher		15.00	40.00	100.00
203E1(☆)	Richmond	T-B	Keesee-Seay	3,736,000	30.00	90.00	200.00
203E3	Richmond	E-B	Keesee-Seay		25.00	60.00	175.00
203F1	Atlanta	T-B	Pike-McCord		20.00	55.00	150.00
203F2	Atlanta	T-B	Bell-McCord	2,300,000	40.00	115.00	285.00
203F3	Atlanta	E-B	Bell-McCord		30.00	80.00	185.00
203G1(☆)	Chicago	T-B	McCloud-McDougal		15.00	40.00	80.00
203G2	Chicago	T-B	Cramer-McDougal	9,528,000	15.00	40.00	85.00
203G3	Chicago	E-B	Cramer-McDougal		10.00	40.00	75.00

T-B: Teehee-Burke   E-B: Elliott-Burke

Federal Reserve Bank Notes/1918/Blue Seal

No.	Bank	Government Signatures	Bank Signatures	Notes Issued	Very Good	Very Fine	New
203H1	St. Louis	T-B	Attebery-Wells		25.00	75.00	175.00
203H2	St. Louis	T-B	Attebery-Biggs	3,300,000	30.00	90.00	225.00
203H3	St. Louis	E-B	Attebery-Biggs		30.00	125.00	235.00
203H4	St. Louis	E-B	White-Biggs		30.00	90.00	225.00
203I1	Minneapolis	T-B	Cook-Wold		25.00	90.00	200.00
203I3	Minneapolis	E-B	Cook-Young		30.00	90.00	225.00
203J1 (☆)	Kansas City	T-B	Anderson-Miller	2,652,000	20.00	80.00	175.00
203J3	Kansas City	E-B	Helm-Miller		30.00	90.00	225.00
203K1	Dallas	T-B	Talley-Van Zandt	1,252,000	30.00	90.00	225.00
203K3	Dallas	E-B	Talley-Van Zandt		30.00	90.00	225.00
203L1 (☆)	San Francisco	T-B	Clerk-Lynch		25.00	80.00	180.00
203L3	San Francisco	E-B	Clerk-Calkins	3,188,000	25.00	80.00	180.00
203L4 (☆)	San Francisco	E-B	Ambrose-Calkins		25.00	80.00	180.00

T-B: Teehee-Burke
E-B: Elliott-Burke

United States Notes/Red Seal

Face Design: Portrait of Thomas Jefferson.

Back Design: At the age of 20 Thomas Jefferson began building his home, Monticello, on Carter's Mountain. Now a museum, it contains numerous inventions by Jefferson as an architect, musician, and lawyer.

No.	Date	Signatures	Notes Printed	Very Fine	Extra Fine	New
204	1928	Tate-Mellon	55,889,424	10.00	20.00	47.50
204(☆)	1928(☆)	Tate-Mellon		35.00	65.00	135.00
204A	1928A	Woods-Mellon	46,859,136	20.00	50.00	130.00
204A(☆)	1928A(☆)	Woods-Mellon		65.00	175.00	300.00
204B	1928B	Woods-Mills	9,001,632	90.00	225.00	450.00
294B(☆)	1928B(☆)	Woods-Mills		200.00	400.00	750.00
204C	1928C	Julian-Morgenthau	86,584,008	7.50	12.00	30.00
204C(☆)	1928C(☆)	Julian-Morgenthau		45.00	75.00	165.00
204D	1928D	Julian-Morgenthau	146,381,364	6.00	10.00	20.00
204D(☆)	1928D(☆)	Julian-Morgenthau		12.50	20.00	45.00
204E	1928E	Julian-Vinson	5,261,016	9.00	17.50	45.00
204E(☆)	1928E(☆)	Julian-Vinson		250.00	400.00	800.00
204F	1928F	Julian-Snyder	43,349,292	5.00	9.00	20.00
204F(☆)	1928F(☆)	Julian-Snyder		10.00	17.50	37.50
204G	1928G	Clark-Snyder	52,208,000	3.50	7.50	12.00
204G(☆)	1928G(☆)	Clark-Snyder		6.00	12.50	22.00

United States Notes/Red Seal

Face Design: A grey 2 replaces the seal, which is now seen on the right.

Back Design: See preceding note.

No.	Date	Signatures	Notes Printed	Extra Fine	New
205	1953	Priest-Humphrey	45,360,000	4.00	10.00
205(☆)	1953(☆)	Priest-Humphrey	2,160,000	6.00	15.00
205A	1953A	Priest-Anderson	18,000,000	4.00	10.00
205A(☆)	1953A(☆)	Priest-Anderson	720,000	6.00	15.00
205B	1953B	Smith-Dillon	10,800,000	4.00	7.00
205B(☆)	1953B(☆)	Smith-Dillon	720,000	5.00	9.00
205C	1953C	Granahan-Dillon	5,760,000	5.00	7.00
205C(☆)	1953C	Granahan-Dillon	360,000	6.00	10.00

Face Design: Similar to preceding note.

Back Design: "IN GOD WE TRUST" was added to the 1963 issue. The engravers were A. Dintaman, and G.A. Payne.

206	1963	Granahan-Dillon	15,360,000	4.00	6.00
206(☆)	1963(☆)	Granahan-Dillon	640,000	5.00	8.50
206A	1963A	Granahan-Fowler	3,200,000	4.00	6.00
206A(☆)	1963A(☆)	Granahan-Fowler	640,000	5.00	8.50

Federal Reserve Notes/Green Seal

Face Design:
The portrait of
Thomas Jefferson is
based on a painting
by Gilbert Stuart, as
are Nos. 204–206.

Back Design:
The original painting
by John Trumbull of
*The Signing of The
Declaration of
Independence* hangs
in the Trumbull
Gallery at Yale
University. See
No. 1152.

No.	Date	Signatures	Notes Printed
207	1976	Simon-Neff	400,000,000*

*Anticipated annual production for all districts.

Demand Notes/1861

Face Design:
The statue of Freedom, which adorns the top of the Capitol in Washington, was created by Thomas Crawford. The statue as seen here was engraved by Owen G. Hanks. A portrait of Alexander Hamilton is on the right.

Back Design

No.	Payable At	Notes Issued	Good	Very Good	Fine
242A	Boston		300.00	400.00	750.00
242B	New York		300.00	400.00	750.00
242C	Philadelphia	4,360,000*	300.00	400.00	750.00
242D	Cincinnati		1,750.00	3,250.00	4,000.00
242H	St. Louis		2,250.00	3,500.00	4,500.00

A total of $60,030,000, including the $10 and $20 notes of this series, was issued, all without the Treasury Seal and the signatures of the Treasurer and the Register of the Treasury. Officials representing these two offices signed for them, and the words "for the" preceding the titles were sometimes written by hand. These notes are exceedingly rare with the exception of notes payable at New York.

*According to records of 1927, 4,248 notes were outstanding.

United States Notes/Red Seal

Face Design:
Similar to preceding
note with the
addition of the
Treasury Seal and
the deletion of the
words "On Demand."

Back Design:
All the following
notes bear the
signatures of
Chittenden-Spinner.
(Nos. 243 and 243A
have the first
obligation reverse.)

No.	Date		Notes Issued	Very Good	Very Fine	New
243	1862*			40.00	100.00	300.00
243a	1862	("Series" on face)		65.00	125.00	375.00
243b	1862		19,332,714**	50.00	175.00	525.00
244	1863	(One serial number)		50.00	125.00	350.00
244a	1863	(Two serial numbers)		50.00	125.00	300.00

Nos. 243b-244a have the second obligation reverse.

*$100,000 were printed, and this figure is included in the total notes printed.
**20,200,000 notes were printed, 99,726 were outstanding according to records of 1889.

United States Notes

Face Design:
The portrait of
Andrew Jackson was
based on a painting
by Thomas Sully;
Alfred Sealey
executed the
engraving. *The
Pioneer*, an
engraving by Henry
Gugler, occupies the
center of the note.

Back Design

No.	Date	Signatures	Notes Issued	Very Good	Very Fine	New
245	1869	Allison-Spinner	10,116,352	32.50	85.00	325.00

United States Notes

Face Design:
Similar to No. 245
with the exception
of the changes
indicated below.

Back Design:
Engraved by
L. G. Huber.

No.	Date	Signatures	Seal	Notes Issued	Very Good	Very Fine	New
The following have a red ornament behind Washington, D.C.; the seal is on the left.							
246A	1875A	Allison-New	Sm Red-r		25.00	100.00	425.00
246B	1875B	Allison-New	Sm Red-r	9,236,000	25.00	125.00	285.00
247	1875	Allison-New	Sm Red-r		25.00	75.00	250.00
248	1875	Allison-Wyman	Sm Red-r		25.00	60.00	250.00
249	1878	Allison-Gilfillan	Sm Red-r	2,603,200	45.00	185.00	450.00
The following have a large seal on the right.							
250	1880	Scofield-Gilfillan	Brown		20.00	60.00	200.00
251	1880	Bruce-Gilfillan	Brown		20.00	50.00	200.00
252	1880	Bruce-Wyman	Brown		20.00	50.00	200.00
The following have blue serial numbers.							
253	1880	Bruce-Wyman	Lg Red		25.00	80.00	235.00
254	1880	Bruce-Wyman	Lg Red-sp		50.00	145.00	425.00
255	1880	Rosecrans-Jordan	Lg Red	72,992,000	25.00	85.00	285.00
256	1880	Rosecrans-Hyatt	Lg Red	(printed)	45.00	85.00	300.00
257	1880	Rosecrans-Huston	Lg Red-sp		50.00	185.00	475.00
258	1880	Rosecrans-Huston	Brown		25.00	85.00	275.00
259	1880	Rosecrans-Nebeker	Brown		55.00	185.00	475.00
260	1880	Rosecrans-Nebeker	Sm Red-sc		15.00	60.00	200.00
261	1880	Tillman-Morgan	Sm Red-sc		15.00	50.00	200.00
262	1880	Bruce-Roberts	Sm Red-sc		15.00	50.00	200.00
263	1880	Lyons-Roberts	Sm Red-sc		15.00	50.00	185.00

r: with rays   sp: with spikes   sc: with scallops

United States Notes

No.	Date	Signatures	Seal	Notes Printed	Very Good	Very Fine	New

The following have a red *V* and the word "Dollars" added; the serial numbers are red once again.

No.	Date	Signatures	Seal	Notes Printed	Very Good	Very Fine	New
264	1907	Vernon-Treat	Red-sc		12.50	25.00	85.00
265	1907	Vernon-McClung	Red-sc		12.50	25.00	85.00
266	1907	Napier-McClung	Red-sc		13.50	25.00	85.00
267	1907	Napier-Thompson	Red-sc		85.00	250.00	675.00
268	1907	Parker-Burke	Red-sc	440,128,000*	10.00	25.00	85.00
269(☆)	1907	Teehee-Burke	Red-sc		10.00	25.00	85.00
270(☆)	1907	Elliott-Burke	Red-sc		12.50	25.00	100.00
271(☆)	1907	Elliott-White	Red-sc		10.00	20.00	70.00
272(☆)	1907	Speelman-White	Red-sc		10.00	17.50	65.00
273(☆)	1907	Woods-White	Red-sc		15.00	40.00	100.00

*This figure is tabulated from the Bureau of Engraving and Printing Annual Reports. Serial numbers observed indicate that the figure could be higher.
sc: with scallops

National Bank Notes/First Charter Period

Face Design:
Columbus In Sight of Land and *America Presented To The Old World* were both designed by Charles Fenton and engraved by Charles Burt.

Back Design:
The *Landing of Columbus* was taken from a painting by John Vanderlyn; Walter Shirlaw was the engraver.

No.	Date	Signatures	Seal	Very Good	Very Fine	New
274	Orig*	Chittenden-Spinner	Red-r	70.00	200.00	500.00
275	Orig	Colby-Spinner	Red-r	70.00	200.00	525.00
276	Orig	Jeffries-Spinner	Red-r	450.00	1,850.00	4,000.00
277	Orig	Allison-Spinner	Red-r	70.00	175.00	475.00
278	1875	Allison-New	Red-sc	70.00	175.00	475.00
279	1875	Allison-Wyman	Red-sc	70.00	175.00	475.00
280	1875	Allison-Gilfillan	Red-sc	70.00	175.00	475.00
281	1875	Scofield-Gilfillan	Red-sc	70.00	175.00	475.00
282	1875	Bruce-Gilfillan	Red-sc	70.00	175.00	475.00
283	1875	Bruce-Wyman	Red-sc	70.00	175.00	475.00
284	1875	Bruce-Jordan	Red-sc	—	—	—
285	1875	Rosecrans-Huston	Red-sc	70.00	185.00	450.00
286	1875	Rosecrans-Jordan	Red-sc	70.00	185.00	450.00

*The original notes did not have the date printed on the face, which was December 21, 1863.
 r: with rays   sc: with scallops

National Bank Notes/1882/Second Charter Period/First Issue/Brown Seal

Face Design: James A. Garfield was born in Orange, Ohio, on November 18, 1831. After serving in the Ohio Senate, he was elected to the Presidency. He was assassinated seven months later. This portrait was based on an autotype by Edward Bierstadt; the engraving was executed by Lorenzo Hatch.

Back Design: Brown with green numbers.

No.	Signatures	Very Good	Very Fine	New
287	Bruce-Gilfillan	25.00	125.00	350.00
288	Bruce-Wyman	25.00	125.00	350.00
289	Bruce-Jordan	35.00	175.00	385.00
290	Rosecrans-Jordan	25.00	125.00	350.00
291	Rosecrans-Hyatt	25.00	125.00	350.00
292	Rosecrans-Huston	25.00	125.00	350.00
293	Rosecrans-Nebeker	25.00	125.00	350.00
294	Rosecrans-Morgan	200.00	550.00	1,000.00
295	Tillman-Morgan	25.00	125.00	360.00
296	Tillman-Roberts	25.00	125.00	375.00
297	Bruce-Roberts	25.00	125.00	360.00
298	Lyons-Roberts	25.00	125.00	350.00
299	Vernon-Treat	40.00	90.00	425.00

National Bank Notes/1882/Second Charter Period/Second Issue/Blue Seal

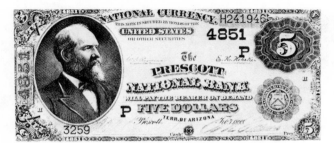

Face Design:
Similar to
preceding note.

Back Design: Green.

No.	Signatures	Very Good	Very Fine	New
300	Rosecrans-Huston	35.00	150.00	325.00
301	Rosecrans-Nebeker	35.00	150.00	325.00
302	Rosecrans-Morgan	200.00	550.00	900.00
303	Tillman-Morgan	35.00	150.00	325.00
304	Tillman-Roberts	40.00	175.00	425.00
305	Bruce-Roberts	40.00	175.00	425.00
306	Lyons-Roberts	40.00	150.00	325.00
307	Vernon-Treat	40.00	175.00	425.00
308	Napier-McClung	200.00	475.00	850.00

National Bank Notes/1882/Second Charter Period/Third Issue/Blue Seal

Face Design: Similar
to preceding note.

Back Design: Green.

No.	Signatures	Very Good	Very Fine	New
309	Tillman-Morgan	40.00	200.00	450.00
310	Tillman-Roberts	90.00	350.00	750.00
311	Lyons-Roberts	40.00	185.00	350.00
312	Bruce-Roberts	90.00	365.00	750.00
313	Vernon-Treat	65.00	275.00	500.00
314	Napier-McClung	65.00	275.00	500.00
315	Teehee-Burke		Possible existence	

National Bank Notes/1902/Third Charter Period

Face Design:
Benjamin Harrison,
twenty-third
President, was born
on August 20, 1833.
His great grandfather
was a signer of the
Declaration of
Independence, his
grandfather was our
ninth President, and
his father served in
the House of Rep-
resentatives. This
note was designed
by Ostrander Smith
and engraved by
George F.C. Smillie.

Back Design: The
design is the same
for all three issues;
however, the second
issue only has
"1902–1908" added.
G.F.C. Smillie was
the engraver.

No.	Signatures	Very Good	Very Fine	New
	First Issue—Red Seal			
316	Lyons-Roberts	50.00	150.00	300.00
317	Lyons-Treat	50.00	200.00	400.00
318	Vernon-Treat	85.00	235.00	475.00
	Second Issue—Blue Seal			
319	Lyons-Roberts	25.00	35.00	90.00
320	Lyons-Treat	25.00	40.00	90.00
321	Vernon-Treat	25.00	35.00	90.00
322	Vernon-McClung	25.00	35.00	90.00
323	Napier-McClung	25.00	40.00	90.00
324	Napier-Thompson	55.00	100.00	250.00
325	Napier-Burke	30.00	50.00	125.00
326	Parker-Burke	30.00	50.00	125.00
327	Teehee-Burke	75.00	200.00	485.00
	Third Issue—Blue Seal			
328	Lyons-Roberts	25.00	30.00	80.00
329	Lyons-Treat	25.00	30.00	80.00
330	Vernon-McClung	25.00	30.00	80.00

National Bank Notes

No.	Signatures	Very Good	Very Fine	New
331	Vernon-Treat	25.00	30.00	80.00
332	Napier-McClung	25.00	35.00	80.00
333	Napier-Thompson	40.00	125.00	225.00
334	Napier-Burke	25.00	35.00	75.00
335	Parker-Burke	25.00	35.00	75.00
336	Teehee-Burke	25.00	35.00	75.00
337	Elliott-Burke	25.00	35.00	75.00
338	Elliott-White	25.00	35.00	75.00
339	Speelman-White	25.00	35.00	75.00
340	Woods-White	25.00	50.00	135.00
341	Woods-Tate	30.00	75.00	150.00
342	Jones-Woods	175.00	600.00	1,000.00

National Gold Bank Notes/Red Seal

Face Design:
See No. 282 for
complete description.

Back Design:
The gold coin
vignette was
engraved by James
Smillie.

The following notes all bear the signatures of Allison-Spinner.

No.	Date	Issuing Bank	City	Notes Issued*	Good	Very Good
343	1870	First National Gold Bank	San Francisco	33,000	300.00	465.00
344	1872	National Gold Bank and Trust Company	San Francisco	17,840	325.00	525.00
345	1872	National Gold Bank of D.O. Mills and Company	Sacramento	7,960	350.00	575.00
346	1873	First National Gold Bank	Santa Barbara	2,000	5 Known	
347	1873	First National Gold Bank	Stockton	4,000	350.00	575.00
348	1874	Farmers National Gold Bank	San Jose	8,028	350.00	575.00

*3,451 notes are outstanding.

Silver Certificates/1886

Face Design:
Lorenzo Hatch
engraved this portrait
of Ulysses S. Grant.

Back Design:
The silver dollars
bear the motto "IN
GOD WE TRUST."
The official adoption
of this phrase on
our paper money did
not come until 1957.

No.	Signatures	Seal	Notes Issued	Very Good	Very Fine	New
349	Rosecrans-Jordan	Red Small		75.00	400.00	2,200.00
350	Rosecrans-Hyatt	Red Small		75.00	400.00	2,300.00
351	Rosecrans-Hyatt	Red Large		75.00	400.00	2,300.00
352	Rosecrans-Huston	Red Large	34,080,000	75.00	400.00	2,300.00
353	Rosecrans-Huston	Brown Large		75.00	400.00	2,600.00
354	Rosecrans-Nebeker	Brown Large		75.00	435.00	2,600.00
355	Rosecrans-Nebeker	Brown Large		75.00	500.00	2,800.00

1891 Series

Face Design: Similar
to preceding note.

Back Design

No.	Signatures	Seal	Notes Printed	Very Good	Very Fine	New
356	Rosecrans-Nebeker	Red sc		30.00	150.00	500.00
357	Tillman-Morgan	Red	31,556,000	30.00	150.00	500.00

sc: scallops

Silver Certificates/1896/Red Seal

This painting measuring approximately four feet across was the original design for Nos. 358-360. Mr. Shirlaw was paid $800 for his efforts.

Face Design: Mr. Shirlaw's central vignette was retained; Thomas F. Morris redesigned the remaining portions, and G.F.C. Smillie executed the engraving.

Back Design: Thomas F. Morris created this design. The female head in the center which greatly resembles the designer's wife, was engraved by G.F.C. Smillie. The portraits of Grant and Sherman were engraved by Lorenzo Hatch.

This is the third note of the educational series.

No.	Signatures	Notes Printed	Very Good	Very Fine	New
358	Tillman-Morgan		90.00	300.00	1500.00
359	Bruce-Roberts	35,012,000*	90.00	300.00	1550.00
360	Lyons-Roberts		125.00	325.00	1600.00

This note is considered by many to be one of the most beautiful notes printed by the Bureau. One man felt differently. As head of the Watch and Ward Society, Anthony Comstock felt the figure representing Electricity on the face displayed just a little too much flesh. He forced the Treasury Department to stop printing these "dirty dollars" and had the Treasury recall as many notes as possible. As a result these exquisite notes are scarce in new condition.

---

*34,932,000 issued.

Silver Certificates/1899/Blue Seal

Face Design: The handsome Indian portrait is that of Chief Running Antelope. The war bonnet used for this portrait is the Pawnee type. G.F.C. Smillie was the engraver.

Back Design: Engraved by E.M. Hall, E.E. Myers, R. Ponickau, and G.U. Rose, Jr.

No.	Signatures	Notes Issued	Very Good	Very Fine	New
361	Lyons-Roberts		35.00	100.00	325.00
362	Lyons-Treat		35.00	100.00	325.00
363	Vernon-Treat		35.00	85.00	350.00
364(☆)	Vernon-McClung		35.00	85.00	350.00
365(☆)	Napier-McClung		35.00	85.00	350.00
366	Napier-Thompson	556,054,000	100.00	325.00	800.00
367(☆)	Parker-Burke		35.00	85.00	350.00
368(☆)	Teehee-Burke		35.00	85.00	350.00
369(☆)	Elliot-Burke		35.00	85.00	350.00
370(☆)	Elliot-White		35.00	85.00	350.00
371	Speelman-White		35.00	85.00	350.00

Face Design: The porthole portrait of Lincoln was based on a photograph by Mathew Brady.

Back Design: The obverse of the Great Seal of the United States as seen here was engraved by R. Ponickau.

No.	Signatures	Notes Printed	Very Good	Very Fine	New
372(☆)	Speelman-White	6,316,000	35.00	165.00	400.00

Treasury or Coin Notes/1890

Face Design: Southampton, Virginia, was the place of George H. Thomas's birth on July 11, 1816. Twenty-four years later he graduated from West Point, where he served as an instructor from 1851 to 1854. Thomas won numerous victories for the Union Army during the Civil War. His portrait was engraved by L.G. Hatch.

Back Design

No.	Signatures	Seal	Notes Printed	Very Good	Very Fine	New
373	Rosecrans-Huston	Brown ⎤		90.00	350.00	900.00
374	Rosecrans-Nebeker	Brown	7,200,000	90.00	400.00	1,050.00
375	Rosecrans-Nebeker	Red ⎦		90.00	350.00	900.00

1891 Series—Red Seal

Face Design: Similar to preceding note.

Back Design

No.	Signatures	Notes Printed	Very Good	Very Fine	New
376	Rosecrans-Nebeker ⎤		65.00	150.00	475.00
377	Tillman-Morgan		65.00	150.00	450.00
378	Bruce-Roberts	17,260,000*	65.00	150.00	450.00
379	Lyons-Roberts ⎦		65.00	300.00	800.00

*16,948,000 notes were issued.

Federal Reserve Notes/1914/Red Seal

Face Design:
The number and letter in the seal to the left of Lincoln signify the Federal Reserve district.

Back Design:
Columbus is seen sighting land on the left, and the *Landing of the Pilgrims* is seen on the right.

The following bear the signatures of Burke-McAdoo.

No.	Bank	Very Good	Very Fine	New
380A	Boston	20.00	50.00	150.00
380B	New York	15.00	50.00	115.00
380C	Philadelphia	15.00	50.00	115.00
380D	Cleveland	15.00	50.00	115.00
380E	Richmond	15.00	50.00	125.00
380F	Atlanta	15.00	50.00	125.00
380G	Chicago	15.00	50.00	115.00
380H	St. Louis	15.00	50.00	115.00
380I	Minneapolis	15.00	50.00	125.00
380J	Kansas City	15.00	50.00	115.00
380K	Dallas	15.00	50.00	125.00
380L	San Francisco	25.00	65.00	185.00

The first day of issue for the above was November 16, 1914.

Federal Reserve Notes/1914/Blue Seal

No.	Bank	Signatures	Notes Printed	Notes Issued	Very Fine	New
381A1(☆)	Boston	Burke-McAdoo			12.50	30.00
381A2(☆)	Boston	Burke-Glass	92,008,000	90,400,000	17.50	40.00
381A3	Boston	Burke-Houston			12.50	30.00
381A4	Boston	White-Mellon			12.50	30.00
381B1	New York	Burke-McAdoo			10.00	27.50
381B2	New York	Burke-Glass	297,852,000	297,852,000	15.00	37.50
381B3(☆)	New York	Burke-Houston			10.00	27.50
381B4	New York	White-Mellon			12.50	30.00
381C1	Philadelphia	Burke-McAdoo			10.00	27.50
381C2	Philadelphia	Burke-Glass	103,824,000	103,824,000	15.00	37.50
381C3(☆)	Philadelphia	Burke-Houston			12.50	30.00
381C4	Philadelphia	White-Mellon			12.50	30.00
381D1	Cleveland	Burke-McAdoo			15.00	35.00
381D2	Cleveland	Burke-Glass	73,216,000	73,216,000	15.00	37.50
381D3	Cleveland	Burke-Houston			12.50	30.00
381D4	Cleveland	White-Mellon			12.50	30.00
381E1	Richmond	Burke-McAdoo			15.00	37.50
381E2	Richmond	Burke-Glass	49,444,000	45,932,000	17.50	40.00
381E3	Richmond	Burke-Houston			15.00	37.50
381E4	Richmond	White-Mellon			12.50	30.00
381F1	Atlanta	Burke-McAdoo			12.50	30.00
381F2	Atlanta	Burke-Glass	55,000,000	54,476,000	20.00	50.00
381F3	Atlanta	Burke-Houston			12.50	30.00
381F4	Atlanta	White-Mellon			12.50	30.00
381G1	Chicago	Burke-McAdoo			12.50	30.00
381G2	Chicago	Burke-Glass	164,876,000	164,876,000	15.00	35.00
381G3(☆)	Chicago	Burke-Houston			12.50	30.00
381G4	Chicago	White-Mellon			10.00	27.50
381H1	St. Louis	Burke-McAdoo			12.50	30.00
381H2	St. Louis	Burke-Glass	41,704,000	41,704,000	15.00	35.00
381H3	St. Louis	Burke-Houston			12.50	30.00
381H4	St. Louis	White-Mellon			10.00	27.50
381I1	Minneapolis	Burke-McAdoo			12.50	30.00
381I2	Minneapolis	Burke-Glass	30,116,000	29,280,000	20.00	50.00
381I3	Minneapolis	Burke-Houston			15.00	35.00
381I4	Minneapolis	White-Mellon			12.50	30.00

Federal Reserve Notes/1914/Blue Seal

No.	Bank	Signatures	Notes Printed	Notes Issued	Very Fine	New
381J1	Kansas City	Burke-McAdoo			12.50	30.00
381J2	Kansas City	Burke-Glass	44,396,000	43,928,000	17.50	42.50
381J3(☆)	Kansas City	Burke-Houston			12.50	30.00
381J4	Kansas City	White-Mellon			10.00	27.50
381K1	Dallas	Burke-McAdoo			22.50	55.00
381K2	Dallas	Burke-Glass	29,416,000	28,536,000	20.00	50.00
381K3	Dallas	Burke-Houston			12.50	30.00
381K4	Dallas	White-Mellon			10.00	27.50
381L1	San Francisco	Burke-McAdoo			15.00	35.00
381L2	San Francisco	Burke-Glass	92,168,000	91,848,000	20.00	50.00
381L3	San Francisco	Burke-Houston			15.00	35.00
381L4	San Francisco	White-Mellon			15.00	35.00

Federal Reserve Bank Notes/Blue Seal

Face Design:
Portrait of Abraham Lincoln.

Back Design:
Similar to No. 380.

No.	Bank	Date	Gov't. Sigs.	Bank Signatures	Notes Issued	Very Good	Very Fine	New
382A(☆)	Boston*	1918	T-B	Bullen-Morss	440,000	185.00	750.00	1,250.00
382B	New York	1918	T-B	Hendricks-Strong	6,400,000	20.00	40.00	120.00
382C1	Philadelphia	1918	T-B	Hardt-Passmore	1,600,000	20.00	40.00	120.00
382C2	Philadelphia	1918	T-B	Dyer-Passmore		20.00	45.00	135.00
382D1(☆)	Cleveland	1918	T-B	Baxter-Fancher		20.00	40.00	120.00
382D2	Cleveland	1918	T-B	Davis-Fancher		27.50	65.00	130.00
382D3	Cleveland	1918	E-B	Davis-Fancher		15.00	50.00	110.00
382F1	Atlanta	1915	T-B	Bell-Wellborn		90.00	300.00	500.00
382F2	Atlanta	1915	T-B	Pike-McCord		60.00	150.00	275.00
382F3	Atlanta	1918	T-B	Pike-McCord		20.00	50.00	110.00
382F4	Atlanta	1918	T-B	Bell-Wellborn		20.00	50.00	110.00
382F5	Atlanta	1918	E-B	Bell-Wellborn		20.00	50.00	120.00
382G1	Chicago	1915	T-B	McLallen-McDougal		20.00	50.00	100.00
382G2	Chicago	1918	T-B	McCloud-McDougal		20.00	50.00	110.00
382G3	Chicago	1918	T-B	Cramer-McDougal		22.50	75.00	150.00
382H1	St. Louis	1918	T-B	Attebery-Wells	1,524,000	27.50	75.00	150.00
382H2	St. Louis	1918	T-B	Attebery-Biggs		27.50	75.00	150.00
382H3	St. Louis	1918	E-B	White-Biggs		27.50	75.00	150.00
382I	Minneapolis	1918	T-B	Cook-Wold		50.00	150.00	350.00
382J1	Kansas City	1915	T-B	Anderson-Miller	4,802,000	27.50	75.00	165.00
382J2	Kansas City	1915	T-B	Cross-Miller		27.50	75.00	165.00
382J3	Kansas City	1915	T-B	Helm-Miller		50.00	140.00	275.00
382J4(☆)	Kansas City	1918	T-B	Anderson-Miller		30.00	75.00	175.00
382J5	Kansas City	1918	E-B	Helm-Miller		30.00	75.00	175.00
382K1	Dallas	1915	T-B	Hoopes-Van Zandt	328,000	50.00	135.00	275.00
382K2	Dallas	1915	T-B	Talley-Van Zandt		60.00	175.00	325.00
382K3	Dallas	1918	T-B	Talley-Van Zandt	500,000	30.00	85.00	175.00
382L1	San Francisco	1915	T-B	Clerk-Lynch	336,000	42.50	140.00	300.00
382L2	San Francisco	1918	T-B	Clerk-Lynch	500,000	42.50	125.00	250.00
382L3	San Francisco	1914**	T-B	Clerk-Lynch		150.00	400.00	1,200.00

*375 notes are outstanding T-B: Teehee-Burke E-B: Elliott-Burke
**This note bears the incorrect date of May 18; it should be May 20.

United States Notes/Red Seal

Face Design

Back Design:
On May 30, 1922, 57 years after the idea was conceived, the Lincoln Memorial was dedicated. When President Lincoln died in 1865 there were 36 states, which are symbolized by the 36 columns surrounding this edifice. Henry Bacon was the architect, and Daniel C. French carved the 19-foot statue of Lincoln.

No.	Date	Signatures	Notes Printed	Very Fine	Extra Fine	New
383	1928	Woods-Mellon	267,209,616	10.00	17.50	35.00
383(☆)	1928(☆)	Woods-Mellon		20.00	35.00	75.00
383A	1928A	Woods-Mills	58,194,600	17.50	27.50	60.00
383A(☆)	1928A(☆)	Woods-Mills		165.00	250.00	350.00
383B	1928B	Julian-Morgenthau	147,827,340	8.50	15.00	30.00
383B(☆)	1928B(☆)	Julian-Morgenthau		25.00	40.00	85.00
383C	1928C	Julian-Morgenthau	214,735,765	8.50	15.00	27.50
383C(☆)	1928C(☆)	Julian-Morgenthau		20.00	35.00	75.00
383D	1928D	Julian-Vinson	9,297,120	20.00	40.00	90.00
383D(☆)	1928D(☆)	Julian-Vinson		50.00	135.00	275.00
383E	1928E	Julian-Snyder	109,952,760	8.50	15.00	27.50
383E(☆)	1928E(☆)	Julian-Snyder		15.00	25.00	50.00
383F	1928F	Clark-Snyder	104,194,704	8.50	15.00	27.50
383F(☆)	1928F(☆)	Clark-Snyder		12.50	25.00	45.00

United States Notes/Red Seal

Face Design:
The red seal is now on
the right.

Back Design:
See preceding note.

No.	Date	Signatures	Notes Printed	Very Fine	Extra Fine	New
384	1953	Priest-Humphrey	120,880,000	8.50	12.50	20.00
384(☆)	1953(☆)	Priest-Humphrey	5,760,000	12.50	30.00	80.00
384A	1953A	Priest-Anderson	90,280,000	—	10.00	15.00
384A(☆)	1953A(☆)	Priest-Anderson	5,400,000	7.50	12.00	25.00
384B	1953B	Smith-Dillon	44,640,000	7.50	10.00	15.00
384B(☆)	1953B(☆)	Smith-Dillon	2,160,000	7.50	10.00	22.00
384C	1953C	Granahan-Dillon	8,640,000	6.00	8.00	15.00
384C(☆)	1953C(☆)	Granahan-Dillon	320,000	7.50	9.00	20.00

The motto "IN GOD WE TRUST" was added to the 1963 issue.

385	1963	Granahan-Dillon	63,360,000	—	6.00	10.00
385(☆)	1963(☆)	Granahan-Dillon	3,840,000	—	8.50	15.00

Silver Certificates/Blue Seal

Face Design:
Blue 5 to the left of
Lincoln.

Back Design:
Similar to No. 383.

No.	Date	Signature	Notes Printed	Very Fine	Extra Fine	New
386	1934	Julian-Morgenthau	393,088,368	7.00	10.00	25.00
386(☆)	1934(☆)	Julian-Morgenthau		12.50	25.00	50.00
386A	1934A	Julian-Morgenthau	656,265,948	—	8.00	17.50
386A(☆)	1934A(☆)	Julian-Morgenthau		10.00	17.50	37.50

The following three notes have yellow seals. They were issued for use in North Africa during World War II.

No.	Date	Signature	Notes Printed	Very Fine	Extra Fine	New
387	1934	Julian-Morgenthau		none reported to date		
387A	1934A	Julian-Morgenthau	16,710,000	12.00	17.50	35.00
387A(☆)	1934A(☆)	Julian-Morgenthau		55.00	85.00	115.00
387B	1934B	Julian-Vinson	59,128,500	12.50	20.00	40.00
387B(☆)	1934B(☆)	Julian-Vinson		20.00	50.00	115.00
387C	1934C	Julian-Snyder	403,328,964	8.00	10.00	20.00
387C(☆)	1934C(☆)	Julian-Snyder		8.50	17.50	40.00
387D	1934D	Clark-Snyder	486,146,148	6.00	8.50	17.50
387D(☆)	1934D(☆)	Clark-Snyder		8.00	15.00	32.50

Face Design:
The 5 on the left is
now grey, and the
blue seal is smaller.
The back design is
the same.

No.	Date	Signature	Notes Printed	Very Fine	Extra Fine	New
388	1953	Priest-Humphrey	339,600,000	—	7.50	15.00
388(☆)	1953(☆)	Priest-Humphrey	15,120,000	7.50	15.00	30.00
388A	1953A	Priest-Humphrey	232,400,000	—	8.00	12.50
388A(☆)	1953A(☆)	Priest-Humphrey	12,960,000	—	8.00	20.00
388B	1953B	Smith-Dillon	73,000,000*	—	8.00	15.00
388B(☆)	1953B(☆)	Smith-Dillon	3,240,000	150.00	200.00	300.00
388C	1953C	Granahan-Dillon	90,640,000	Never released		

*Only 14,196,000 notes were released.

Federal Reserve Bank Notes/1929/Brown Seal

Face Design

Back Design:
Similar to No. 383.

All the following notes bear the signatures of Jones-Woods.

No.	Bank	Notes Printed	Very Fine	Extra Fine	New
389A	Boston	3,180,000	15.00	25.00	45.00
389B	New York	2,100,000	15.00	25.00	45.00
389C	Philadelphia	3,096,000	15.00	25.00	45.00
389D	Cleveland	4,236,000	15.00	25.00	45.00
389E	Richmond	Not issued	—	—	—
389F	Atlanta	1,884,000	20.00	35.00	75.00
389G	Chicago	5,988,000	12.50	20.00	35.00
389H	St. Louis	276,000	65.00	150.00	275.00
389I	Minneapolis	684,000	25.00	55.00	125.00
389J	Kansas City	2,460,000	15.00	30.00	55.00
389K	Dallas	996,000	20.00	50.00	75.00
389L	San Francisco	360,000	150.00	165.00	1,200.00

National Bank Notes/1929/Brown Seal

Face Design: Type I

Face Design: Type II
has the bank charter
number printed a
second time near the
serial number.

Back Design:
Similar to No. 383.

Both types bear the signatures of Jones-Woods.

		Type I			Type II		
No.	**Rarity***	**Very Fine**	**Extra Fine**	**New**	**Very Fine**	**Extra Fine**	**New**
	1	17.50	30.00	50.00	20.00	35.00	55.00
	2	17.50	32.50	55.00	20.00	35.00	65.00
	3	20.00	37.50	65.00	25.00	40.00	80.00
	4	25.00	45.00	80.00	30.00	55.00	95.00
390	5	30.00	52.50	100.00	40.00	65.00	120.00
	6	40.00	65.00	125.00	55.00	80.00	150.00
	7	65.00	80.00	165.00	80.00	125.00	200.00
	8	100.00	150.00	250.00	200.00	300.00	400.00
	9	450.00	650.00	1,000.00	600.00	850.00	1,250.00

The Chase National Bank (now The Chase Manhattan Bank) issued 6,346,530 Type I $5 notes. This
was the largest amount of this denomination to be issued by any national bank.
The total issue for both types for all banks was 170,229,387.

*Rarity table is on page 41.

Federal Reserve Notes/Green Seal

Face Design: The number in the seal indicates the Federal Reserve district.

Back Design: Similar to No. 383.

1928 Series, signatures of Tate-Mellon

No.	Bank	Notes Printed	Very Fine	Extra Fine	New
391A	Boston	8,025,300	8.00	20.00	40.00
391B	New York	14,701,884	8.00	15.00	35.00
391C	Philadelphia	11,819,712	8.00	15.00	35.00
391D	Cleveland	9,049,500	8.00	17.50	40.00
391E	Richmond	6,027,600	8.00	20.00	45.00
391F	Atlanta	10,964,400	8.00	17.50	37.50
391G	Chicago	12,326,052	7.00	15.00	35.00
391H	St. Louis	4,675,200	9.00	22.00	50.00
391I	Minneapolis	4,284,300	12.50	25.00	50.00
391J	Kansas City	4,480,800	12.50	22.00	50.00
391K	Dallas	8,137,824	12.50	22.00	45.00
391L	San Francisco	9,792,000	9.00	20.00	40.00

Federal Reserve Notes/Green Seal

1928A Series, signatures of Woods-Mellon

No.	Bank	Notes Printed	Very Fine	Extra Fine	New
392A	Boston	9,404,352	7.50	17.50	37.50
392B	New York	42,878,196	7.50	15.00	30.00
392C	Philadelphia	10,806,012	7.50	16.50	35.00
392D	Cleveland	6,822,000	7.50	17.50	37.50
392E	Richmond	2,409,900	7.50	20.00	42.50
392F	Atlanta	3,537,600	7.50	17.50	40.00
392G	Chicago	37,882,176	7.50	15.00	30.00
392H	St. Louis	2,731,824	7.50	20.00	40.00
392I	Minneapolis	652,800	12.50	25.00	50.00
392J	Kansas City	3,572,400	7.50	20.00	42.50
392K	Dallas	2,564,400	7.50	20.00	45.00
392L	San Francisco	6,565,500	7.50	17.50	37.50

1928B Series, signatures of Woods-Mellon (letter replaces number in seal).

No.	Bank	Notes Printed	Very Fine	Extra Fine	New
393A	Boston	28,430,724	7.50	17.50	30.00
393B	New York	51,157,536	7.50	15.00	27.50
393C	Philadelphia	25,698,396	7.50	15.00	30.00
393D	Cleveland	24,874,272	7.50	15.00	32.50
393E	Richmond	15,151,932	7.50	20.00	35.00
393F	Atlanta	13,386,420	7.50	20.00	35.00
393G	Chicago	17,157,036	7.50	15.00	30.00
393H	St. Louis	20,251,716	7.50	15.00	35.00
393I	Minneapolis	6,954,060	12.50	25.00	40.00
393J	Kansas City	10,677,636	7.50	17.50	35.00
393K	Dallas	4,334,400	12.50	27.50	42.50
393L	San Francisco	28,840,080	7.50	17.50	30.00

1928C, signatures of Woods-Mills

No.	Bank	Notes Printed	Very Fine	Extra Fine	New
394D	Cleveland	3,293,640	75.00	125.00	250.00
394F	Atlanta	2,056,200	100.00	150.00	300.00
394L	San Francisco	266,304	115.00	185.00	400.00

Federal Reserve Notes/Green Seal

1928D Series, signatures of Woods-Woodin

No.	Bank	Notes Printed	Very Fine	Extra Fine	New
395F	Atlanta	1,281,600	200.00	385.00	750.00

1934 Series, signatures of Julian-Morgenthau.

The words "Redeemable in Gold" are no longer included in the obligation. The green seal comes in two varieties on this note, one lighter than the other. The lighter seal is worth slightly more than the prices listed.

396A	Boston	30,510,036	7.50	15.00	35.00
396B	New York	47,888,760	7.50	15.00	30.00
396C	Philadelphia	47,327,760	7.50	15.00	30.00
396D	Cleveland	62,273,508	7.50	15.00	30.00
396E	Richmond	62,128,452	7.50	15.00	30.00
396F	Atlanta	50,548,608	7.50	15.00	30.00
396G	Chicago	31,299,156	7.50	15.00	30.00
396H	St. Louis	48,737,280	7.50	15.00	30.00
396I	Minneapolis	16,795,392	10.00	25.00	47.50
396J	Kansas City	31,854,432	7.50	15.00	45.00
396K	Dallas	33,332,208	7.50	15.00	45.00
396L	San Francisco	39,324,168	7.50	15.00	37.50
396LL	San Francisco*	9,416,000	30.00	50.00	90.00

*This note bearing a brown seal and HAWAII overprint was issued for use in the Pacific during World War II.

Federal Reserve Notes/Green Seal

1934A Series, signatures of Julian-Morgenthau

No.	Bank	Notes Printed	Very Fine	Extra Fine	New
397A	Boston	23,231,568	6.50	12.00	25.00
397B	New York	143,199,336	6.50	12.00	20.00
397C	Philadelphia	30,691,632	6.50	12.00	25.00
397D	Cleveland	1,610,676	6.50	15.00	27.50
397E	Richmond	6,555,168	6.50	15.00	25.00
397F	Atlanta	22,811,916	6.50	15.00	25.00
397G	Chicago	88,376,376	6.50	15.00	20.00
397H	St. Louis	7,843,452	6.50	15.00	27.50
397L	San Francisco	72,118,452	6.50	15.00	25.00
397LL	San Francisco*	Included in 396LL	10.00	20.00	40.00

*This note, bearing a brown seal and "HAWAII" overprint, was issued for use in the Pacific during World War II.

1934B Series, signatures of Julian-Vinson

No.	Bank	Notes Printed	Very Fine	Extra Fine	New
398A	Boston	3,457,800	6.50	15.00	32.50
398B	New York	14,099,580	6.50	12.00	25.00
398C	Philadelphia	8,306,820	6.50	12.00	30.00
398D	Cleveland	11,348,184	6.50	12.00	30.00
398E	Richmond	5,902,848	6.50	15.00	32.50
398F	Atlanta	4,314,048	6.50	15.00	30.00
398G	Chicago	9,070,932	6.50	12.00	25.00
398H	St. Louis	4,307,712	6.50	15.00	35.00
398I	Minneapolis	2,482,500	6.50	15.00	40.00
398J	Kansas City	73,800	17.50	30.00	60.00
398K	Dallas	No record	—	—	—
398L	San Francisco	9,910,296	6.50	12.00	25.00

Federal Reserve Notes/Green Seal

1934C Series, signatures of Julian-Snyder

No.	Bank	Notes Printed	Extra Fine	New
399A	Boston	14,463,600	10.00	20.00
399B	New York	74,383,248	10.00	17.50
399C	Philadelphia	22,879,212	10.00	17.50
399D	Cleveland	19,898,256	10.00	17.50
399E	Richmond	23,800,524	10.00	17.50
399F	Atlanta	23,572,968	10.00	17.50
399G	Chicago	60,598,812	10.00	17.50
399H	St. Louis	20,393,340	10.00	20.00
399I	Minneapolis	5,089,200	10.00	25.00
399J	Kansas City	8,313,504	10.00	22.00
399K	Dallas	5,107,800	12.50	25.00
399L	San Francisco	9,451,944	10.00	22.50

1934D Series, signatures of Clark-Snyder

No.	Bank	Notes Printed	Extra Fine	New
400A	Boston	12,660,552	10.00	17.50
400B	New York	50,976,576	10.00	15.00
400C	Philadelphia	12,106,740	10.00	17.50
400D	Cleveland	8,969,052	10.00	17.50
400E	Richmond	13,333,032	10.00	17.50
400F	Atlanta	9,599,352	10.00	17.50
400G	Chicago	36,601,680	10.00	17.50
400H	St. Louis	8,093,412	10.00	17.50
400I	Minneapolis	3,594,900	10.00	20.00
400J	Kansas City	6,538,740	10.00	17.50
400K	Dallas	4,139,016	12.50	25.00
400L	San Francisco	11,704,200	10.00	17.50

1950 Series, signatures of Clark-Snyder. Both seals are now somewhat smaller.

No.	Bank	Notes Printed	New
401A	Boston	30,672,000	15.00
401A(☆)	Boston	408,000	20.00
401B	New York	106,768,000	12.50
401B(☆)	New York	1,464,000	12.50
401C	Philadelphia	44,784,000	15.00
401C(☆)	Philadelphia	600,000	17.50
401D	Cleveland	54,000,000	15.00
401D(☆)	Cleveland	744,000	17.50
401E	Richmond	47,088,000	15.00

Federal Reserve Notes/Green Seal

No.	Bank	Notes Printed	New
401E(☆)	Richmond	684,000	15.00
401F	Atlanta	52,416,000	15.00
401F(☆)	Atlanta	696,000	15.00
401G	Chicago	85,104,000	15.00
401G(☆)	Chicago	1,176,000	12.50
410H	St. Louis	36,864,000	15.00
410H(☆)	St. Louis	552,000	15.00
401I	Minneapolis	11,796,000	17.50
401I(☆)	Minneapolis	144,000	22.50
401J	Kansas City	25,428,000	15.00
401J(☆)	Kansas City	360,000	20.00
401K	Dallas	22,848,000	15.00
401K(☆)	Dallas	372,000	20.00
401L	San Francisco	55,008,000	15.00
401L(☆)	San Francisco	744,000	17.50

Federal Reserve Notes/Green Seal

1950A Series, signatures of Priest-Humphrey

No.	Bank	Notes Printed	New	No.	Bank	Notes Printed	New
402A	Boston	53,568,000	12.50	402G	Chicago	129,296,000	12.50
402A(☆)	Boston	2,808,000	17.50	402G(☆)	Chicago	6,264,000	17.50
402B	New York	186,472,000	12.50	402H	Saint Louis	54,936,000	12.50
402B(☆)	New York	9,216,000	17.50	402H(☆)	Saint Louis	3,384,000	20.00
402C	Philadelphia	69,616,000	12.50	402I	Minneapolis	11,232,000	15.00
402C(☆)	Philadelphia	4,320,000	15.00	402I(☆)	Minneapolis	864,000	22.50
402D	Cleveland	45,360,000	12.50	402J	Kansas City	29,952,000	12.50
402D(☆)	Cleveland	2,376,000	17.50	402J(☆)	Kansas City	1,088,000	20.00
402E	Richmond	76,672,000	12.50	402K	Dallas	24,984,000	15.00
402E(☆)	Richmond	5,400,000	17.50	402K(☆)	Dallas	1,368,000	20.00
402F	Atlanta	86,464,000	12.50	402L	San Francisco	90,712,000	12.50
402F(☆)	Atlanta	5,040,000	17.50	402L(☆)	San Francisco	—	—

1950B Series, signatures of Priest-Anderson

No.	Bank	Notes Printed	New	No.	Bank	Notes Printed	New
403A	Boston	30,880,000	12.50	403G	Chicago	104,320,000	12.50
403A(☆)	Boston	2,520,000	12.50	403G(☆)	Chicago	6,120,000	12.50
403B	New York	85,960,000	12.50	403H	Saint Louis	25,840,000	12.50
403B(☆)	New York	4,680,000	15.00	403H(☆)	Saint Louis	1,440,000	17.50
403C	Philadelphia	43,560,000	12.50	403I	Minneapolis	20,880,000	12.50
403C(☆)	Philadelphia	2,880,000	15.00	403I(☆)	Minneapolis	792,000	20.00
403D	Cleveland	38,800,000	12.50	403J	Kansas City	32,400,000	12.50
403D(☆)	Cleveland	2,880,000	15.00	403J(☆)	Kansas City	2,520,000	17.50
403E	Richmond	52,920,000	12.50	403K	Dallas	52,120,000	12.50
403E(☆)	Richmond	2,080,000	15.00	403K(☆)	Dallas	3,240,000	15.00
403F	Atlanta	80,560,000	12.50	403L	San Francisco	56,080,000	12.50
403F(☆)	Atlanta	3,960,000	12.50	403L(☆)	San Francisco	3,600,000	15.00

1950C Series, signatures of Smith-Dillon

No.	Bank	Notes Printed	New	No.	Bank	Notes Printed	New
404A	Boston	20,880,000	12.50	404G	Chicago	56,880,000	12.50
404A(☆)	Boston	720,000	17.50	404G(☆)	Chicago	3,240,000	15.00
404B	New York	47,440,000	12.50	404H	Saint Louis	22,680,000	12.50
404B(☆)	New York	2,880,000	15.00	404H(☆)	Saint Louis	720,000	17.50
404C	Philadelphia	29,520,000	12.50	404I	Minneapolis	12,960,000	15.00
404C(☆)	Philadelphia	1,800,000	15.00	404I(☆)	Minneapolis	720,000	17.50
404D	Cleveland	33,840,000	12.50	404J	Kansas City	24,760,000	12.50
404D(☆)	Celveland	1,800,000	15.00	404J(☆)	Kansas City	1,800,000	15.00
404E	Richmond	33,480,000	12.50	404K	Dallas	3,960,000	12.50
404E(☆)	Richmond	2,160,000	15.00	404K(☆)	Dallas	360,000	20.00
404F	Atlanta	54,360,000	12.50	404L	San Francisco	25,920,000	12.50
404F(☆)	Atlanta	3,240,000	15.00	404L(☆)	San Francisco	1,440,000	15.00

Federal Reserve Notes/Green Seal

1950D Series, signatures of Granahan-Dillon

No.	Bank	Notes Printed	New	No.	Bank	Notes Printed	New
405A	Boston	25,200,000	10.00	405G	Chicago	67,240,000	10.00
405A(☆)	Boston	1,080,000	15.00	405G(☆)	Chicago	3,600,000	12.50
405B	New York	102,160,000	10.00	405H	Saint Louis	20,160,000	10.00
405B(☆)	New York	5,040,000	12.50	405H(☆)	Saint Louis	720,000	17.50
405C	Philadelphia	21,520,000	10.00	405I	Minneapolis	7,920,000	12.50
405C(☆)	Philadelphia	1,080,000	15.00	405I(☆)	Minneapolis	360,000	20.00
405D	Cleveland	23,400,000	10.00	405J	Kansas City	11,160,000	10.00
405D(☆)	Cleveland	1,080,000	15.00	405J(☆)	Kansas City	720,000	17.50
405E	Richmond	42,490,000	10.00	405K	Dallas	7,200,000	12.50
405E(☆)	Richmond	1,080,000	15.00	405K(☆)	Dallas	360,000	20.00
405F	Atlanta	35,200,000	10.00	405L	San Francisco	53,280,000	10.00
405F(☆)	Atlanta	1,800,000	15.00	405L(☆)	San Francisco	3,600,000	12.50

1950E Series, signatures of Granahan-Fowler

No.	Bank	Notes Printed	New
406B	New York	82,000,000	10.00
406B(☆)	New York	6,678,000	12.50
406G	Chicago	14,760,000	15.00
406G(☆)	Chicago	1,080,000	17.50
406L	San Francisco	24,400,000	12.00
406L(☆)	San Francisco	1,800,000	17.50

Federal Reserve Notes/Green Seal

1963 Series, signatures of Granahan-Dillon. "IN GOD WE TRUST" added to back design.

No.	Bank	Notes Printed	New	No.	Bank	Notes Printed	New
407A	Boston	4,480,000	12.50	407G	Chicago	22,400,000	8.50
407A(☆)	Boston	640,000	17.50	407G(☆)	Chicago	3,200,000	15.00
407B	New York	12,160,000	8.50	407H	St. Louis	14,080,000	8.50
407B(☆)	New York	1,280,000	12.50	407H(☆)	St. Louis	1,920,000	12.50
407C	Philadelphia	8,320,000	8.50	407I	Minneapolis	None printed	
407C(☆)	Philadelphia	1,920,000	12.50	407I(☆)	Minneapolis	None printed	
407D	Cleveland	10,240,000	8.50	407J	Kansas City	1,920,000	15.00
407D(☆)	Cleveland	1,920,000	12.50	407J(☆)	Kansas City	640,000	17.50
407E	Richmond	None Printed		407K	Dallas	5,760,000	12.50
407E(☆)	Richmond	None Printed		407K(☆)	Dallas	1,920,000	12.50
407F	Atlanta	17,920,000	8.50	407L	San Francisco	18,560,000	8.50
407F(☆)	Atlanta	2,560,000	15.00	407L(☆)	San Francisco	1,920,000	12.50

1063A Series, signatures of Granahan-Fowler

No.	Bank	Notes Printed	New	No.	Bank	Notes Printed	New
408A	Boston	77,440,000	8.50	408G	Chicago	213,440,000	8.50
408A(☆)	Boston	5,760,000	12.50	408G(☆)	Chicago	16,640,000	10.00
408B	New York	98,080,000	8.50	408H	St. Louis	56,960,000	8.50
408B(☆)	New York	7,680,000	10.00	408H(☆)	St. Louis	5,120,000	12.50
408C	Philadelphia	106,400,000	8.50	408I	Minneapolis	32,640,000	8.50
408C(☆)	Philadelphia	10,240,000	10.00	408I(☆)	Minneapolis	3,200,000	15.00
408D	Cleveland	83,840,000	8.50	408J	Kansas City	55,040,000	8.50
408D(☆)	Cleveland	7,040,000	10.00	408J(☆)	Kansas City	5,760,000	12.50
408E	Richmond	118,560,000	8.50	408K	Dallas	64,000,000	8.50
408E(☆)	Richmond	10,880,000	10.00	408K(☆)	Dallas	3,840,000	15.00
408F	Atlanta	117,920,000	8.50	408L	San Francisco	128,900,000	8.50
408F(☆)	Atlanta	9,600,000	10.00	408L(☆)	San Francisco	12,153,000	10.00

Federal Reserve Notes/Green Seal

1969 Series, signatures of Elston-Kennedy

No.	Bank	Notes Printed	New
409A	Boston	51,200,000	7.50
409A(☆)	Boston	1,920,000	8.50
409B	New York	198,560,000	7.50
409B(☆)	New York	8,960,000	8.50
409C	Philadelphia	69,120,000	7.50
409C(☆)	Philadelphia	2,560,000	8.50
409D	Cleveland	56,320,000	7.50
409D(☆)	Cleveland	2,560,000	8.50
409E	Richmond	84,480,000	7.50
409E(☆)	Richmond	3,200,000	8.50
409F	Atlanta	84,480,000	7.50
409F(☆)	Atlanta	3,840,000	8.50
409G	Chicago	125,600,000	7.50
409G(☆)	Chicago	5,120,000	10.00
409H	St. Louis	27,520,000	7.50
409H(☆)	St. Louis	1,280,000	8.50
409I	Minneapolis	16,640,000	7.50
409I(☆)	Minneapolis	640,000	12.50
409J	Kansas City	48,640,000	7.50
409J(☆)	Kansas City	3,192,000	8.50
409K	Dallas	39,680,000	7.50
409K(☆)	Dallas	1,920,000	8.50
409L	San Francisco	103,840,000	7.50
409L(☆)	San Francisco	4,480,000	8.50

1969A Series, signatures of Kabis-Connally

No.	Bank	Notes Printed	New
410A	Boston	23,040,000	7.50
410A(☆)	Boston	1,280,000	8.50
410B	New York	62,240,000	7.50
410B(☆)	New York	2,394,000	8.50
410C	Philadelphia	41,160,000	7.50
410C(☆)	Philadelphia	1,920,000	8.50
410D	Cleveland	21,120,000	7.50
410D(☆)	Cleveland	640,000	12.50
410E	Richmond	37,920,000	7.50
410E(☆)	Richmond	1,120,000	8.50
410F	Atlanta	25,120,000	7.50
410F(☆)	Atlanta	480,000	
410G	Chicago	60,800,000	7.50
410G(☆)	Chicago	1,920,000	8.50
410H	St. Louis	15,360,000	7.50
410H(☆)	St. Louis	640,000	12.50
410I	Minneapolis	8,960,000	7.50
410I(☆)	Minneapolis	—	—
410J	Kansas City	17,920,000	7.50
410J(☆)	Kansas City	640,000	12.50
410K	Dallas	21,120,000	7.50
410K(☆)	Dallas	640,000	12.50
410L	San Francisco	44,800,000	7.50
410L(☆)	San Francisco	1,920,000	8.50

124/ FIVE DOLLARS

Federal Reserve Notes/Green Seal

1969B Series, signatures of Banuelos-Connally

1969C Series, signatures of Banuelos-Shultz

No.	Bank	Notes Printed	New	No.	Bank	Notes Printed	New
411A	Boston	5,760,000	6.50	412A	Boston	50,720,000	
411A(☆)	Boston	None printed		412A(☆)	Boston	1,920,000	
411B	New York	34,560,000	6.50	412B	New York	120,000,000	
411B(☆)	New York	634,000	7.50	412B(☆)	New York	2,400,000	
411C	Philadelphia	5,120,000	6.50	412C	Philadelphia	53,760,000	
411C(☆)	Philadelphia	None printed		412C(☆)	Philadelphia	1,280,000	
411D	Cleveland	12,160,000	6.50	412D	Cleveland	43,680,000	
411D(☆)	Cleveland	None printed		412D(☆)	Cleveland	1,120,000	
411E	Richmond	15,360,000	6.50	412E	Richmond	73,760,000	
411E(☆)	Richmond	640,000	7.50	412E(☆)	Richmond	640,000	
411F	Atlanta	18,560,000	6.50	412F	Atlanta	81,440,000	
411F(☆)	Atlanta	640,000	7.50	412F(☆)	Atlanta	3,200,000	
411G	Chicago	27,040,000	6.50	412G	Chicago	54,400,000	
411G(☆)	Chicago	480,000	10.00	412G(☆)	Chicago	None printed	
411H	St. Louis	5,120,000	6.50	412H	St. Louis	37,760,000	
411H(☆)	St. Louis	None printed		412H(☆)	St. Louis	1,820,000	
411I	Minneapolis	8,320,000	6.50	412I	Minneapolis	14,080,000	
411I(☆)	Minneapolis	None printed		412I(☆)	Minneapolis	None printed	
411J	Kansas City	8,320,000	6.50	412J	Kansas City	41,120,000	
411J(☆)	Kansas City	640,000	7.50	412J(☆)	Kansas City	1,920,000	
411K	Dallas	12,160,000	6.50	412K	Dallas	41,120,000	
411K(☆)	Dallas	None printed		412K(☆)	Dallas	1,920,000	
411L	San Francisco	23,160,000	6.50	412L	San Francisco	80,800,000	
411L(☆)	San Francisco	640,000	7.50	412L(☆)	San Francisco	3,680,000	

1974 Series, signatures of Neff-Simon

Demand Notes/1861

Face Design:
On the left is a
portrait of Lincoln
engraved by F.
Girsch and to the
right is a female
figure representing
Art.

Back Design

No.	Payable at	Notes Issued	Good	Very Good	Fine
463A	Boston		400.00	650.00	1,000.00
463B	New York		425.00	650.00	1,000.00
463C	Philadelphia	2,003,000*	450.00	700.00	1,500.00
463D	Cincinnati		Extremely Rare		
463H	St. Louis		Extremely Rare		

A total of $60,030,000, including the $10 and $20 notes of this series, was issued, all without the
Treasury Seal and the signatures of the Treasurer and the Register of the Treasury. Officials
representing these two offices signed for them, and the words "for the" preceding the titles were
sometimes written by hand. These notes are exceedingly rare, an illustration of one is seen below.

(Courtesy of Coin
Galleries of
Westchester, Ltd.)

*3,000 notes were technically reissued; 1998½ notes were outstanding according to records of
1903.

United States Notes/Red Seal

Face Design:
Similar to preceding
note, with the addition
of the Treasury Seal
and the deletion of
the words "On
Demand."

Back Design:
First obligation.

The following bear the signatures of Chittenden-Spinner.

No.	Date	Very Good	Very Fine	New
464	1862	75.00	235.00	600.00

Face Design

Back Design:
Second obligation.

No.	Date	Very Good	Very Fine	New
464a	1862	85.00	250.00	700.00
465	1863 (one serial number)	85.00	250.00	750.00
465a	1863 (two serial numbers)	85.00	250.00	750.00

A total of 11,800,505 notes were printed.

United States Notes

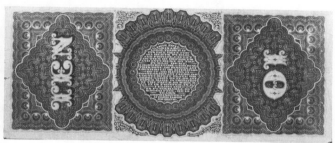

Face Design: The portrait of Daniel Webster was engraved by Alfred Sealey; the small eagle was engraved by Henry Gugler. If you turn this note upside down you will see why this note has been called the "Jackass Note." *Introduction of the Old World to the New World* occupies the right side; the engraving also is known as *Pocahontas Presented at Court.*

Back Design

No.	Date	Signatures	Seal	Notes Issued	Very Good	Very Fine	New
466	*1869*	Allison-Spinner	Red	8,522,124	55.00	285.00	650.00

The following have the seal on the left and a red "TEN" on the right.

No.	Date	Signatures	Seal	Notes Issued	Very Good	Very Fine	New
467	1875	Allison-New	Sm Red-r	2,366,000	40.00	110.00	350.00
467A	1875A	Allison-New	Sm Red-r		40.00	150.00	425.00
468	1878	Allison-Gilfillan	Sm Red-r	2,600,000	40.00	165.00	475.00

The back for Nos. 467–468 is illustrated on p. 128.

r: with rays

United States Notes

Face Design:
Similar to No. 466.

Back Design for
Nos. 467–482.

The large seal is used once again, "TEN" is deleted and the serial numbers are red.

No.	Date	Signatures	Seal	Notes Printed	Very Good	Very Fine	New
469	1880	Scofield-Gilfillan	Brown		35.00	90.00	285.00
470	1880	Bruce-Gilfillan	Brown		35.00	90.00	285.00
471	1880	Bruce-Wyman	Brown		35.00	90.00	285.00

The following have blue serial numbers.

No.	Date	Signatures	Seal	Notes Printed	Very Good	Very Fine	New
472	1880	Bruce-Wyman	Lg. Red		35.00	90.00	285.00
473	1880	Rosecrans-Jordan	Lg. Red		35.00	115.00	315.00
474	1880	Rosecrans-Hyatt	Lg. Red		35.00	125.00	325.00
475	1880	Rosecrans-Hyatt	Lg. Red-sp	43,340,000	40.00	135.00	475.00
476	1880	Rosecrans-Huston	Lg. Red-sp		40.00	145.00	525.00
477	1880	Rosecrans-Huston	Brown		35.00	110.00	315.00
478	1880	Rosecrans-Nebeker	Brown		40.00	175.00	415.00
479	1880	Rosecrans-Nebeker	Sm. Red-sc		30.00	80.00	285.00
480	1880	Tillman-Morgan	Sm. Red-sc		30.00	80.00	285.00
481	1880	Bruce-Roberts	Sm. Red-sc		30.00	80.00	285.00
482	1880	Lyons-Roberts	Sm. Red-sc		30.00	80.00	285.00

r: with rays   sp: with spikes   sc: with scallops

United States Notes/1901/Red Seal

Face design: This "Buffalo Bill," with portraits of Lewis and Clark and the bison in the center, was undoubtedly issued to stimulate interest in the Lewis and Clark Centennial Exposition held in Portland, Oregon in 1905. The two portraits were engraved by G.F.C. Smillie. Ostrander Smith based his bison design on a sketch by Charles Knight. Marcus W. Baldwin executed the engraving. The same bison is seen on the 30¢ stamp of 1923.

Back Design

Proof impressions were made with the signatures of Napier-Thompson.

No.	Signature	Notes Printed	Very Good	Very Fine	New
483	Lyons-Roberts		35.00	80.00	425.00
484	Lyons-Treat		35.00	80.00	400.00
485	Vernon-Treat		35.00	80.00	400.00
486(☆)	Vernon-McClung		35.00	80.00	400.00
487	Napier-McClung	148,958,000	35.00	80.00	400.00
488	Parker-Burke		35.00	80.00	400.00
489	Teehee-Burke		35.00	80.00	400.00
490(☆)	Elliott-White		35.00	80.00	400.00
491(☆)	Speelman-White		35.00	80.00	375.00

United States Notes/1923/Red Seal

Face Design: Andrew Jackson

Back Design

No.	Signature	Notes Printed	Very Good	Very Fine	New
492(☆)	Speelman-White	696,000	75.00	375.00	1500.00

About fifty notes in new condition are known, including the first note, A1A.

Compound Interest Treasury Notes/6%

Face Design:
Portrait of Salmon P.
Chase and *The Eagle
of the Capitol.*

Back Design:
Redemption values in
center.

Act of March 3, 1863

No.	Signatures	Notes Printed	Notes Issued	Outstanding	Fine
493	Chittenden-Spinner	92,420	84,940	164	2,500.00

Act of June 30, 1864

No.	Signatures	Notes Printed	Notes Issued	Outstanding	Fine
494	Chittenden-Spinner	1,947,776	1,769,784		2,200.00
495	Colby-Spinner		1,754,000*	2,007	2,000.00

*New figure submitted by Walter Breen.

Interest-bearing Note/5%

Face Design:
Portrait of Salmon
P. Chase.

Back Design:
Obligation and
warning to
counterfeiters.

Act of March 3, 1863

No.	Signatures	Notes Issued	Outstanding in 1895	Fine	Very Fine
496	Chittenden-Spinner	620,000	503½	2,600.00	3,250.00

National Bank Notes/First Charter Period

Face Design:
Similar to No. 512.

Back Design:
The same vignette of
DeSoto discovering
the Mississippi
engraved by F.
Girsch is seen on
No. 1,370.

No.	Date	Signatures	Seal	Very Good	Very Fine	New
497	Orig*	Chittenden-Spinner	Red-r	50.00	225.00	750.00
498	Orig*	Colby-Spinner	Red-r	50.00	200.00	725.00
499	Orig*	Jeffries-Spinner	Red-r	325.00	1,250.00	3,250.00
500	Orig*	Allison-Spinner	Red-r	50.00	175.00	725.00
501	1875	Allison-New	Red-sc	50.00	175.00	725.00
502	1875	Allison-Wyman	Red-sc	50.00	175.00	725.00
503	1875	Allison-Gilfillan	Red-sc	50.00	175.00	725.00
504	1875	Scofield-Gilfillan	Red-sc	50.00	175.00	725.00
505	1875	Bruce-Gilfillan	Red-sc	50.00	175.00	725.00
506	1875	Bruce-Wyman	Red-sc	50.00	250.00	875.00
507	1875	Rosecrans-Huston	Red-sc	50.00	250.00	725.00
508	1875	Rosecrans-Nebeker	Red-sc	50.00	225.00	725.00

*The original notes had no date printed on the face.
 r: with rays   sc: with scallops

National Bank Notes/Second Charter Period/1882

Face Design:
Franklin and Electricity 1752 was engraved by Alfred Jones and Louis Delnoce for the American Bank Note Company. *America Seizing Lightning,* another American Bank Note engraving, is seen on the right. The Winnemucca, Nevada, note illustrated is the only note of this issue to emanate from a Nevada bank.

Back Design:
Similar to No. 288.

First Issue—Brown Seal

No.	Signatures	Very Good	Very Fine	New
509	Bruce-Gilfillan	35.00	150.00	300.00
510	Bruce-Wyman	35.00	150.00	300.00
511	Bruce-Jordan	35.00	200.00	400.00
512	Rosecrans-Jordan	35.00	150.00	300.00
513	Rosecrans-Hyatt	35.00	150.00	300.00
514	Rosecrans-Huston	35.00	150.00	300.00
515	Rosecrans-Nebeker	35.00	150.00	300.00
516	Rosecrans-Morgan	135.00	700.00	1,250.00
517	Tillman-Morgan	35.00	150.00	300.00
518	Tillman-Roberts	40.00	150.00	350.00
519	Bruce-Roberts	35.00	150.00	300.00
520	Lyons-Roberts	35.00	150.00	300.00
521	Lyons-Treat	50.00	225.00	425.00
522	Vernon-Treat	40.00	185.00	400.00

National Bank Notes/Second Charter Period/1882

Face Design:
Similar to
preceding note.

Back Design:
William P.
Fessenden, Secre-
tary of the Treasury,
is on the left; a
symbolic figure of
Mechanics is on
the right.

Second Issue—Blue Seal

No.	Signatures	Very Good	Very Fine	New
523	Rosecrans-Huston	40.00	170.00	350.00
524	Rosecrans-Nebeker	40.00	170.00	350.00
525	Rosecrans-Morgan	175.00	600.00	975.00
526	Tillman-Morgan	40.00	170.00	350.00
527	Tilman-Roberts	40.00	170.00	350.00
528	Bruce-Roberts	65.00	185.00	350.00
529	Lyons-Roberts	40.00	160.00	350.00
530	Vernon-Treat	70.00	200.00	300.00
531	Vernon-McClung	150.00	275.00	415.00
532	Napier-McClung	150.00	275.00	400.00

National Bank Notes/Second Charter Period/1882

Face Design:
Similar to
preceding note.

Back Design:
"Ten Dollars"
replaces
"1882–1908."

Third Issue—Blue Seal

No.	Signatures	Very Good	Very Fine	New
533	Tillman-Morgan	90.00	325.00	800.00
534	Tillman-Roberts	70.00	265.00	600.00
535	Bruce-Roberts	80.00	325.00	775.00
536	Lyons-Roberts	60.00	165.00	600.00
537	Vernon-Treat	80.00	350.00	625.00
538	Napier-McClung	65.00	265.00	600.00
539	Teehee-Burke	80.00	315.00	750.00

National Bank Notes/Third Charter Period/1902

Face Design:
This portrait of
William McKinley
was engraved by
G.F.C.Smillie based
on a photograph by
Courtney.

Back Design:
The design is the
same for all three
issues. Only the
second issue has
"1902–1908" added.
G.F.C. Smillie was
the engraver.

First Issue—Red Seal

No.	Signatures	Very Good	Very Fine	New
540	Lyons-Roberts	50.00	125.00	365.00
541	Lyons-Treat	50.00	175.00	365.00
542	Vernon-Treat	50.00	200.00	400.00

Second Issue—Blue Seal

No.	Signatures	Very Good	Very Fine	New
543	Lyons-Roberts	40.00	70.00	115.00
544	Lyons-Treat	40.00	70.00	115.00
545	*Vernon-Treat*	40.00	70.00	115.00
546	Vernon-McClung	40.00	70.00	115.00
547	Napier-McClung	40.00	70.00	125.00
548	Napier-Thompson	50.00	120.00	175.00
549	Napier-Burke	50.00	75.00	145.00
550	Parker-Burke	50.00	75.00	145.00
551	Teehee-Burke	85.00	150.00	200.00

National Bank Notes/Third Charter Period/1902

Face Design:
Similar to
preceding note.

Third Issue—Blue Seal

No.	Signatures	Very Good	Very Fine	New
552	Lyons-Roberts	35.00	50.00	100.00
553	Lyons-Treat	35.00	50.00	100.00
554	Vernon-Treat	35.00	50.00	100.00
555	Vernon-McClung	35.00	50.00	100.00
556	Napier-McClung	35.00	50.00	100.00
557	Napier-Thompson	40.00	125.00	235.00
558	Napier-Burke	35.00	50.00	115.00
559	Parker-Burke	35.00	50.00	115.00
560	Teehee-Burke	35.00	50.00	115.00
561	Elliott-Burke	35.00	50.00	115.00
562	Elliott-White	35.00	50.00	115.00
563	Speelman-White	35.00	50.00	115.00
564	Woods-White	35.00	70.00	200.00
565	Woods-Tate	40.00	110.00	265.00
566	Jones-Woods	225.00	625.00	1,150.00

National Gold Bank Notes

Face Design: Similar to National bank notes; see No. 512.

The back design is the same for all denominations.

The following bear the signatures of Allison-Spinner and have red seals.

No.	Date	Issuing Bank	City	Notes Issued*	Good	Very Good
567	1870	First National Gold Bank	San Francisco	18,004	400.00	550.00
568	1872	National Gold Bank & Trust Co.	San Francisco	12,669	425.00	600.00
569	1872	National Gold Bank of D.O. Mills and Co.	Sacramento	3,723	465.00	700.00
570	1873	First National Gold Bank	Stockton	15,000	400.00	550.00
571	1873	First National Gold Bank	Santa Barbara	2,400	Unknown	
572	1874	Farmers' National Gold Bank	San Jose	8,547	425.00	575.00
573	1874	First National Gold Bank	Petaluma	6,000	425.00	600.00
574	1875	First National Gold Bank	Petaluma	1,089	525.00	775.00
574a	1875	Same as above, unique on white paper		—	—	
575	1875	First National Gold Bank	Oakland	4,800	465.00	.650.00
576	1875	Union National Gold Bank	Oakland	1,500	625.00	975.00
577	1875	First National Gold Bank	Stockton**	779	—	—

*2,481 notes are outstanding.
**This note bears the signature of Scofield-Gilfillan.

Silver Certificates

Face Design:
Robert Morris, U.S.
Senator 1789-1795.
The engraving is by
Charles Schlect.

Back Design

The following notes dated 1878 bear the signatures of Scofield-Gilfillan, and have red seals. Proof impressions were made with the signatures of Allison-Gilfillan.

No.	Countersigned by	Payable at	Notes Issued	Very Good	Very Fine	New
578	W.G. White*	New York		—	—	—
579	J.C. Hopper*	New York	20,000	600.00	2,500.00	
580	T. Hillhouse*	New York			Unknown	
581	T. Hillhouse	New York	16,000		2 Known	
582	R.M. Anthony*	San Francisco	3,400		Unknown	
583	A.U. Wyman*	Washington, D.C.	4,000		2 Known	
583a	A.U. Wyman	Washington, D.C.	182,000	600.00	2,250.00	—

The following two notes also bear the Scofield-Gilfillan signatures, but they have brown seals and are dated 1880.

No.	Countersigned by	Payable at	Notes Issued	Very Good	Very Fine	New
584	T. Hillhouse	New York	384,000	750.00	1,750.00	—
585	A.U. Wyman	Washington, D.C.	196,000	750.00	2,650.00	—

1,734 notes of the 1878 series were outstanding in 1893. The signatures for Nos. 578 and 579 were reversed in the first edition of this catalog

* Autographed countersignatures

Silver Certificates/1880

Face Design:
A larger seal above
an added *X*.

Back Design:
Similar to No. 585.

No.	Signatures	Seal	Notes Issued	Very Good	Very Fine	New
586	Scofield-Gilfillan	Brown	2,772,000	100.00	400.00	2,000.00
587	Bruce-Gilfillan	Brown	1,120,000	100.00	400.00	2,250.00
588	Bruce-Wyman	Brown		100.00	400.00	1,800.00
589*	Bruce-Wyman	Red	304,000	165.00	550.00	3,250.00

*This note does not have the *X* in the center.

Silver Certificates/1886

Face Design:
Thomas A. Hendricks
held the
Vice-Presidency for
nine months. He died
on November 25,
1885, in Indianapolis,
where he had spent
most of his academic
and political life. His
portrait was engraved
by Charles Schlecht.

Back Design

No.	Signatures	Seal	Notes Printed	Very Good	Very Fine	New
590	Rosecrans-Jordan	Red		60.00	150.00	600.00
591	Rosecrans-Hyatt	Red		60.00	175.00	600.00
592	Rosecrans-Hyatt	Lg Red		60.00	175.00	600.00
593	Rosecrans-Huston	Lg Red	14,204,000	60.00	185.00	650.00
594	Rosecrans-Huston	Brown		60.00	150.00	600.00
595	Rosecrans-Nebeker	Brown		60.00	150.00	600.00
596	Rosecrans-Nebeker	Red		85.00	475.00	1,350.00

Silver Certificates

Face Design:
Similar to No. 590.

Back Design

No.	Signatures	Seal	Notes Printed	Very Good	Very Fine	New
			Series of 1891			
597	Rosecrans-Nebeker	Red		30.00	75.00	275.00
598	Tillman-Morgan	Red	34,420,000	30.00	75.00	275.00
599	Bruce-Roberts	Red		30.00	90.00	300.00
600	Lyons-Roberts	Red		30.00	90.00	275.00
			Series of 1908			
601	Vernon-Treat	Blue		30.00	85.00	385.00
601a	Vernon-McClung	Blue	8,408,000	30.00	85.00	350.00
602	Parker-Burke	Blue		30.00	85.00	350.00

The three notes above are similar to Nos. 597-600, with a large X added to the face.

Refunding Certificates

Face Design:
This portrait of
Benjamin Franklin
seems to be based on
the painting by James
Barton Longacre.

Back Design

Both types are dated April 1, 1879, and bear the signatures of Scofield-Gilfillan.

No.	Notes Issued	Notes Outstanding	Notes Known	Very Fine
603	5,850	2	2	—
604	3,995,425	800	200	1,750.00

Face Design

Back Design

Gold Certificates/Gold Seal

Face Design:
Michael Hillegas, the
first United States
Treasurer, was born
in Philadelphia on
April 22, 1729, and
died there on
September 29, 1804.
His portrait was
engraved by
G.F.C. Smillie.

Back Design:
Bright yellow.
Engraved by H.L.
Chorlton, E.M. Hall,
and G.U. Rose, Jr.

No.	Date	Signatures	Notes Issued	Very Good	Very Fine	New
605	1907	Vernon-Treat	19,296,230*	30.00	60.00	175.00
606	1907	Vernon-McClung	17,600,000*	30.00	60.00	175.00
607	1907	Napier-McClung		30.00	60.00	175.00
608	1907	Napier-Thompson		35.00	115.00	450.00
609	1907	Parker-Burke	18,763,802*	30.00	50.00	150.00
610(☆)	1907	Teehee-Burke	38,344,500*	30.00	50.00	150.00
611(☆)	1922	Speelman-White	180,604,000**	22.50	35.00	115.00

*Estimated figures based on observed serial numbers. Walter Breen reports 1,880,000 notes
were issued in September, 1913; it is possible they bore the signatures of Napier-Thompson.
**Notes printed

Treasury Notes/1890

Face Design:
General Philip
Sheridan was born in
Albany, New York, on
March 6, 1831.
Sheridan graduated
from West Point in
1853 and fought in
the Civil War. This
portrait is based on
an engraving by L.
Hatch.

Back Design:
Engraved by D.M.
Cooper, W.A.
Copenhaver, W.H.
Dougal, E.M. Hall,
A.L. Helm, W.G.
Phillips, and D.M.
Russell.

No.	Signatures	Seal	Notes Printed	Very Good	Very Fine	New
612	Rosecrans-Huston	Brown		95.00	300.00	975.00
613	Rosecrans-Nebeker	Brown	4,600,000	95.00	325.00	1,050.00
614	Rosecrans-Nebeker	Red		95.00	300.00	975.00

1891 Series

Face Design:
Similar to No. 614.

Back Design:
Engraved by J.A.
Allen, D.M. Cooper,
W.H. Dougal, E.M.
Hall, A.L. Helm, J.R.
Hill, E.E. Myers, E.G.
Rose, and G.U. Rose,
Jr.

No.	Signatures	Seal	Notes Printed	Very Good	Very Fine	New
615	Rosecrans-Nebeker	Red		85.00	185.00	500.00
616	Tillman-Morgan	Red	6,028,000*	85.00	185.00	500.00
617	Bruce-Roberts	Red		85.00	185.00	500.00

*5,868,000 notes were issued.

Federal Reserve Notes/1914/Red Seal

Face Design:
Portrait of Andrew
Jackson; the
engraver was G.F.C.
Smillie.

Back Design:
Vignettes depicting
Farming and
Industry. See No.
620.

The following bear the signatures of Burke-McAdoo

No.	Bank	Very Good	Very Fine	New
618A	Boston	25.00	85.00	200.00
618B	New York	20.00	70.00	145.00
618C	Philadelphia	20.00	70.00	145.00
618D	Cleveland	20.00	70.00	130.00
618E	Richmond	20.00	70.00	145.00
618F	Atlanta	20.00	70.00	145.00
618G	Chicago	20.00	70.00	135.00
618H	St. Louis	20.00	70.00	145.00
618I	Minneapolis	20.00	70.00	145.00
618J	Kansas City	20.00	70.00	145.00
618K	Dallas	25.00	85.00	200.00
618L	San Francisco	25.00	85.00	200.00

The first day of issue for the above was November 16, 1914.

Federal Reserve Notes/1914/Blue Seal

No.	Bank	Signatures	Notes Printed	Notes Issued	Very Fine	New
619A1	Boston	Burke-McAdoo			20.00	35.00
619A2	Boston	Burke-Glass	69,756,000	69,756,000	30.00	50.00
619A3	Boston	Burke-Houston			20.00	35.00
619A4	Boston	White-Mellon			20.00	35.00
619B1	New York	Burke-McAdoo			20.00	37.50
619B2	New York	Burke-Glass	176,728,000	176,728,000	30.00	50.00
619B3(☆)	New York	Burke-Houston			20.00	35.00
619B4	New York	White-Mellon			20.00	35.00
619C1	Philadelphia	Burke-McAdoo			20.00	35.00
619C2	Philadelphia	Burke-Glass	56,616,000	56,616,000	30.00	50.00
619C3	Philadelphia	Burke-Houston			20.00	35.00
619C4	Philadelphia	White-Mellon			20.00	35.00
619D1	Cleveland	Burke-McAdoo			20.00	35.00
619D2	Cleveland	Burke-Glass	43,856,000	43,856,000	30.00	50.00
619D3(☆)	Cleveland	Burke-Houston			20.00	35.00
619D4	Cleveland	White-Mellon			20.00	35.00
619E1	Richmond	Burke-McAdoo			20.00	37.50
619E2	Richmond	Burke-Glass	27,528,000	27,528,000	30.00	50.00
619E3	Richmond	Burke-Houston			22.00	40.00
619E4	Richmond	White-Mellon			20.00	37.50
619F1	Atlanta	Burke-McAdoo			20.00	37.50
619F2	Atlanta	Burke-Glass	31,400,000	31,400,000	32.50	55.00
619F3	Atlanta	Burke-Houston			22.00	40.00
619F4	Atlanta	White-Mellon			22.00	40.00

Federal Reserve Notes/1914/Blue Seal

No.	Bank	Signatures	Notes Printed	Notes Issued	Very Fine	New
619G1	Chicago	Burke-McAdoo			20.00	35.00
619G2(☆)	Chicago	Burke-Glass	84,804,000	84,804,000	27.50	45.00
619G3(☆)	Chicago	Burke-Houston			20.00	35.00
619G4	Chicago	White-Mellon			20.00	35.00
619H1(☆)	St. Louis	Burke-McAdoo			20.00	37.50
619H2(☆)	St. Louis	Burke-Glass	21,508,000	21,508,000	30.00	50.00
619H3(☆)	St. Louis	Burke-Houston			20.00	35.00
619H4	St. Louis	White-Mellon			20.00	35.00
619I1	Minneapolis	Burke-McAdoo			20.00	37.50
619I2	Minneapolis	Burke-Glass	14,376,000	14,376,000	30.00	50.00
619I3(☆)	Minneapolis	Burke-Houston			20.00	35.00
619I4	Minneapolis	White-Mellon			20.00	35.00
619J1	Kansas City	Burke-McAdoo			20.00	37.50
619J2	Kansas City	Burke-Glass	16,448,000	16,448,000	35.00	60.00
619J3(☆)	Kansas City	Burke-Houston			22.00	40.00
619J4	Kansas City	White-Mellon			22.00	40.00
619K1	Dallas	Burke-McAdoo			22.00	40.00
619K2	Dallas	Burke-Glass	13,400,000	12,988,000	30.00	47.50
619K3	Dallas	Burke-Houston			22.00	40.00
619K4	Dallas	White-Mellon			22.00	40.00
619L1	San Francisco	Burke-McAdoo			20.00	37.50
619L2	San Francisco	Burke-Glass	41,432,000	41,432,000	35.00	62.50
619L3	San Francisco	Burke-Houston			30.00	47.50
619L4	San Francisco	White-Mellon			20.00	37.50

Federal Reserve Bank Notes/Blue Seal

Face Design:
Portrait of Andrew
Jackson.

Back Design:
Vignettes depicting
Farming and
Industry.

No.	Bank	Date	Gov't. Sig.	Bank Signatures	Notes Issued	Very Good	Very Fine	New
620B	New York*	1918	T-B	Hendricks-Strong	200,000	110.00	265.00	575.00
620F1	Atlanta	1915	T-B	Bell-Wellborn ⎤		175.00	350.00	675.00
620F2	Atlanta	1918	E-B	Bell-Wellborn ⎦	300,000	115.00	300.00	600.00
620G1	Chicago	1915	T-B	McLallen-McDougal ⎤		85.00	200.00	465.00
620G2	Chicago	1918	T-B	McCloud-McDougal ⎦	300,000	85.00	200.00	465.00
620H(☆)	St. Louis**	1918	T-B	Attebery-Wells	100,000	185.00	400.00	925.00
620J1	Kansas City	1915	T-B	Anderson-Miller ⎤		85.00	200.00	465.00
620J2	Kansas City	1915	T-B	Cross-Miller		85.00	200.00	465.00
620J3	Kansas City	1915	T-B	Cross-Miller***	504,000	85.00	200.00	465.00
620J4	Kansas City	1915	T-B	Helm-Miller ⎦		85.00	200.00	465.00
620K1	Dallas	1915	T-B	Hoopes-Van Zandt		85.00	200.00	465.00
620K2	Dallas	1915	T-B	Gilbert-Van Zandt		175.00	500.00	1,100.00
620K3	Dallas	1915	T-B	Talley-Van Zandt	240,000	85.00	200.00	465.00

*343 notes are outstanding
**237 notes are outstanding
***At the time of signing, Cross apparently was the Acting Secretary of the bank.
  T-B: Teehee-Burke   E-B: Elliott-Burke

Silver Certificates/Blue Seal

Face Design:
Portrait of Alexander
Hamilton.

Back Design

No.	Date	Signatures	Notes Printed	Very Fine	Extra Fine	New
621	1933	Julian-Woodin (only 156,000 were released)	216,000	500.00	850.00	2,300.00
621A	1933A	Julian-Morgenthau (only 28,000 were released)	336,000*	—	—	—

1934 Series

Face Design: The seal is now on the right and a blue *10* is on the left.

Back Design: Similar to No. 621.

No.	Date	Signatures	Notes Printed	Very Fine	Extra Fine	New
622	1934	Julian-Morgenthau	9,132,000	15.00	22.50	40.00
622(☆)	1934(☆)	Julian-Morgenthau		20.00	45.00	100.00
623	1934	Julian-Morgenthau ⎤	21,860,000	500.00	950.00	2,250.00
623A	1934A	Julian-Morgenthau ⎦		17.50	27.50	42.50
623A(☆)	1934A(☆)	Julian-Morgenthau		45.00	75.00	115.00

623, 623A, and 623A(☆) have yellow seals. They were issued for use in North Africa during World War II.

No.	Date	Signatures	Notes Printed	Very Fine	Extra Fine	New
624A	1934A	Julian-Morgenthau	42,346,428	12.50	20.00	40.00
624A(☆)	1934A(☆)	Julian-Morgenthau		20.00	30.00	80.00

*Treasury Department Cash Division figures.

Silver Certificates/Blue Seal

No.	Date	Signatures	Notes Printed	Very Fine	Extra Fine	New
624B	1934B	Julian-Vinson	337,740	75.00	200.00	525.00
624B(☆)	1934B(☆)	Julian-Vinson		425.00	600.00	1,350.00
624C	1934C	Julian-Snyder	20,032,632	15.00	20.00	30.00
624C(☆)	1934C(☆)	Julian-Snyder		20.00	30.00	50.00
624D	1934D	Clark-Snyder	11,801,112	12.50	17.50	27.50
624D(☆)	1934D(☆)	Clark-Snyder		20.00	30.00	65.00

1953 Series

Face Design:
The *10* to the left of Hamilton is now grey.

Back Design:
Similar to No. 621.

No.	Date	Signatures	Notes Printed	Very Fine	Extra Fine	New
625	1953	Priest-Humphrey	10,440,000	12.50	20.00	30.00
625(☆)	1953(☆)	Priest-Humphrey	576,000	17.50	30.00	65.00
625A	1953A	Priest-Anderson	1,080,000	12.50	20.00	35.00
625A(☆)	1953A(☆)	Priest-Anderson	144,000	20.00	30.00	65.00
625B	1953B	Smith-Dillon	720,000	15.00	22.00	42.50

Federal Reserve Bank Notes/1929/Brown Seal

Face Design:
Portrait of Alexander
Hamilton.

Back Design:
Similar to No. 621.

The following bear the signatures of Jones-Woods.

No.	Bank	Notes Printed	Very Fine	Extra Fine	New
626A	Boston	1,680,000	20.00	30.00	45.00
626B	New York	5,556,000	15.00	22.50	40.00
626C	Philadelphia	1,416,000	20.00	30.00	45.00
626D	Cleveland	2,412,000	17.50	25.00	42.50
626E	Richmond	1,356,000	20.00	32.50	50.00
626F	Atlanta	1,056,000	20.00	35.00	50.00
626G	Chicago	3,156,000	17.50	22.50	37.50
626H	St. Louis	1,584,000	20.00	32.50	50.00
626I	Minneapolis	588,000	25.00	45.00	75.00
626J	Kansas City	1,284,000	20.00	35.00	50.00
626K	Dallas	504,000	30.00	50.00	90.00
626L	San Francisco	1,080,000	20.00	40.00	70.00

National Bank Notes/1929/Brown Seal

Face Design:
Type I.

Face Design:
Type II has the bank
charter number
printed a second time
near the serial
number.

Back Design:
Similar to No. 621.

Both types bear the signatures of Jones-Woods.

No.	Rarity*	Type I			Type II		
		Very Fine	Extra Fine	New	Very Fine	Extra Fine	New
	1	17.50	30.00	50.00	20.00	35.00	55.00
	2	17.50	32.50	55.00	20.00	35.00	65.00
	3	20.00	37.50	65.00	25.00	40.00	80.00
	4	25.00	45.00	80.00	30.00	55.00	95.00
627	5	30.00	52.50	100.00	40.00	65.00	120.00
	6	40.00	65.00	125.00	55.00	80.00	150.00
	7	65.00	80.00	160.00	80.00	125.00	200.00
	8	100.00	150.00	250.00	200.00	300.00	400.00
	9	480.00	650.00	1,000.00	600.00	850.00	1,250.00

The total issue for both types was 124,236,394.

---

*Rarity table is on page 41.

Federal Reserve Notes/1928/Green Seal

Face Design: The number in the seal indicates the Federal Reserve district.

Back Design: Similar to No. 621.

1928 Series, signatures of Tate-Mellon

No.	Bank	Notes Printed	Very Fine	Extra Fine	New
628A	Boston	9,804,552	15.00	27.50	50.00
628B	New York	11,295,796	15.00	27.50	45.00
628C	Philadelphia	8,114,412	15.00	27.50	45.00
628D	Cleveland	7,570,680	15.00	27.50	45.00
628E	Richmond	4,534,800	15.00	30.00	50.00
628F	Atlanta	6,807,720	15.00	30.00	50.00
628G	Chicago	8,130,000	15.00	25.00	45.00
628H	St. Louis	4,124,100	15.00	30.00	50.00
628I	Minneapolis	3,874,440	15.00	30.00	52.50
628J	Kansas City	3,620,400	15.00	30.00	55.00
628K	Dallas	4,855,500	20.00	30.00	55.00
628L	San Francisco	7,086,900	15.00	25.00	45.00

1928A Series, signatures of Woods-Mellon

No.	Bank	Notes Printed	Very Fine	Extra Fine	New
629A	Boston	2,893,440	15.00	25.00	40.00
629B	New York	18,631,056	15.00	25.00	37.50
629C	Philadelphia	2,710,680	15.00	25.00	40.00
629D	Cleveland	5,610,000	15.00	25.00	37.50
629E	Richmond	552,300	15.00	25.00	45.00
629F	Atlanta	3,033,480	15.00	25.00	40.00
629G	Chicago	8,715,000	15.00	25.00	37.50
629H	St. Louis	531,600	15.00	25.00	45.00
629I	Minneapolis	102,600	17.50	30.00	52.50
629J	Kansas City	410,400	17.50	30.00	50.00
629K	Dallas	961,800	20.00	35.00	55.00
629L	San Francisco	2,547,900	15.00	25.00	37.50

Federal Reserve Notes

1928B Series, signatures of Woods-Mellon.
Letter replaces number in Federal Reserve Seal.

No.	Bank	Notes Printed	Very Fine	Extra Fine	New
630A	Boston	33,218,088	12.50	20.00	27.50
630B	New York	44,458,308	12.50	20.00	27.50
630C	Philadelphia	22,689,216	12.50	20.00	27.50
630D	Cleveland	17,418,024	12.50	20.00	27.50
630E	Richmond	12,714,504	12.50	22.50	32.50
630F	Atlanta	5,246,700	12.50	22.50	35.00
630G	Chicago	38,035,000	12.50	20.00	27.50
630H	St. Louis	10,814,664	15.00	22.50	30.00
630I	Minneapolis	5,294,460	15.00	25.00	40.00
630J	Kansas City	7,748,040	15.00	25.00	40.00
630K	Dallas	3,396,096	17.50	30.00	42.50
630L	San Francisco	22,695,300	12.50	17.50	27.50

1928C Series, signatures of Woods-Mills

No.	Bank	Notes Printed	Very Fine	Extra Fine	New
631B	New York	2,902,678	15.00	25.00	50.00
631D	Cleveland	4,230,428	15.00	25.00	50.00
631E	Richmond	304,800	15.00	30.00	60.00
631F	Atlanta	688,380	15.00	30.00	65.00
631G	Chicago	2,423,400	15.00	25.00	50.00

Federal Reserve Notes/Green Seal

1934 Series, signatures of Julian-Morgenthau

No.	Bank	Notes Printed	Very Fine	Extra Fine	New
632A	Boston	46,276,152	15.00	20.00	30.00
632B	New York	117,298,008	—	17.50	25.00
632C	Philadelphia	34,770,768	15.00	20.00	30.00
632D	Cleveland	28,764,108	15.00	20.00	35.00
632E	Richmond	16,437,252	15.00	20.00	37.50
632F	Atlanta	20,656,872	15.00	25.00	37.50
632G	Chicago	69,962,064	—	17.50	27.50
632H	St. Louis	22,593,204	15.00	25.00	37.50
632I	Minneapolis	16,840,980	15.00	27.50	45.00
632J	Kansas City	22,627,824	15.00	25.00	40.00
632K	Dallas	21,403,488	15.00	25.00	40.00
632L	San Francisco	37,402,308	15.00	20.00	30.00

1934A series, signatures of Julian-Morgenthau

No.	Bank	Notes Printed	Very Fine	Extra Fine	New
633A	Boston	104,540,088	12.00	17.50	30.00
633B	New York	281,940,996	12.00	17.50	30.00
633C	Philadelphia	95,338,032	12.00	17.50	30.00
633D	Cleveland	93,332,004	12.00	17.50	30.00
633E	Richmond	101,037,912	12.00	17.50	30.00
633F	Atlanta	85,478,160	12.00	17.50	30.00
633G	Chicago	177,285,960	12.00	17.50	30.00
633H	St. Louis	50,694,312	12.00	20.00	32.50
633I	Minneapolis	16,340,016	12.00	20.00	35.00
633J	Kansas City	31,069,978	12.00	20.00	32.50
633K	Dallas	28,263,156	12.00	20.00	32.50
633L	San Francisco	125,537,592	12.00	17.50	25.00
633LL	San Francisco (Hawaii)	10,424,000	17.50	27.50	50.00

Federal Reserve Notes/Green Seal

1934B Series, signatures of Julian-Vinson

No.	Bank	Notes Printed	Extra Fine	New
634A	Boston	3,999,600	15.00	30.00
634B	New York	34,815,948	15.00	25.00
634C	Philadelphia	10,339,020	15.00	25.00
634D	Cleveland	1,394,700	15.00	32.50
634E	Richmond	4,018,272	15.00	30.00
634F	Atlanta	6,746,076	20.00	30.00
634G	Chicago	18,130,836	15.00	25.00
634H	St. Louis	6,849,348	17.50	35.00
634I	Minneapolis	2,254,800	22.50	40.00
634J	Kansas City	3,835,764	17.50	35.00
634K	Dallas	3,085,200	17.50	35.00
634L	San Francisco	9,076,800	15.00	30.00

1934C Series, signatures of Julian-Snyder

No.	Bank	Notes Printed	Extra Fine	New
635A	Boston	42,431,404	15.00	25.00
635B	New York	115,675,644	12.50	20.00
635C	Philadelphia	46,874,760	15.00	25.00
635D	Cleveland	332,400	35.00	75.00
635E	Richmond	37,422,600	15.00	25.00
635F	Atlanta	44,838,264	15.00	25.00
635G	Chicago	105,875,412	12.50	20.00
635H	St. Louis	36,541,404	15.00	25.00
635I	Minneapolis	11,944,848	17.50	37.50
635J	Kansas City	20,874,072	15.00	25.00
635K	Dallas	25,642,620	15.00	25.00
635L	San Francisco	49,164,480	15.00	25.00

1934D Series, signatures of Clark-Snyder

No.	Bank	Notes Printed	Extra Fine	New
636A	Boston	19,917,900	15.00	20.00
636B	New York	64,067,904	15.00	20.00
636C	Philadelphia	18,432,000	15.00	20.00
636D	Cleveland	20,291,316	15.00	20.00
636E	Richmond	18,090,312	15.00	20.00
636F	Atlanta	17,064,816	15.00	20.00
636G	Chicago	55,943,844	15.00	20.00
636H	St. Louis	15,828,048	15.00	20.00
636I	Minneapolis	5,237,220	20.00	35.00
636J	Kansas City	7,992,000	20.00	30.00
636K	Dallas	7,178,196	20.00	30.00
636L	San Francisco	23,956,584	15.00	25.00

Federal Reserve Notes/Green Seal

1950 Series, signatures of Clark-Snyder

No.	Bank	Notes Printed	Extra Fine	New
637A	Boston	70,992,000	12.50	20.00
637A(☆)	Boston	1,008,000		25.00
637B	New York	218,576,000	12.50	20.00
637B(☆)	New York	2,568,000		20.00
637C	Philadelphia	76,320,000	12.50	20.00
637C(☆)	Philadelphia	1,008,000		25.00
637D	Cleveland	76,032,000	12.50	20.00
637D(☆)	Cleveland	1,008,000		25.00
637E	Richmond	61,776,000	12.50	20.00
637E(☆)	Richmond	876,000		25.00
637F	Atlanta	63,792,000	12.50	20.00
637F(☆)	Atlanta	864,000		25.00
637G	Chicago	161,056,000	12.50	20.00
637G(☆)	Chicago	2,088,000		20.00
637H	St. Louis	47,808,000	12.50	25.00
637H(☆)	St. Louis	648,000		27.50
637I	Minneapolis	18,864,000	17.50	25.00
637I(☆)	Minneapolis	252,000		30.00
637J	Kansas City	36,332,000	15.00	25.00
637J(☆)	Kansas City	456,000		27.50
637K	Dallas	33,264,000	15.00	25.00
637K(☆)	Dallas	480,000		27.50
637L	San Francisco	76,896,000	12.50	20.00
637L(☆)	San Francisco	1,152,000		25.00

1950A Series, signatures of Priest-Humphrey

No.	Bank	Notes Printed	Extra Fine	New
638A	Boston	104,248,000	12.00	17.50
638A(☆)	Boston	5,112,000		17.50
638B	New York	356,664,000	12.00	17.50
638B(☆)	New York	16,992,000		17.50
638C	Philadelphia	71,920,000	12.00	20.00
638C(☆)	Philadelphia	3,672,000		20.00
638D	Cleveland	75,088,000	12.00	20.00
638D(☆)	Cleveland	3,672,000		20.00
638E	Richmond	82,144,000	12.00	20.00
638E(☆)	Richmond	4,392,000		20.00
638F	Atlanta	73,288,000	12.00	20.00
638F(☆)	Atlanta	3,816,000		20.00
638G	Chicago	235,064,000	12.00	17.50

Federal Reserve Notes/Green Seal

1950A Series, signatures of Priest-Humphrey

No.	Bank	Notes Printed	Extra Fine	New
638G(☆)	Chicago	11,160,000		20.00
638H	St. Louis	46,512,000	12.00	20.00
638H(☆)	St. Louis	2,880,000		20.00
638I	Minneapolis	8,136,000	15.00	25.00
638I(☆)	Minneapolis	432,000		30.00
638J	Kansas City	25,488,000	12.00	20.00
638J(☆)	Kansas City	2,304,000		20.00
638K	Dallas	21,816,000	12.00	20.00
638K(☆)	Dallas	1,584,000		25.00
638L	San Francisco	101,584,000	12.00	17.50
638L(☆)	San Francisco	6,408,000		17.50

1950B Series, signatures of Priest-Anderson

No.	Bank	Notes Printed	Extra Fine	New
639A	Boston	49,240,000		15.00
639A(☆)	Boston	2,880,000		17.50
639B	New York	170,840,000		15.00
639B(☆)	New York	8,280,000		15.00
639C	Philadelphia	66,880,000		15.00
639C(☆)	Philadelphia	3,240,000		17.50
639D	Cleveland	55,360,000		15.00
639D(☆)	Cleveland	2,880,000		17.50
639E	Richmond	51,120,000		15.00
639E(☆)	Richmond	2,880,000		17.50
639F	Atlanta	66,520,000		15.00
639F(☆)	Atlanta	2,880,000		17.50
639G	Chicago	165,080,000		15.00
639G(☆)	Chicago	6,480,000		15.00
639H	St. Louis	33,040,000		15.00
639H(☆)	St. Louis	1,800,000		20.00
639I	Minneapolis	13,320,000		20.00
639I(☆)	Minneapolis	720,000		25.00
639J	Kansas City	33,480,000		15.00
639J(☆)	Kansas City	2,520,000		17.50
639K	Dallas	26,280,000		17.50
639K(☆)	Dallas	1,440,000		20.00
639L	San Francisco	55,000,000		15.00
639L(☆)	San Francisco	2,880,000		17.50

Federal Reserve Notes/Green Seal

No.	Bank	Notes Printed	New	No.	Bank	Notes Printed	New
1950C Series, signatures of Smith-Dillon				1950D Series, signatures of Granahan-Dillon			
640A	Boston	51,120,000	17.00	641A	Boston	38,800,000	16.00
640A(☆)	Boston	2,160,000	20.00	641A(☆)	Boston	1,800,000	20.00
640B	New York	126,520,000	17.00	641B	New York	150,320,000	16.00
640B(☆)	New York	6,840,000	15.00	641B(☆)	New York	6,840,000	17.50
640C	Philadelphia	25,200,000	17.00	641C	Philadelphia	19,080,000	16.00
640C(☆)	Philadelphia	720,000	22.50	641C(☆)	Philadelphia	1,080,000	20.00
640D	Cleveland	33,120,000	17.00	641D	Cleveland	24,120,000	16.00
640D(☆)	Cleveland	1,800,000	20.00	641D(☆)	Cleveland	360,000	25.00
640E	Richmond	45,640,000	17.00	641E	Richmond	33,840,000	16.00
640E(☆)	Richmond	1,800,000	20.00	641E(☆)	Richmond	720,000	22.50
640F	Atlanta	38,880,000	17.00	641F	Atlanta	36,000,000	16.00
640F(☆)	Atlanta	1,800,000	20.00	641F(☆)	Atlanta	1,440,000	20.00
640G	Chicago	69,400,000	17.00	641G	Chicago	115,480,000	16.00
640G(☆)	Chicago	3,600,000	17.50	641G(☆)	Chicago	5,040,000	17.50
640H	St. Louis	23,040,000	17.00	641H	St. Louis	10,440,000	16.00
640H(☆)	St. Louis	1,080,000	20.00	641H(☆)	St. Louis	720,000	22.50
640I	Minneapolis	9,000,000	20.00	641I	Minneapolis	No Record	—
640I(☆)	Minneapolis	720,000	22.50	641I(☆)	Minneapolis	None Printed	
640J	Kansas City	23,320,000	17.00	641J	Kansas City	15,480,000	16.00
640J(☆)	Kansas City	800,000	22.50	641J(☆)	Kansas City	1,080,000	20.00
640K	Dallas	17,640,000	17.00	641K	Dallas	18,280,000	16.00
640K(☆)	Dallas	720,000	22.50	641K(☆)	Dallas	800,000	22.50
640L	San Francisco	35,640,000	17.00	641L	San Francisco	62,560,000	16.00
640L(☆)	San Francisco	1,800,000	20.00	641L(☆)	San Francisco	3,600,000	17.50

1950E Series, signatures of Granahan-Fowler

1963 Series, signatures of Granahan-Dillon.
"IN GOD WE TRUST" now on back

No.	Bank	Notes Printed	New	No.	Bank	Notes Printed	New
642B	New York	12,600,000	12.00	643A	Boston	5,760,000	16.00
642B(☆)	New York	2,621,000	20.00	643B	New York	24,960,000	16.00
642G	Chicago	65,080,000	12.00	643C	Philadelphia	6,400,000	16.00
642G(☆)	Chicago	4,320,000	20.00	643D	Cleveland	7,040,000	16.00
642L	San Francisco	17,280,000	15.00	643E	Richmond	4,480,000	18.00
642L(☆)	San Francisco	720,000	25.00	643F	Atlanta	10,880,000	16.00
				643G	Chicago	35,200,000	16.00
				643H	St. Louis	13,440,000	16.00
				643I	Minneapolis	None Printed	—
				643J	Kansas City	3,840,000	20.00
				643K	Dallas	5,120,000	18.00
				643L	San Francisco	14,080,000	16.00

Federal Reserve Notes/Green Seal

1963A Series, signatures of Granahan-Fowler.

1969 Series, signatures of Elston-Kennedy

No.	Bank	Notes Printed	New	No.	Bank	Notes Printed	New
644A	Boston	131,360,000	14.00	645A	Boston	74,880,000	12.50
644A(☆)	Boston	6,400,000	15.00	645A(☆)	Boston	2,560,000	15.00
644B	New York	199,360,000	14.00	645B	New York	247,360,000	12.50
644B(☆)	New York	9,600,000	15.00	645B(☆)	New York	10,240,000	12.50
644C	Philadelphia	100,000,000	14.00	645C	Philadelphia	56,960,000	12.50
644C(☆)	Philadelphia	4,480,000	15.00	645C(☆)	Philadelphia	2,560,000	15.00
644D	Cleveland	72,960,000	14.00	645D	Cleveland	57,600,000	12.50
644D(☆)	Cleveland	3,840,000	15.00	645D(☆)	Cleveland	2,560,000	15.00
644E	Richmond	114,720,000	14.00	645E	Richmond	56,960,000	12.50
644E(☆)	Richmond	5,120,000	15.00	645E(☆)	Richmond	2,560,000	15.00
644F	Atlanta	80,000,000	14.00	645F	Atlanta	53,760,000	12.50
644F(☆)	Atlanta	3,840,000	15.00	645F(☆)	Atlanta	2,560,000	15.00
644G	Chicago	195,520,000	14.00	645G	Chicago	142,240,000	12.50
644G(☆)	Chicago	9,600,000	15.00	645G(☆)	Chicago	6,400,000	15.00
644H	St. Louis	43,520,000	14.00	645H	St. Louis	22,400,000	12.50
644H(☆)	St. Louis	1,920,000	17.50	645H(☆)	St. Louis	640,000	20.00
644I	Minneapolis	16,640,000	14.00	645I	Minneapolis	12,800,000	12.50
644I(☆)	Minneapolis	640,000	22.50	645I(☆)	Minneapolis	280,000	20.00
644J	Kansas City	31,360,000	14.00	645J	Kansas City	31,360,000	12.50
644J(☆)	Kansas City	1,920,000	17.50	645J(☆)	Kansas City	1,280,000	15.00
644K	Dallas	51,200,000	14.00	645K	Dallas	30,080,000	12.50
644K(☆)	Dallas	1,920,000	17.50	645K(☆)	Dallas	1,280,000	15.00
644L	San Francisco	87,200,000	14.00	645L	San Francisco	56,320,000	12.50
644L(☆)	San Francisco	5,120,000	15.00	645L(☆)	San Francisco	3,185,000	15.00

1969A Series, signatures of Kabis-Connally

No.	Bank	Notes Printed	New	No.	Bank	Notes Printed	New
646A	Boston	41,120,000	12.50	646G	Chicago	80,160,000	12.50
646A(☆)	Boston	1,920,000	15.00	646G(☆)	Chicago	3,560,000	15.00
646B	New York	111,840,000	12.50	646H	St. Louis	15,360,000	12.50
646B(☆)	New York	3,840,000	15.00	646H(☆)	St. Louis	640,000	20.00
646C	Philadelphia	24,320,000	12.50	646I	Minneapolis	8,320,000	12.50
646C(☆)	Philadelphia	1,920,000	15.00	646I(☆)	Minneapolis	—	—
646D	Cleveland	23,680,000	12.50	646J	Kansas City	10,880,000	12.50
646D(☆)	Cleveland	1,276,000	15.00	646J(☆)	Kansas City	—	—
646E	Richmond	25,600,000	12.50	646K	Dallas	20,480,000	12.50
646E(☆)	Richmond	640,000	20.00	646K(☆)	Dallas	640,000	20.00
646F	Atlanta	20,480,000	12.50	646L	San Francisco	27,520,000	12.50
646F(☆)	Atlanta	640,000	20.00	646L(☆)	San Francisco	1,280,000	15.00

Federal Reserve Notes/Green Seal

1969B Series, signatures of Banuelos-Connally   1969C Series, signatures of Banuelos-Shultz.

No.	Bank	Notes Printed	New	No.	Bank	Notes Printed	New
647A	Boston	16,640,000	11.00	648A	Boston	44,800,000	—
647A(☆)	Boston	None Printed		648A(☆)	Boston	640,000	15.00
647B	New York	60,320,000	11.00	648B	New York	203,200,000	—
647B(☆)	New York	1,920,000	12.50	648B(☆)	New York	7,040,000	12.50
647C	Philadelphia	16,000,000	11.00	648C	Philadelphia	69,920,000	—
647C(☆)	Philadelphia	None Printed		648C(☆)	Philadelphia	1,280,000	—
647D	Cleveland	12,800,000	11.00	648D	Cleveland	46,880,000	—
647D(☆)	Cleveland	None Printed		648D(☆)	Cleveland	2,400,000	—
647E	Richmond	12,160,000	11.00	648E	Richmond	45,600,000	—
647E(☆)	Richmond	640,000	17.50	648E(☆)	Richmond	1,120,000	—
647F	Atlanta	13,440,000	11.00	648F	Atlanta	46,240,000	—
647F(☆)	Atlanta	640,000	17.50	648F(☆)	Atlanta	1,920,000	—
647G	Chicago	32,640,000	11.00	648G	Chicago	55,200,000	—
647G(☆)	Chicago	1,268,000	15.00	648G(☆)	Chicago	880,000	15.00
647H	St. Louis	8,960,000	11.00	648H	St. Louis	29,800,000	—
647H(☆)	St. Louis	1,280,000	15.00	648H(☆)	St. Louis	1,280,000	—
647I	Minneapolis	3,200,000	11.00	648I	Minneapolis	11,520,000	—
647I(☆)	Minneapolis	None Printed		648I(☆)	Minneapolis	640,000	15.00
647J	Kansas City	5,120,000	11.00	648J	Kansas City	23,040,000	—
647J(☆)	Kansas City	640,000	17.50	648J(☆)	Kansas City	640,000	15.00
647K	Dallas	5,760,000	11.00	648K	Dallas	24,960,000	—
647K(☆)	Dallas	None Printed		648K(☆)	Dallas	640,000	15.00
647L	San Francisco	23,840,000	11.00	648L	San Francisco	56,960,000	—
647L(☆)	San Francisco	640,000	17.50	648L(☆)	San Francisco	640,000	15.00

1974 Series, signatures of Neff-Simon.

Gold Certificate/Gold Seal

Face Design:
Engraved by H.K.
Earle, H.S. Nutter,
F. Pauling, and
W.B. Wells.

Back Design:
See No. 621.

No.	Date	Signatures	Notes Printed	Very Fine	Extra Fine	New
699	1928	Woods-Mellon	130,812,000	25.00	40.00	85.00
699(☆)	1928(☆)	Woods-Mellon		75.00	135.00	225.00
699A	1928A	Woods-Mills	2,544,000	Never released		

Demand Notes/1861

LARGE SIZE

Face Design:
Symbolic figure of
Liberty holds sword
and shield.

Back Design

(Photograph courtesy
William T. Anton, Jr.)

No.	Payable at	Notes Issued	Good	Very Good	Fine
700A	Boston		4,000.00	8,000.00	—
700B	New York		2,500.00	6,250.00	—
700C	Philadelphia	910,000*	3,000.00	7,000.00	—
700D	Cincinnati		Extremely Rare		
700E	St. Louis		Unknown		

Treasurer F.E. Spinner was presented with the first sheet of second emission $20 demand notes; unsigned and canceled, the sheet was cut. Spinner gave two notes to government officials and retained the note illustrated and the remaining note. A total of $60,030,000, including $5 and $10 notes of this series, was issued, all without the Treasury Seal and the signatures of the Treasurer and the Register of the Treasury. Officials representing these two offices signed for them, and the words "for the" preceding the titles were sometimes written by hand. These notes are exceedingly rare.

*610 notes were outstanding according to records of 1927.

United States Notes/Red Seal

Face Design: Similar to preceding note with the addition of the Treasury Seal and the deletion of the words "On Demand."

Back Design: First obligation.

Back Design: Second obligation.

The following bear the signatures of Chittenden-Spinner.

No.	Date	Notes Printed	Very Good	Very Fine	New
701	1862*		125.00	350.00	925.00
701a	1862**	3,895,984	110.00	425.00	1,125.00
702	1863**		70.00	350.00	900.00

*First Obligation
**Second obligation

United States Notes/Red Seal

Face Design:
The portrait of
Alexander Hamilton
was engraved by
Charles Burt. *Liberty*
on the right was
designed by
S.A. Schoff.

Back Design

No.	Date	Signatures	Notes Issued	Very Good	Very Fine	New
703	1869	Allison-Spinner	3,658,120	185.00	650.00	2,000.00

United States Notes

Face Design:
Similar to No. 703
with the exception
of the changes
indicated below.

Back Design

No.	Date	Signatures	Seal	Notes Issued	Very Good	Very Fine	New
		The following have *XX* in red on the left and right.					
704	1875	Allison-New	Sm. Red-r	12,500,000	110.00	275.00	850.00
705	1878	Allison-Gilfillan	Sm. Red-r	1,740,000	110.00	315.00	900.00

United States Notes

No.	Date	Signatures	Seal	Notes Printed	Very Good	Very Fine	New
				The following are without *XX;* the serial numbers are now blue.			
706	1880	Scofield-Gilfillan	Brown		75.00	165.00	375.00
707	1880	Bruce-Gilfillan	Brown		75.00	165.00	375.00
708	1880	Bruce-Wyman	Brown		75.00	150.00	325.00
709	1880	Bruce-Wyman	Lg. Red		75.00	185.00	375.00
710	1880	Rosecrans-Jordan	Lg. Red		75.00	200.00	375.00
711	1880	Rosecrans-Hyatt	Lg. Red		75.00	165.00	325.00
712	1880	Rosecrans-Hyatt	Lg. Red-sp		75.00	225.00	550.00
713	1880	Rosecrans-Huston	Lg. Red-sp		75.00	225.00	550.00
714	1880	Rosecrans-Huston	Brown		75.00	225.00	425.00
715	1880	Rosecrans-Nebeker	Brown		175.00	300.00	600.00
716	1880	Rosecrans-Nebeker	Sm. Red-sc		65.00	125.00	300.00
717	1880	Tillman-Morgan	Sm. Red-sc		65.00	150.00	300.00
718	1880	Bruce-Roberts	Sm. Red-sc		65.00	150.00	325.00
719	1880	Lyons-Roberts	Sm. Red-sc		65.00	150.00	300.00
720	1880	Vernon-Treat	Sm. Red-sc	404,000	65.00	165.00	375.00
721	1880	Vernon-McClung	Sm. Red-sc	408,000	65.00	165.00	375.00
			The following have red serial numbers once again.				
722(☆)1880		Teehee-Burke	Sm. Red-sc	400,000*	65.00	150.00	325.00
723(☆)1880		Elliott-White	Sm. Red-sc		65.00	100.00	285.00

The official total for Nos. 706–723 is 20,792,000, however, higher serial numbers have been recorded by Walter Breen who believes the total could be 21,252,000.

*This figure might prove to be incomplete.
 r: with rays   sp: with spikes   sc: with scallops

Compound Interest Treasury Note/6%

Act of March 3, 1863. The face and back designs are similar to the following note.

No.	Signatures	Notes Printed	Issued	Outstanding	Fine
724	Chittenden-Spinner	152,000	0	0	

Face Design: The portrait of Abraham Lincoln probably was engraved by Henry Gugler. The two vignettes are entitled *Victory and Mortar Firing.*

Back Design

No.	Signatures	Notes Printed	Issued	Outstanding	Fine
725	Chittenden-Spinner	696,000	677,600		—
726	Colby-Spinner	1,228,128	1,181,492	1,715	2,750.00

Interest-bearing Note/5%

Face Design:
Similar to No. 725.

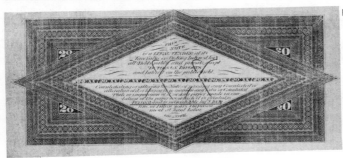

Back Design

Act of March 3, 1863

No.	Signatures	Notes Issued	Outstanding	Fine	Very Fine
727*	Chittenden-Spinner	822,000	602	2,000.00	4,750.00

*14 are known.

National Bank Notes/First Charter Period

Face Design: Felix O.C. Darley painted the original version of the *Battle of Lexington, 1775,* engraved here by Louis Delnoce. *Loyalty* on the right was engraved by Alfred Jones.

Back Design: The *Baptism of Pocahontas* by John G. Chapman was engraved by Charles Burt.

No.	Date	Signatures	Seal	Very Good	Very Fine	New
728	Orig*	Chittenden-Spinner	Red-r	225.00	800.00	1,750.00
729	Orig*	Colby-Spinner	Red-r	225.00	725.00	1,700.00
730	Orig*	Jeffries-Spinner	Red-r	—	—	—
731	Orig*	Allison-Spinner	Red-r	225.00	725.00	1,700.00
732	1875	Allison-New	Red-sc	225.00	725.00	1,700.00
733	1875	Allison-Wyman	Red-sc	225.00	725.00	1,700.00
734	1875	Allison-Gilfillan	Red-sc	225.00	725.00	1,700.00
735	1875	Scofield-Gilfillan	Red-sc	225.00	725.00	1,700.00
736	1875	Bruce-Gilfillan	Red-sc	225.00	725.00	1,700.00
737	1875	Bruce-Wyman	Red-sc	225.00	725.00	1,700.00
738	1875	Rosecrans-Huston	Red-sc	225.00	725.00	1,700.00
739	1875	Rosecrans-Nebeker	Red-sc	225.00	800.00	1,750.00
740	1875	Tillman-Morgan	Red-sc		Unknown	

A total of 340,082 notes are outstanding for all the above.

*The original notes did not have a date printed on the face.
 r: with rays   sc: with scallops

National Bank Notes/1882/Second Charter Period

Face Design:
Similar to
No. 735.

Back Design

First Issue—Brown Seal

No.	Signatures	Very Good	Very Fine	New
741	Bruce-Gilfillan	85.00	175.00	400.00
742	Bruce-Wyman	85.00	175.00	400.00
743	Bruce-Jordan	125.00	275.00	575.00
744	Rosecrans-Jordan	85.00	175.00	400.00
745	Rosecrans-Hyatt	85.00	175.00	400.00
746	Rosecrans-Huston	85.00	175.00	400.00
747	Rosecrans-Nebeker	85.00	175.00	400.00
748	Rosecrans-Morgan	225.00	800.00	2,250.00
749	Tillman-Morgan	85.00	175.00	400.00
750	Tillman-Roberts	85.00	175.00	400.00
751	Bruce-Roberts	85.00	175.00	400.00
752	Lyons-Roberts	85.00	175.00	400.00
753	Lyons-Treat	165.00	450.00	800.00
754	Vernon-Treat	115.00	300.00	575.00

National Bank Notes/1882/Second Charter Period

Face Design:
Similar to No. 735.

Back Design: Green

Second Issue—Blue Seal

No.	Signatures	Very Good	Very Fine	New
755	Rosecrans-Huston	145.00	315.00	525.00
756	Rosecrans-Nebeker	135.00	215.00	450.00
757	Rosecrans-Morgan	300.00	875.00	2,000.00
758	Tillman-Morgan	135.00	215.00	450.00
759	Tillman-Roberts	135.00	215.00	525.00
760	Bruce-Roberts	135.00	300.00	550.00
761	Lyons-Roberts	135.00	215.00	450.00
762	Vernon-Treat	145.00	300.00	525.00
763	Napier-McClung	145.00	400.00	675.00

Face Design:
Similar to No. 735.

Back Design:
Denomination
replaces dates.

No.	Signatures	Very Good	Very Fine	New
764	Tillman-Morgan	165.00	475.00	1,000.00
765	Tillman-Roberts	200.00	600.00	1,200.00
766	Bruce-Roberts	200.00	600.00	1,200.00
767	Lyons-Roberts	150.00	375.00	950.00
768	Lyons-Treat	185.00	525.00	1,100.00
769	Vernon-Treat	185.00	525.00	1,100.00
770	Napier-McClung	165.00	475.00	975.00
771	Parker-Burke		Rare	
772	Teehee-Burke	100.00	500.00	1,200.00

National Bank Notes/1902/Third Charter Period

Face Design: Hugh McCulloch held the office of Secretary of the Treasury twice, 1865–1869 and 1884–1885. Ostrander Smith designed this note, and Charles Burt executed the engraving.

Back Design: The design is the same for all three issues. The second has "1902–1908" added. *Union and Civilization* was engraved by G.F.C. Smillie.

First Issue—Red Seal

No.	Signatures	Very Good	Very Fine	New
773	Lyons-Roberts	85.00	135.00	450.00
774	Lyons-Treat	125.00	200.00	500.00
775	Vernon-Treat	165.00	225.00	600.00

Second Issue—Blue Seal

No.	Signatures	Very Good	Very Fine	New
776	Lyons-Roberts	45.00	75.00	115.00
777	Lyons-Treat	45.00	75.00	115.00
778	Vernon-Treat	45.00	75.00	115.00
779	Vernon-McClung	45.00	75.00	115.00
780	Napier-McClung	45.00	115.00	185.00
781	Napier-Thompson	45.00	80.00	125.00
782	Napier-Burke	45.00	80.00	145.00
783	Parker-Burke	45.00	80.00	145.00
784	Teehee-Burke	85.00	150.00	215.00

National Bank Notes/1902/Third Charter Period

Face Design:
Similar to
preceding note.
Peter Huntoon
classifies this
illustrated note as
a five-star rarity.

Third Issue—Blue Seal

No.	Signatures	Very Good	Very Fine	New
785	Lyons-Roberts	50.00	65.00	125.00
786	Lyons-Treat	50.00	65.00	125.00
787	Vernon-Treat	50.00	65.00	125.00
788	Vernon-McClung	50.00	65.00	125.00
789	Napier-McClung	50.00	65.00	125.00
790	Napier-Thompson	60.00	135.00	300.00
791	Napier-Burke	55.00	70.00	130.00
792	Parker-Burke	55.00	70.00	130.00
793	Teehee-Burke	55.00	75.00	135.00
794	Elliott-Burke	55.00	70.00	130.00
795	Elliott-White	55.00	70.00	130.00
796	Speelman-White	55.00	100.00	150.00
797	Woods-White	55.00	150.00	375.00
798	Woods-Tate	125.00	350.00	600.00
798a	Jones-Woods		Rare	

National Gold Bank Notes/Red Seal

Face Design:
See No. 735 for
complete description.

Back Design

The signatures of Bruce-Gilfillan appear on Nos. 800 and 800a, Scofield-Gilfillan on 804 and 804a, and Allison-Spinner on the remaining notes.

No.	Date	Issuing Bank	City	Notes Issued	Good	Very Good
799	1870*	First National Gold Bank	San Francisco	11,248	750.00	1,200.00
800	1875	First National Gold Bank	San Francisco	3,600	900.00	1,400.00
800a	1875	Same as above on white paper			3 Known	
801	1872	National Gold Bank of D.O. Mills & Company	Sacramento	3,641	750.00	1,000.00
802	1873*	First National Gold Bank	Stockton	5,000	725.00	950.00
802a	1875	First National Gold Bank	Stockton	293	—	—
803	1874	Farmers' National Gold Bank	San Jose	2,849	725.00	975.00
804	1874*	First National Gold Bank	Petaluma	2,000	750.00	1,000.00
804a	1875	First National Gold Bank	Petaluma	363	—	—
805	1875*	First National Gold Bank	Oakland	1,600	800.00	1,075.00
805a	1875	First National Gold Bank	Oakland	12	—	—
806	1875	Union National Gold Bank	Oakland	500	1,000.00	1,450.00
807	1873*	First National Gold Bank	Santa Barbara	800	1 Known	

506 notes are outstanding for Nos. 799-807.

*Original Series

Silver Certificates

Face Design: Sinnepuxcent, Maryland, was the place of Stephen Decatur's birth. Decatur chose a naval career, and as a commander he was killed in a duel by James Baron in 1820. Decatur's portrait was engraved by Lorenzo Hatch.

Back Design

The following notes bear the signatures of Scofield-Gilfillan and have red seals with the exception of No. 813, which has a brown seal.

No.	Date	Countersigned by	Payable at	Notes Issued	Very Good	Fine	New
808	1878	W.G. White*	New York	20,000	—	—	—
809	1878	J.C. Hopper*	New York		500.00	1,750.00	—
809a	1878	T. Hillhouse	New York	22,000		Unique	
810	1878	R.M. Anthony*	San Francisco	3,300		Unknown	
811	1878	A.U. Wyman*	Washington, D.C.	4,000		Unique	
812	1878	A.U. Wyman**	Washington, D.C.	88,000	500.00	1,500.00	—
813	1880	T. Hillhouse	New York	182,000	500.00	1,500.00	—

No.	Date	Signatures	Seal	Notes Issued	Very Good	Very Fine	New
814	1880	Scofield-Gilfillan	Brown	1,216,000	125.00	500.00	2,000.00
815	1880	Bruce-Gilfillan	Brown	556,000	175.00	500.00	2,000.00
816	1880	Bruce-Wyman	Brown	1,972,000	125.00	500.00	2,000.00
817	1880	Bruce-Wyman	Red	124,000	200.00	800.00	2,750.00

Proof impressions of the above were made with the signatures of Rosecrans-Jordan.

*Autographed countersignatures.
**At least 10 notes are known.

Silver Certificates/1886

Face Design:
Lorenzo Hatch
engraved the portrait
of Daniel Manning,
Secretary of the
Treasury, 1885-1887.
The allegorical
figures of Agriculture
and Industry are seen
on the left and right.

Back Design:
Engraved by
D.M. Cooper and
G.U. Rose.

No.	Signatures	Seal	Notes Printed	Very Good	Very Fine	New
818	Rosecrans-Hyatt	Red		135.00	550.00	2,000.00
819	Rosecrans-Huston	Brown	1,712,000*	135.00	550.00	2,000.00
820	Rosecrans-Nebeker	Brown		165.00	600.00	2,150.00
821	Rosecrans-Nebeker	Red		185.00	650.00	3,000.00

1891 Series

Face Design:
Similar to No. 821.

Back Design

822	Rosecrans-Nebeker	Red		85.00	285.00	800.00
823	Tillman-Morgan	Red		85.00	285.00	800.00
824	Bruce-Roberts	Red		85.00	285.00	800.00
825	Lyons-Roberts	Red	11,028,000	85.00	285.00	800.00
826	Parker-Burke	Blue		85.00	285.00	875.00
827	Teehee-Burke	Blue		85.00	285.00	875.00

Nos. 826 & 827 have *XX* in blue on the face.

*1,682,000 notes were issued.

Gold Certificates/Act of March 3, 1863/First Issue

No. *827a*

Face Design:
An eagle with wings spread is entitled *E Pluribus Unum.* The engraving is by Charles Skinner.

Back Design:
20 on the left and right. Of 100,000 notes printed, 48,000 were issued; 9 were outstanding in 1895, and 2 are known.

Series 1882

Face Design:
Portrait of President James Garfield, engraved by Charles Burt.

Back Design:
M.W. Baldwin's *Ocean Telegraph* commemorated the completion of the Atlantic Cable in August 1858.

No.	Signatures	Seal	Notes Issued	Very Good	Very Fine	New
828	Bruce-Gilfillan	Brown	14,000*	1,200.00	4,000.00	—
Autographed countersignature of Thomas C. Acton.						
829	Bruce-Gilfillan	Brown	586,000*	1,100.00	3,500.00	—
Printed countersignature of Thomas C. Acton.						
830	Bruce-Gilfillan	Brown	72,000	—	—	—
831	Bruce-Wyman	Brown	608,000	750.00	1,200.00	2,350.00
832	Rosecrans-Huston	Lg. Brown	200,000	900.00	1,600.00	—
833	Lyons-Roberts	Sm. Red	16,544,000	125.00	225.00	500.00

*These notes are payable at New York; less than 20 are known for both types combined.

Gold Certificates

Face Design:
Portrait of George
Washington.

Back Design:
The Great Seal of the
United States as seen
here was engraved
by R. Ponickau.

No.	Date	Signatures	Seal	Notes Issued	Very Good	Very Fine	New
834	1905	Lyons-Roberts	Red	1,664,000	200.00	700.00	2,000.00
835	1905	Lyons-Treat	Red	3,012,000	200.00	675.00	1,750.00
836	1906	Vernon-Treat	Gold	6,232,000*	50.00	100.00	325.00
837	1906	Vernon-McClung	Gold		50.00	100.00	325.00
838(☆)	1906	Napier-McClung	Gold	14,400,000*	50.00	100.00	325.00
839	1906	Napier-Thompson**	Gold		70.00	145.00	475.00
840(☆)	1906	Parker-Burke	Gold	9,914,587*	50.00	100.00	325.00
841	1906	Teehee-Burke	Gold	17,544,000	50.00	100.00	325.00
842(☆)	1922	Speelman-White	Gold	87,120,000	37.50	60.00	235.00

*Treasury ledgers are incomplete therefore these figures are based on observed serial numbers and conjecture for No. 838.
**Walter Breen reports that 660,000 notes were issued in September 1913. It is possible that they bore the signatures of Napier-Thompson.

Treasury Notes/1890

Face Design: John Marshall served as Secretary of State under John Adams and later as Chief Justice of the Supreme Court. He was born in Virginia in 1755, and he died in Philadelphia in 1835. His portrait was engraved by Charles Schlecht.

Back Design

No.	Signatures	Seal	Notes Printed	Very Good	Very Fine	New
843	Rosecrans-Huston	Brown		225.00	800.00	4,700.00
844	Rosecrans-Nebeker	Brown	1,292,000	275.00	800.00	4,850.00
845	Rosecrans-Nebeker	Red		225.00	800.00	4,700.00

Treasury Notes/1891

Face Design:
Similar to No. 845.

Back Design

No.	Signatures	Seal	Notes Printed	Very Good	Very Fine	New
846	Tillman-Morgan*	Red		375.00	1,000.00	8,500.00
847	Bruce-Roberts	Red	1,148,000**		Unique	

*23 notes are outstanding; 12 are known.
**496,000 notes were issued.

Federal Reserve Notes/1914/Red Seal

Face Design:
Stephen Grover
Cleveland. G.F.C.
Smillie was the
engraver.

Back Design: The
three methods of
transportation are
depicted.

The following bear the signatures of Burke-McAdoo

No.	Bank	Very Good	Very Fine	New
848A	Boston	50.00	100.00	225.00
848B	New York	50.00	85.00	200.00
848C	Philadelphia	50.00	85.00	200.00
848D	Cleveland	50.00	85.00	200.00
848E	Richmond	50.00	85.00	200.00
848F	Atlanta	50.00	85.00	200.00
848G	Chicago	50.00	85.00	200.00
848H	St. Louis	50.00	85.00	200.00
848I	Minneapolis	50.00	85.00	200.00
848J	Kansas City	50.00	85.00	200.00
848K	Dallas	50.00	85.00	200.00
848L	San Francisco	50.00	100.00	225.00

The first day of issue for the above was November 16, 1914.

Federal Reserve Notes/1914/Blue Seal

No.	Bank	Signatures	Notes Printed	Notes Issued	Very Fine	New
849A1	Boston	Burke-McAdoo			25.00	50.00
849A2	Boston	Burke-Glass	26,024,000	25,760,000	35.00	75.00
849A3(☆)	Boston	Burke-Houston			25.00	50.00
849A4	Boston	White-Mellon			25.00	50.00
849B1	New York	Burke-McAdoo			25.00	50.00
849B2	New York	Burke-Glass	59,848,000	58,704,000	35.00	75.00
849B3	New York	Burke-Houston			25.00	50.00
849B4	New York	White-Mellon			25.00	50.00
849C1	Philadelphia	Burke-McAdoo			25.00	50.00
849C2	Philadelphia	Burke-Glass	30,088,000	30,088,000	35.00	75.00
849C3	Philadelphia	Burke-Houston			25.00	50.00
849C4	Philadelphia	White-Mellon			25.00	50.00
849D1	Cleveland	Burke-McAdoo			25.00	50.00
849D2	Cleveland	Burke-Glass	38,544,000	38,544,000	35.00	85.00
849D3	Cleveland	Burke-Houston			25.00	50.00
849D4	Cleveland	White-Mellon			25.00	50.00
849E1	Richmond	Burke-McAdoo			35.00	75.00
849E2	Richmond	Burke-Glass	17,336,000	16,944,000	35.00	75.00
849E3	Richmond	Burke-Houston			25.00	50.00
849E4	Richmond	White-Mellon			25.00	50.00
849F1	Atlanta	Burke-McAdoo			25.00	50.00
849F2	Atlanta	Burke-Glass	16,384,000	15,956,000	45.00	100.00
849F3	Atlanta	Burke-Houston			25.00	50.00
849F4	Atlanta	White-Mellon			25.00	50.00
849G1	Chicago	Burke-McAdoo			25.00	50.00
849G2	Chicago	Burke-Glass	46,776,000	46,776,000	35.00	85.00
849G3	Chicago	Burke-Houston			25.00	50.00
849G4	Chicago	White-Mellon			25.00	50.00
849H1	St. Louis	Burke-McAdoo			30.00	65.00
849H2	St. Louis	Burke-Glass	10,748,000	10,748,000	35.00	85.00
849H3	St. Louis	Burke-Houston			27.50	60.00
849H4	St. Louis	White-Mellon			27.50	60.00

Federal Reserve Notes/1914/Blue Seal

No.	Bank	Signatures	Notes Printed	Notes Issued	Very Fine	New
849I1	Minneapolis	Burke-McAdoo			25.00	55.00
849I2	Minneapolis	Burke-Glass	6,872,000	6,600,000	35.00	85.00
849I3	Minneapolis	Burke-Houston			25.00	50.00
849I4	Minneapolis	White-Mellon			25.00	55.00
849J1	Kansas City	Burke-McAdoo			25.00	50.00
849J2	Kansas City	Burke-Glass	9,172,000	9,172,000	45.00	100.00
849J3	Kansas City	Burke-Houston			25.00	55.00
849J4	Kansas City	White-Mellon			25.00	50.00
849K1	Dallas	Burke-McAdoo			25.00	50.00
849K2	Dallas	Burke-Glass	7,064,000	6,872,000	35.00	85.00
849K3	Dallas	Burke-Houston			25.00	50.00
849K4	Dallas	White-Mellon			25.00	50.00
849L1	San Francisco	Burke-McAdoo			35.00	75.00
849L2	San Francisco	Burke-Glass	35,756,000	35,756,000	45.00	100.00
849L3	San Francisco	Burke-Houston			25.00	50.00
849L4	San Francisco	White-Mellon			25.00	50.00

Federal Reserve Bank Notes/Blue Seal

Face Design:
Portrait of Grover
Cleveland.

Back Design:
Similar to No. 848.

No.	Bank	Date	Gov't. Sig.	Bank Signatures	Notes Issued	Very Good	Very Fine	New
850F1	Atlanta	1915	T-B	Bell-Welborn (Bell as Cashier)		135.00	375.00	900.00
850F2	Atlanta	1915	T-B	Bell-Wellborn (Bell as Secretary)	24,000	135.00	375.00	900.00
850F3	Atlanta	1915	T-B	Pike-McCord			Unique	
850F4	Atlanta	1918	E-B	Bell-Wellborn	96,000	100.00	300.00	800.00
850G	Chicago*	1915	T-B	McLallen-McDougal	84,000	135.00	350.00	850.00
850H	St. Louis**	1918	T-B	Attebery-Wells	24,000	265.00	750.00	—
850J1	Kansas City	1915	T-B	Anderson-Miller	180,000	125.00	250.00	750.00
850J2	Kansas City	1915	T-B	Cross-Miller		125.00	250.00	750.00
850K1	Dallas	1915	T-B	Hoopes-Van Zandt		185.00	600.00	2,000.00
850K2	Dallas	1915	T-B	Gilbert-Van Zandt	100,000***	—	900.00	3,750.00
850K3	Dallas	1915	T-B	Talley-Van Zandt		185.00	625.00	2,000.00

* 170 notes are outstanding
**93 notes are outstanding.
***230 notes are outstanding; 2 are known for 850K2.
  T-B: Teehee-Burke   E-B: Elliott-Burke

Federal Reserve Bank Notes/1929/Brown Seal

SMALL SIZE

Face Design:
Portrait of
Andrew Jackson.

Back Design

The following bear the signatures of Jones-Woods.

No.	Bank	Notes Printed	Very Fine	Extra Fine	New
851A	Boston	972,000	32.50	45.00	60.00
851B	New York	2,568,000	27.50	35.00	50.00
851C	Philadelphia	1,008,000	27.50	37.50	55.00
851D	Cleveland	1,020,000	27.50	37.50	55.00
851E	Richmond	1,632,000	27.50	35.00	55.00
851F	Atlanta	960,000	32.50	45.00	65.00
851G	Chicago	2,028,000	27.50	35.00	50.00
851H	St. Louis	444,000	37.50	57.50	85.00
851I	Minneapolis	864,000	30.00	45.00	70.00
851J	Kansas City	612,000	30.00	45.00	75.00
851K	Dallas	468,000	32.50	45.00	80.00
851L	San Francisco	888,000	30.00	45.00	70.00

National Bank Notes/1929/Brown Seal

Face Design:
Portrait of Andrew
Jackson. Type I.

Face Design:
Type II has the bank
charter number
printed a second time
near the serial
number.

Back Design:
Similar to No. 851.

Both types bear the signatures of Jones-Woods.

No.	Rarity*	Type I			Type II		
		Very Fine	Extra Fine	New	Very Fine	Extra Fine	New
	1	25.00	35.00	55.00	25.00	40.00	60.00
	2	30.00	40.00	60.00	30.00	45.00	65.00
	3	35.00	45.00	65.00	35.00	50.00	75.00
	4	45.00	55.00	80.00	45.00	60.00	100.00
852	5	50.00	65.00	100.00	55.00	70.00	125.00
	6	65.00	85.00	125.00	75.00	100.00	150.00
	7	80.00	100.00	160.00	100.00	145.00	200.00
	8	95.00	150.00	250.00	200.00	300.00	400.00
	9	450.00	650.00	1,000.00	600.00	850.00	1,250.00

The total issue for both types was 22,531,578.

*Rarity table on page 41.

Federal Reserve Notes/Green Seal

Face Design

Back Design:
Similar to No. 851.

1928 Series, signatures of Tate-Mellon

No.	Bank	Notes Printed	Extra Fine	New
853A	Boston	3,790,880	30.00	50.00
853B	New York	12,797,200	30.00	47.50
853C	Philadelphia	3,787,200	30.00	50.00
853D	Cleveland	10,626,900	30.00	47.50
853E	Richmond	4,119,600	30.00	60.00
853F	Atlanta	3,842,388	30.00	60.00
853G	Chicago	10,891,740	30.00	50.00
853H	St. Louis	2,523,300	30.00	65.00
853I	Minneapolis	2,633,100	35.00	65.00
853J	Kansas City	2,584,500	35.00	65.00
853K	Dallas	1,568,500	35.00	65.00
853L	San Francisco	8,404,800	30.00	55.00

1928A Series, signatures of Woods-Mellon

No.	Bank	Notes Printed	Extra Fine	New
854A	Boston	1,293,900	30.00	50.00
854B	New York	1,055,800	30.00	50.00
854C	Philadelphia	1,717,200	30.00	50.00
854D	Cleveland	625,200	32.50	60.00
854E	Richmond	1,534,500	32.50	55.00
854F	Atlanta	1,442,400	32.50	55.00
854G	Chicago	822,000	32.50	60.00
854H	St. Louis	573,300	32.50	65.00
854I	Minneapolis		None Issued	
854J	Kansas City	113,900	35.00	75.00
854K	Dallas	1,032,000	35.00	65.00
854L	San Francisco		None Issued	

Federal Reserve Notes/Green Seal

1928B Series, signatures of Woods-Mellon

No.	Bank	Notes Printed	Extra Fine	New
855A	Boston	7,749,636	27.50	45.00
855B	New York	19,448,436	25.00	40.00
855C	Philadelphia	8,095,548	25.00	40.00
855D	Cleveland	11,684,196	25.00	40.00
855E	Richmond	4,413,900	27.50	45.00
855F	Atlanta	2,390,240	32.50	50.00
855G	Chicago	17,220,276	25.00	40.00
855H	St. Louis	3,834,600	32.50	50.00
855I	Minneapolis	3,298,920	32.50	50.00
855J	Kansas City	4,941,252	32.50	50.00
855K	Dallas	2,406,060	32.50	50.00
855L	San Francisco	9,689,124	27.50	45.00

1928C Series, signatures of Woods-Mills

No.	Bank	Notes Printed	Extra Fine	New
856G	Chicago	3,363,300	55.00	115.00
856L	San Francisco	1,420,200	60.00	125.00

Federal Reserve Notes/Green Seal

1934 Series, signatures of Julian-Morgenthau

No.	Bank	Notes Printed	Very Fine	Extra Fine	New
857A	Boston	37,673,068	—	27.50	40.00
857B	New York	27,573,264	—	27.50	40.00
857C	Philadelphia	53,209,968	—	27.50	40.00
857D	Cleveland	48,301,416	—	27.50	40.00
857E	Richmond	36,259,224	—	27.50	40.00
857F	Atlanta	41,547,660	—	27.50	40.00
857G	Chicago	20,777,832	—	27.50	40.00
857H	St. Louis	27,174,552	—	27.50	40.00
857I	Minneapolis	16,795,116	25.00	30.00	47.50
857J	Kansas City	28,865,304	25.00	30.00	45.00
857K	Dallas	20,852,160	25.00	30.00	45.00
857L	San Francisco	32,203,956	—	27.50	40.00
857LL	San Francisco*	11,246,000	100.00	250.00	500.00

1934A Series, signature of Julian-Morgenthau

No.	Bank	Notes Printed	Very Fine	Extra Fine	New
858A	Boston	3,302,416	—	27.50	40.00
858B	New York	102,555,538	—	27.50	40.00
858C	Philadelphia	3,371,316	—	27.50	45.00
858D	Cleveland	23,475,108	—	27.50	40.00
858E	Richmond	46,816,224	—	27.50	40.00
858F	Atlanta	6,756,816	—	27.50	40.00
858G	Chicago	91,141,452	—	27.50	40.00
858H	St. Louis	3,701,568	—	27.50	45.00
858I	Minneapolis	1,162,500	25.00	30.00	50.00
858J	Kansas City	3,221,184	25.00	30.00	47.50
858K	Dallas	2,531,700	—	27.50	47.50
858L	San Francisco	94,454,112	—	27.50	40.00
858LL	San Francisco*	Included in 857LL	30.00	50.00	75.00

*These notes bear brown seals and "HAWAII" overprints. They were issued for use in the Pacific during World War II.

Federal Reserve Notes/Green Seal

1934B Series, signatures of Julian-Vinson

No.	Bank	Notes Printed	Extra Fine	New
859A	Boston	3,904,800	30.00	45.00
859B	New York	14,876,436	25.00	40.00
859C	Philadelphia	3,271,452	27.50	45.00
859D	Cleveland	2,814,600	30.00	47.50
859E	Richmond	9,451,632	25.00	40.00
859F	Atlanta	6,887,640	25.00	40.00
859G	Chicago	9,084,600	25.00	40.00
859H	St. Louis	5,817,300	30.00	45.00
859I	Minneapolis	2,304,800	32.50	50.00
859J	Kansas City	3,524,244	30.00	45.00
859K	Dallas	2,807,388	35.00	50.00
859L	San Francisco	5,289,540	25.00	40.00

1934C Series, signatures of Julian-Snyder

Structural changes on the White House were seen for the first time on $20 notes commencing July 20, 1948, during the printing of the 1934C series. Two additional chimneys, a second floor balcony, and larger trees and shrubbery are visible in the revised vignette.

No.	Bank	Notes Printed	Extra Fine	New
860A	Boston	7,397,352	27.50	42.50
860B	New York	18,668,148	27.50	40.00
860C	Philadelphia	11,590,752	27.50	40.00
860D	Cleveland	17,912,424	27.50	40.00
860E	Richmond	22,526,568	27.50	40.00
860F	Atlanta	18,858,876	27.50	40.00
860G	Chicago	26,031,660	27.50	37.50
860H	St. Louis	13,276,984	27.50	40.00
860I	Minneapolis	3,490,200	30.00	50.00
860J	Kansas City	9,675,468	27.50	42.50
860K	Dallas	10,205,364	27.50	42.50
860L	San Francisco	20,580,828	25.00	37.50

Federal Reserve Notes/Green Seal

1934 D Series, signatures of Clark-Snyder

No.	Bank	Notes Printed	Extra Fine	New
861A	Boston	4,520,000	27.50	40.00
861B	New York	27,894,260	25.00	37.50
861C	Philadelphia	6,022,428	27.50	40.00
861D	Cleveland	8,981,688	25.00	37.50
861E	Richmond	14,055,984	25.00	37.50
861F	Atlanta	7,495,440	27.50	40.00
861G	Chicago	15,187,596	25.00	37.50
861H	St. Louis	5,923,248	27.50	40.00
861I	Minneapolis	2,422,416	35.00	47.50
861J	Kansas City	4,211,904	32.50	45.00
861K	Dallas	3,707,364	32.50	45.00
861L	San Francisco	12,015,228	27.50	37.50

1950 Series, signatures of Clark-Snyder

No.	Bank	Notes Printed	Extra Fine	New
862A	Boston	23,184.000	25.00	32.50
862B	New York	80,064,000	25.00	32.50
862C	Philadelphia	29,520,000	25.00	32.50
862D	Cleveland	51,120,000	25.00	32.50
862E	Richmond	67,536,000	25.00	32.50
862F	Atlanta	39,312,000	25.00	32.50
862G	Chicago	70,464,000	25.00	32.50
862H	St. Louis	27,352,000	25.00	32.50
862I	Minneapolis	9,216,000	27.50	40.00
862J	Kansas City	22,752,000	25.00	32.50
862K	Dallas	22,656,000	25.00	32.50
862L	San Francisco	70,272,000	25.00	32.50

Federal Reserve Notes/Green Seal

1950A Series, signatures of Priest-Humphrey

No.	Bank	Notes Printed	Extra Fine	New
863A	Boston	19,656,000	25.00	32.50
863B	New York	82,568,000	22.50	27.50
863C	Philadelphia	16,560,000	25.00	32.50
863D	Cleveland	50,320,000	25.00	30.00
863E	Richmond	69,544,000	22.50	27.50
863F	Atlanta	27,648,000	25.00	32.50
863G	Chicago	73,720,000	22.50	27.50
863H	St. Louis	22,680,000	25.00	32.50
863I	Minneapolis	5,544,000	25.00	35.00
863J	Kansas City	22,968,000	25.00	30.00
863K	Dallas	10,728,000	25.00	32.50
863L	San Francisco	85,528,000	22.50	27.50

1950B Series, signatures of Priest-Anderson

No.	Bank	Notes Printed	Extra Fine	New
864A	Boston	5,040,000	25.00	32.50
864B	New York	49,960,000	22.50	27.50
864C	Philadelphia	7,920,000	25.00	35.00
864D	Cleveland	38,160,000	22.50	27.50
864E	Richmond	42,120,000	22.50	30.00
864F	Atlanta	40,240,000	22.50	30.00
864G	Chicago	80,560,000	22.50	27.50
864H	St. Louis	19,440,000	22.50	27.50
864I	Minneapolis	12,240,000	22.50	27.50
864J	Kansas City	28,440,000	22.50	27.50
864K	Dallas	11,880,000	22.50	27.50
864L	San Francisco	51,040,000	22.50	27.50

Federal Reserve Notes/Green Seal

1950C Series, signatures of Smith-Dillon

No.	Bank	Notes Printed	New
865A	Boston	7,200,000	35.00
865B	New York	43,200,000	27.50
865C	Philadelphia	7,560,000	35.00
865D	Cleveland	28,440,000	27.50
865E	Richmond	37,000,000	27.50
865F	Atlanta	19,080,000	27.50
865G	Chicago	29,160,000	27.50
865H	St. Louis	12,960,000	27.50
865I	Minneapolis	6,480,000	35.00
865J	Kansas City	18,360,000	32.50
865K	Dallas	9,000,000	35.00
865L	San Francsico	45,360,000	27.50

1950D Series, signatures of Granahan-Dillon

No.	Bank	Notes Printed	New
866A	Boston	9,320,000	30.00
866B	New York	64,280,000	30.00
866C	Philadelphia	5,400,000	32.50
866D	Cleveland	23,760,000	30.00
866E	Richmond	30,240,000	30.00
866F	Atlanta	22,680,000	30.00
866G	Chicago	67,960,000	30.00
866H	St. Louis	6,120,000	30.00
866I	Minneapolis	3,240,000	35.00
866J	Kansas City	8,200,000	30.00
866K	Dallas	6,480,000	32.50
866L	San Francisco	69,400,000	30.00

1950E Series, signatures of Granahan-Fowler

No.	Bank	Notes Printed	New
867B	New York	8,640,000	32.50
867G	Chicago	9,360,000	32.50
867L	San Francisco	8,640,000	32.50

1963 Series, signatures of Granahan-Dillon.
"IN GOD WE TRUST" now on back

No.	Bank	Notes Printed	New
868A	Boston	2,560,000	32.50
868B	New York	16,640,000	27.50
868C	Philadelphia	None	
868D	Cleveland	7,680,000	30.00
868E	Richmond	4,480,000	30.00
868F	Atlanta	10,240,000	27.50
868G	Chicago	2,560,000	32.50
868H	St. Louis	3,200,000	32.50
868I	Minneapolis	None	
868J	Kansas City	3,840,000	32.50
868K	Dallas	2,560,000	35.00
868L	San Francisco	7,040,000	30.00

1963A Series, signatures of Granahan-Fowler.

No.	Bank	Notes Printed	New
869A	Boston	23,680,000	25.00
869A(☆)	Boston	1,280,000	30.00
869B	New York	93,600,000	25.00
869B(☆)	New York	3,840,000	27.50
869C	Philadelphia	17,920,000	25.00
869C(☆)	Philadelphia	640,000	30.00
869D	Cleveland	68,480,000	25.00
869D(☆)	Cleveland	2,560,000	27.50
869E	Richmond	128,800,000	25.00
869E(☆)	Richmond	5,760,000	25.00
869F	Atlanta	42,880,000	25.00
869F(☆)	Atlanta	1,920,000	27.50
869G	Chicago	156,320,000	25.00
869G(☆)	Chicago	7,040,000	25.00
869H	St. Louis	34,560,000	25.00
869H(☆)	St. Louis	1,920,000	27.50
869I	Minneapolis	10,240,000	25.00
869I(☆)	Minneapolis	640,000	30.00
869J	Kansas City	37,120,000	25.00
869J(☆)	Kansas City	1,920,000	27.50
869K	Dallas	38,400,000	25.00
869K(☆)	Dallas	1,280,000	30.00
869L	San Francisco	169,120,000	25.00
869L(☆)	San Francisco	8,320,000	25.00

Federal Reserve Notes/Green Seal

1969 Series, signatures of Elston-Kennedy				1969A Series, signatures of Kabis-Connally			
No.	**Bank**	**Notes Printed**	**New**	**No.**	**Bank**	**Notes Printed**	**New**
870A	Boston	19,200,000	22.50	871A	Boston	13,440,000	22.50
870A(☆)	Boston	1,280,000	25.00	871A(☆)	Boston	None Printed	—
870B	New York	106,400,000	22.50	871B	New York	69,760,000	22.50
870B(☆)	New York	5,106,000	—	871B(☆)	New York	2,460,000	—
860C	Philadelphia	10,880,000	22.50	871C	Philadelphia	13,440,000	22.50
870C(☆)	Philadelphia	1,280,000	25.00	871C(☆)	Philadelphia	None Printed	—
870D	Cleveland	60,160,000	22.50	871D	Cleveland	29,440,000	22.50
870D(☆)	Cleveland	2,560,000	25.00	871D(☆)	Cleveland	640,000	27.50
870E	Richmond	66,560,000	22.50	861E	Richmond	42,400,000	22.50
870E(☆)	Richmond	2,560,000	25.00	871E(☆)	Richmond	1,920,000	25.00
870F	Atlanta	36,480,000	22.50	871F	Atlanta	13,440,000	22.50
870F(☆)	Atlanta	1,280,000	25.00	871F(☆)	Atlanta	None Printed	—
870G	Chicago	107,680,000	22.50	871G	Chicago	81,640,000	22.50
870G(☆)	Chicago	3,202,000	—	871G(☆)	Chicago	1,920,000	25.00
870H	St. Louis	19,200,000	22.50	871H	St. Louis	14,080,000	22.50
870H(☆)	St. Louis	640,000	30.00	871H(☆)	St. Louis	640,000	27.50
870I	Minneapolis	12,160,000	22.50	871I	Minneapolis	7,040,000	22.50
870I(☆)	Minneapolis	640,000	30.00	871I(☆)	Minneapolis	None Printed	—
870J	Kansas City	39,040,000	22.50	871J	Kansas City	16,040,000	22.50
870J(☆)	Kansas City	1,280,000	25.00	871J(☆)	Kansas City	None Printed	—
870K	Dallas	25,600,000	22.50	871K	Dallas	14,720,000	22.50
870K(☆)	Dallas	640,000	30.00	871K(☆)	Dallas	640,000	27.50
870L	San Francisco	103,840,000	22.50	871L	San Francisco	50,560,000	22.50
870L(☆)	San Francisco	5,120,000	—	871L(☆)	San Francisco	1,280,000	25.00

Federal Reserve Notes/Green Seal

1969B Series, signatures of Banuelos-Connally | 1969C Series, signatures of Banuelos-Shultz.

872A	Boston	None	—	873A	Boston	17,280,000	—
872B	New York	39,200,000	22.50	873A(☆)	Boston	640,000	25.00
872C	Philadelphia	None	—	873B	New York	135,200,000	—
872D	Cleveland	6,400,000	22.50	873B(☆)	New York	1,640,000	—
872E	Richmond	27,520,000	22.50	873C	Philadelphia	40,960,000	—
872F	Atlanta	14,080,000	22.50	873C(☆)	Philadelphia	640,000	25.00
872F(☆)	Atlanta	640,000	27.50	873D	Cleveland	57,760,000	—
872G	Chicago	14,240,000	22.50	873D(☆)	Cleveland	480,000	25.00
872G(☆)	Chicago	1,112,000	—	873E	Richmond	80,160,000	—
872H	St. Louis	5,120,000	22.50	873E(☆)	Richmond	1,920,000	—
872I	Minneapolis	2,560,000	22.50	873F	Atlanta	35,840,000	—
872J	Kansas City	3,840,000	22.50	873F(☆)	Atlanta	640,000	25.00
872J(☆)	Kansas City	640,000	27.50	873G	Chicago	78,720,000	—
872K	Dallas	12,160,000	22.50	873G(☆)	Chicago	640,000	25.00
872L	San Francisco	26,000,000	22.50	873H	St. Louis	33,920,000	—
872L(☆)	San Francisco	640,000	27.50	873H(☆)	St. Louis	640,000	25.00
				873I	Minneapolis	14,080,000	—
				873I(☆)	Minneapolis	640,000	25.00
				873J	Kansas City	32,000,000	—
				873J(☆)	Kansas City	640,000	25.00
				873K	Dallas	31,360,000	—
				873K(☆)	Dallas	1,920,000	—
1974 Series, signatures of Neff-Simon				873L	San Francisco	82,080,000	—
				873L(☆)	San Francisco	1,120,000	—

Gold Certificate/Gold Seal

Face Design

Back Design:
See No. 851.

No.	Date	Signatures	Notes Printed	Very Fine	Extra Fine	New
925	1928	Woods-Mellon	66,204,000	30.00	50.00	100.00
925(☆)	1928(☆)	Woods-Mellon		125.00	200.00	315.00
925A	1928A	Woods-Mills	1,500,000	Never released		

Interest-Bearing Treasury Notes/6%/Two-Year Notes   # LARGE SIZE

Face Design:
From left to right is a portrait of Andrew Jackson, a vignette of Justice, and a portrait of Salmon P. Chase. The color is black and orange.

Back Design

No.
925b   Act of March 2, 1861

This unique note, measuring 7⅜ x 3¾ inches, sold for a bid of $10,000 at the 1970 ANA Convention. The signatures on this note are those of F. E. Spinner, Treasurer, and G. Luff, who signed for the Register. "For the" was handwritten. Notes of this issue were the last to circulate before the first greenbacks of 1861.

In Treasury ledgers at the National Archives I was able to ascertain the delivery of 7,624 notes printed from old plates and 114,316 from new plates. This figure is undoubtedly incomplete.

Denominations of $100, $500 and $1,000 were also issued. Sixty-day notes in denominations of $50 through $5,000 were issued as well.

United States Notes/Red Seal

Face Design: The portrait of Alexander Hamilton was engraved by Joseph P. Ourdan.

Back Design: First obligation.

The following bear the signatures of Chittenden-Spinner.

No.	Date	Notes Printed	Very Good	Very Fine	New
926	1862*		600.00	1,650.00	4,500.00
926a	1862**	601,104	675.00	3,500.00	5,000.00
927	1863**		550.00	1,500.00	2,800.00

*First obligation, an estimated 260,000.
**Second obligation, an estimated 341,104.

United States Note/Red Seal

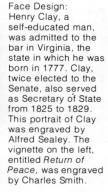

Face Design:
Henry Clay, a
self-educated man,
was admitted to the
bar in Virginia, the
state in which he was
born in 1777. Clay,
twice elected to the
Senate, also served
as Secretary of State
from 1825 to 1829.
This portrait of Clay
was engraved by
Alfred Sealey. The
vignette on the left,
entitled *Return of
Peace,* was engraved
by Charles Smith.

Back Design

No.	Date	Signatures	Notes Issued	Very Good	Very Fine	New
928	1869	Allison-Spinner	604,000*	2,500.00	6,250.00	15,000.00

*Only 24 pieces are outstanding; about 15 are in existence. Notes of this series were recalled due to the abundance of counterfeits bearing plate letter *B*.

United States Notes

Face Design:
Portrait of Benjamin Franklin. The figure of America, with crown bearing *E Pluribus Unum*, was engraved by Charles Burt.

Back Design

No.	Date	Signatures	Seal	Notes Issued	Very Good	Very Fine	New
			The following have an *L* in red on the left and right.				
929	1874	Allison-Spinner	Sm. Red-r	489,200	500.00	1,100.00	4,500.00
930	1875	Allison-Wyman	Sm. Red-r	40,000	400.00	725.00	3,000.00
931	1878	Allison-Gilfillan	Sm. Red-r	210,000	375.00	700.00	2,500.00
		The following are without the *L;* the serial numbers are now blue.					
932	1880	Bruce-Gilfillan	Brown		150.00	365.00	850.00
933	1880	Bruce-Wyman	Brown		150.00	300.00	775.00
934	1880	Rosecrans-Jordan	Lg. Red		165.00	365.00	850.00
935	1880	Rosecrans-Hyatt	Lg. Red		175.00	415.00	1,075.00
936	1880	Rosecrans-Hyatt	Lg. Red-sp	1,280,000	165.00	365.00	850.00
937	1880	Rosecrans-Huston	Lg. Red-sp	(printed)	165.00	365.00	850.00
938	1880	Rosecrans-Huston	Brown		150.00	365.00	850.00
939	1880	Tillman-Morgan	Sm. Red-sc		165.00	315.00	725.00
940	1880	Bruce-Roberts	Sm. Red-sc		165.00	315.00	725.00
941	1880	Lyons-Roberts	Sm. Red-sc		165.00	335.00	850.00

r: with rays   sp: with spikes   sc: with scallops

Compound Interest Treasury Note/6%

Face Design:
Portrait of Alexander
Hamilton. The female
figure on the left
represents Loyalty.

Back Design

Act of March 3, 1863

No.	Signatures	Notes Printed	Issued	Outstanding	Fine	Extra Fine
942	Chittenden-Spinner	55,580	40,180	95*	—	—
943	Colby-Spinner	208,000	0			

Act of June 30, 1864

No.	Signatures	Notes Printed	Issued	Outstanding	Fine	Extra Fine
944	Chittenden-Spinner	880,500	851,200	1,213	4,000.00	11,000.00
945	Colby-Spinner	612,000	306,000**			

The above notes were counterfeited extensively.

*One known.
**Estimated.

Interest-bearing Notes/5%/Act of March 3, 1863

Face Design:
This uniface specimen bearing the portrait of Alexander Hamilton is printed on paper differing from that of the regular issue. The vignette is entitled *Loyalty*.

One-Year Notes

No.	Notes Issued	Outstanding
945a	164,800	131

Two-Year Notes

Face Design:
Caduceus on the left was designed by J.W. Casilear and engraved by Alfred Jones. The two remaining vignettes are entitled *Justice and Shield* and *Loyalty*.

Back Design

(Illustrations courtesy of Amon Carter, Jr.)

No.		Notes Printed	Notes Issued	Outstanding
945b	Without coupons	148,000	136,000	115
945c	With 3 coupons	199,762	118,112	38

Interest-bearing Notes/7-3/10%/Three-Year Notes

Face Design:
The *Great Eagle* as seen on this specimen note was engraved by Alfred Jones for the American Bank Note Company.

Back Design

Act of July 17, 1861

No.	Dated	Serial Number Color	Notes Issued	Outstanding
946	Aug. 19, 1861	Red	71,641	108
947	Oct. 1, 1861	Red	82,365	17
948	Oct. 1, 1861	Blue	527	10

Act of June 30, 1864

Face and Back Design:
Similar to No. 952.

No.	Dated	Notes Printed	Notes Issued	Outstanding
949	Aug. 15, 1864	623,408	363,952	270
950	Mar. 3, 1865	42,268		

Interest-bearing Notes/7-3/10%/Three-Year Notes

Face Design:
The eagle in the center is similar to Henry Gugler's engraving on No. 466.

Back Design

Act of March 3, 1865

No.	Dated	Notes Printed	Notes Issued	Outstanding	Known
951	June 15, 1865	226,324	182,926	56	1
952	July 15, 1865	368,000	343,320	211	6

National Bank Notes/First Charter Period

Face Design:
Washington Crossing the Delaware was engraved by Alfred Jones. *Prayer for Victory*, seen at the right, was engraved by Louis Delnoce. The note illustrated was discovered by Dean Oakes. This is the first known $50 note issued by a Colorado Territory National Bank. See No. 171.

Back Design:
R.W. Wier's mural of the *Embarkation of the Pilgrims* was engraved by W.W. Rice.

No.	Date	Signatures	Seal	Very Good	Very Fine	Extra Fine
953	Orig*	Chittenden-Spinner	Red-r	800.00	2,500.00	3,500.00
954	Orig*	Colby-Spinner	Red-r	800.00	2,500.00	3,500.00
955	Orig*	Allison-Spinner	Red-r	800.00	2,500.00	3,500.00
956	1875	Allison-New	Red-sc	800.00	2,500.00	3,500.00
957	1875	Allison-Wyman	Red-sc		Unique	
958	1875	Allison-Gilfillan	Red-sc	800.00	2,500.00	3,500.00
959	1875	Scofield-Gilfillan	Red-sc	800.00	2,500.00	3,500.00
960	1875	Bruce-Gilfillan	Red-sc	800.00	2,500.00	3,500.00
961	1875	Bruce-Wyman	Red-sc	800.00	2,500.00	3,500.00
962	1875	Rosecrans-Huston	Red-sc	800.00	2,500.00	3,500.00
963	1875	Rosecrans-Nebeker	Red-sc	800.00	2,500.00	3,500.00
964	1875	Tillman-Morgan	Red-sc	800.00	2,500.00	3,500.00

A total of 23,871 notes are outstanding for all the above; about 40 are in existence.

*The original notes did not have a date printed on the face.
 r: with rays   sc: with scallops

National Bank Notes/1882/Second Charter Period

Face Design:
Similar to No. 956.

Back Design:
Similar to No. 288.

First Issue—Brown Seal

No.	Signatures	Very Good	Very Fine	New
965	Bruce-Gilfillan	150.00	325.00	1,500.00
966	Bruce-Wyman	150.00	325.00	1,500.00
967	Bruce-Jordan	175.00	325.00	1,575.00
968	Rosecrans-Jordan	150.00	325.00	1,575.00
969	Rosecrans-Hyatt	150.00	325.00	1,575.00
970	Rosecrans-Houston	150.00	325.00	1,575.00
971	Rosecrans-Nebeker	150.00	325.00	1,575.00
972	Rosecrans-Morgan	600.00	1,050.00	2,750.00
973	Tillman-Morgan	150.00	325.00	1,500.00
974	Tillman-Roberts	150.00	325.00	1,500.00
975	Bruce-Roberts	150.00	325.00	1,500.00
976	Lyons-Roberts	150.00	325.00	1,500.00
977	Vernon-Treat	150.00	325.00	1,500.00

National Bank Notes/1882/Second Charter Period

Back Design

Face Design:
Similar to No. 956.

Second Issue—Blue Seal

No.	Signatures	Very Good	Very Fine	New
978	Rosecrans-Huston	275.00	475.00	1,250.00
979	Rosecrans-Nebeker	275.00	475.00	1,250.00
980	Tillman-Morgan	275.00	475.00	1,250.00
981	Tillman-Roberts	300.00	575.00	1,350.00
982	Bruce-Roberts	275.00	475.00	1,250.00
983	Lyons-Roberts	275.00	475.00	1,250.00
984	Vernon-Treat	275.00	475.00	1250.00
985	Napier-McClung	365.00	725.00	1,500.00

Face Design:
Similar to No. 956.

Back Design

No.	Signatures	Notes Printed	Notes Issued	Known
986	Lyons-Roberts	9,300	8,571	4

National Bank Notes/1902/Third Charter Period

Face Design: John Sherman served as Secretary of the Treasury, 1877–1881, and as Secretary of State 1897–1898. Ostrander Smith was the designer of this note and F.C. Smillie the engraver.

Back Design: The design is the same for all three issues. The second issue has "1902–1908" added. *Mechanics and Navigation* was engraved by G.F.C. Smillie.

No.	Signatures	Very Good	Very Fine	New
	First Issue—Red Seal			
987	Lyons-Roberts	400.00	900.00	1,650.00
988	Lyons-Treat	400.00	1,000.00	1,675.00
989	Vernon-Treat	475.00	1,200.00	1,800.00
	Second Issue—Blue Seal			
990	Lyons-Roberts	200.00	350.00	600.00
991	Lyons-Treat	200.00	350.00	600.00
992	Vernon-Treat	200.00	350.00	600.00
993	Vernon-McClung	200.00	350.00	600.00
994	Napier-McClung	200.00	350.00	600.00
995	Napier-Thompson	300.00	575.00	875.00
996	Napier-Burke	85.00	300.00	600.00
997	Parker-Burke	85.00	300.00	600.00
998	Teehee-Burke	150.00	900.00	1,200.00

National Bank Notes/1902/Third Charter Period

No.	Signatures	Very Good	Very Fine	New
	Third Issue—Blue Seal			
999	Lyons-Roberts	115.00	200.00	500.00
1,000	Lyons-Treat	115.00	200.00	500.00
1,001	Vernon-Treat	115.00	200.00	500.00
1,002	Vernon-McClung	115.00	200.00	500.00
1,003	Napier-McClung	115.00	200.00	500.00
1,004	Napier-Thompson	150.00	350.00	750.00
1,005	Napier-Burke	115.00	200.00	500.00
1,006	Parker-Burke	115.00	200.00	500.00
1,007	Teehee-Burke	115.00	200.00	500.00
1,008	Elliot-Burke	115.00	200.00	500.00
1,009	Elliot-White	115.00	200.00	500.00
1,010	Speelman-White	115.00	200.00	500.00
1,011	Woods-White	150.00	500.00	950.00
1,012	Woods-Tate		Unknown	

National Gold Bank Notes/Red Seal

Face Design:
Similar to No. 956.

Back Design:
Similar to No. 343.

The following notes bear the signatures of Allison-Spinner.

No.	Date	Issuing Bank	City	Notes Issued	Good	Very Good
1,013	1870	First National Gold Bank	San Francisco	2,000	3,000.00	4,000.00
1,013a	1875	First National Gold Bank	San Francisco	620	—	—
1,014	1874	Farmers' National Gold Bank	San Jose	400	4,000.00	5,500.00
1,014a	1872	National Gold Bank and Trust Company	San Francisco	2,856		
1,014b	1872	National Gold Bank of D. O. Mills and Company	Sacramento	604	Unknown	
1,014c	1873	First National Gold Bank	Stockton	867		
1,014d	1873	First National Gold Bank	Santa Barbara	200		
1,014e	1874	First National Gold Bank	Petaluma	400	1 known	
1,014f	1875	Union National Gold Bank	Oakland	100	Unknown	

A total of 113 notes are outstanding for Nos. 1,013-1,014f.

*3 are known.

Silver Certificates

Face Design:
Edward Everett was appointed Professor of Greek at Harvard at the age of 21. In 1824 he was elected to the House of Representatives, and in 1835 he assumed the Governorship of Massachusetts. Later he served as Secretary of State under President Fillmore. His portrait was engraved by Charles Schlecht.

Back Design

Nos. 1015-1017 have red seals, the signatures of Scofield-Gilfillan, and handwritten countersignatures.

No.	Date	Countersigned by	Payable at	Notes Issued	Very Fine	New
1,014g	1878	W.G. White	New York		Unknown	
1,014h	1878	J.C. Hopper	New York	8,000	Unknown	
1,015	1878	T. Hillhouse	New York	8,000	7,000.00	—
1,016	1878	R.M. Anthony*	San Francisco	1,000	Unique	
1,017	1878	A.U. Wyman*	Washington, D.C.	4,000	Unknown	
1,017a	1878	A.U. Wyman	Washington, D.C.	38,000	6,500.00	—

No.	Date	Signatures	Seal	Notes Issued	Good	Very Fine	New
1,018	1880	Scofield-Gilfillan	Brown-r	16,000	—	—	—
1,019	1880	Bruce-Gilfillan	Brown-r	80,000	500.00	1,750.00	3,750.00
1,020	1880	Bruce-Wyman	Brown-r	100,000	500.00	1,850.00	4,250.00
1,021	1880	Rosecrans-Huston	Brown-sp	100,000	500.00	1,850.00	4,250.00
1,022	1880**	Rosecrans-Nebeker	Red	120,000	500.00	1,850.00	—

Revised figures from the first edition were made available by Walter Breen.

r: with rays   sp: with spikes
*Autographed countersignatures.
**5 notes are known

Silver Certificates/1891

Face Design:
Similar to No. 1021.

Back Design:
Engraved by W.A.
Copenhaver,
W.H. Dougal, E.M.
Hall, A.L. Helm, and
G.U. Rose, Jr.

No.	Signatures	Seal	Notes Printed	Very Good	Very Fine	New
1,023	Rosecrans-Nebeker	Red		175.00	325.00	2,000.00
1,024	Tillman-Morgan	Red		175.00	325.00	2,000.00
1,025	Bruce-Roberts	Red		175.00	385.00	2,250.00
1,026	Lyons-Roberts	Red	3,028,000*	175.00	325.00	2,000.00
1,027	Vernon-Treat	Red		175.00	325.00	2,000.00
1,028	Parker-Burke	Blue		175.00	385.00	2,250.00

*2,597,000 notes were issued.

Gold Certificates/1882

Face Design:
Silas Wright was born in Amherst, Massachusetts, on May 24, 1795. He held the offices of state senator, United States Senator, and Governor of New York. Wright died on August 27, 1847, in Canton, New York. Charles Burt's engraving was based on a painting by Alonzo Chappell.

Back Design

No.	Signatures	Seal	Notes Issued	Very Good	Very Fine	New
1,029	Bruce-Gilfillan*	Brown	9,000		Rare	
1,030	Bruce-Gilfillan**	Brown	191,000	600.00	5,000.00	—
1,031	Bruce-Gilfillan	Brown	96,000	—	1,000.00	—
1,032	Bruce-Wyman***	Brown	40,000		Rare	
1,033	Rosecrans-Hyatt	Lg. Red	40,000		Rare	
1,034	Rosecrans-Huston	Lg. Brown	100,000	300.00	850.00	1,650.00
1,035	Lyons-Roberts	Red	1,724,000	125.00	275.00	750.00
1,036	Lyons-Treat	Red	400,000	150.00	375.00	700.00
1,037	Vernon-Treat	Red		165.00	400.00	700.00
1,038	Vernon-McClung	Red		125.00	275.00	700.00
1,039	Napier-McClung	Red		125.00	250.00	700.00

*Autographed countersignature of Thomas C. Acton; payable in New York. 1974 Donlon Sale, $5,700 in AU.

**Printed countersignature of Thomas C. Acton; payable in New York.

***Proof impressions with printed countersignatures of Thomas C. Acton were made.

Gold Certificates/Gold Seal

Face Design:
Portrait of Ulysses S. Grant.

Back Design

No.	Date	Signatures	Notes Printed	Very Good	Very Fine	New
1,040	1913	Parker-Burke	1,604,000	115.00	265.00	650.00
1,041	1913	Teehee-Burke		115.00	265.00	650.00
1,042(☆)	1922	Speelman-White	5,984,000*	90.00	165.00	375.00

*Large and small serial numbers.

Treasury Note/1891/Red Seal

Face Design: William H. Seward (1801-1872) served as Secretary of State from 1860 through 1869 and was responsible for the purchase of Alaska. He negotiated for other purchases such as the Danish West Indies. Only the Alaska purchase was ratified by Congress. New York was the place of Seward's birth and death. His portrait was engraved by Charles Schlecht.

Back Design: Engraved by D.M. Cooper, W.H. Dougal, E.M. Hall, E.E. Myers, and G.U. Rose, Jr.

No.	Signatures	Notes Issued	Very Good	Very Fine	New
1,043	Rosecrans-Nebeker	23,500	2,000.00	12,500.00	22,500.00

23 notes are outstanding, about 15 are known, and 6 are in new condition.

Federal Reserve Notes/1914/Red Seal

Face Design:
Portrait of Ulysses S.
Grant.

Back Design:
The symbolic figure
of Panama stands
between two ships.

The following bear the signatures of Burke-McAdoo.

No.	Bank	Very Good	Very Fine	New
1,044A	Boston	100.00	200.00	450.00
1,044B	New York	100.00	175.00	375.00
1,044C	Philadelphia	100.00	175.00	375.00
1,044D	Cleveland	100.00	175.00	375.00
1,044E	Richmond	100.00	200.00	450.00
1,044F	Atlanta	100.00	200.00	450.00
1,044G	Chicago	100.00	175.00	375.00
1,044H	St. Louis	100.00	200.00	450.00
1,044I	Minneapolis	100.00	200.00	450.00
1,044J	Kansas City	100.00	200.00	450.00
1,044K	Dallas	100.00	200.00	450.00
1,044L	San Francisco	100.00	200.00	450.00

The first day of issue for the above was November 16, 1914.

Federal Reserve Notes/1914/Blue Seal

No.	Bank	Signatures	Notes Printed	Notes Issued	Very Fine	New
1,045A1	Boston	Burke-McAdoo			90.00	135.00
1,045A2	Boston	Burke-Glass			100.00	165.00
1,045A3	Boston	Burke-Houston	1,072,000	1,052,000	90.00	135.00
1,045A4	Boston	White-Mellon			90.00	135.00
1,045B1	New York	Burke-McAdoo			90.00	135.00
1,045B2	New York	Burke-Glass			100.00	165.00
1,045B3	New York	Burke-Houston	5,264,000	5,264,000	95.00	150.00
1,045B4	New York	White-Mellon			90.00	135.00
1,045C1	Philadelphia	Burke-McAdoo			90.00	135.00
1,045C2	Philadelphia	Burke-Glass			100.00	165.00
1,045C3	Philadelphia	Burke-Houston	3,720,000	3,720,000	90.00	135.00
1,045C4	Philadelphia	White-Mellon			90.00	135.00
1,045D1	Cleveland	Burke-McAdoo			90.00	135.00
1,045D2	Cleveland	Burke-Glass			100.00	165.00
1,045D3	Cleveland	Burke-Houston	6,136,000	6,012,000	90.00	135.00
1,045D4	Cleveland	White-Mellon			90.00	135.00
1,045E1	Richmond	Burke-McAdoo			100.00	160.00
1,045E2	Richmond	Burke-Glass			125.00	190.00
1,045E3(☆)	Richmond	Burke-Houston	1,668,000	1,664,000	100.00	165.00
1,045E4	Richmond	White-Mellon			90.00	135.00
1,045F1	Atlanta	Burke-McAdoo			90.00	135.00
1,045F2	Atlanta	Burke-Houston			100.00	165.00
1,045F3	Atlanta	Burke-Glass	1,060,000	868,000	90.00	135.00
1,045F4	Atlanta	White-Mellon			90.00	135.00
1,045G1	Chicago	Burke-McAdoo			90.00	135.00
1,045G2	Chicago	Burke-Glass			100.00	165.00
1,045G3	Chicago	Burke-Houston	3,988,000	3,988,000	90.00	135.00
1,045G4	Chicago	White-Mellon			90.00	135.00
1,045H1	St. Louis	Burke-McAdoo			100.00	160.00
1,045H2	St. Louis	Burke-Glass			135.00	200.00
1,045H3	St. Louis	Burke-Houston	584,000	572,000	100.00	160.00
1,045H4	St. Louis	White-Mellon			100.00	160.00
1,045I1	Minneapolis	Burke-McAdoo			95.00	150.00
1,045I2	Minneapolis	Burke-Glass			135.00	200.00
1,045I3	Minneapolis	Burke-Houston	164,000	160,000	95.00	150.00
1,045I4	Minneapolis	White-Mellon			90.00	135.00

Federal Reserve Notes/1914/Blue Seal

No.	Bank	Signatures	Notes Printed	Notes Issued	Very Fine	New
1,045J1	Kansas City	Burke-McAdoo			90.00	135.00
1,045J2	Kansas City	Burke-Glass	424,000	372,000	100.00	165.00
1,045J3	Kansas City	Burke-Houston			90.00	135.00
1,045J4	Kansas City	White-Mellon			90.00	135.00
1,045K1	Dallas	Burke-McAdoo			95.00	150.00
1,045K2	Dallas	Burke-Glass	240,000	216,000	135.00	200.00
1,045K3	Dallas	Burke-Houston			95.00	150.00
1,045K4	Dallas	White-Mellon			95.00	150.00
1,045L1	San Francisco	Burke-McAdoo			95.00	150.00
1,045L2	San Francisco	Burke-Glass	1,356,000	1,365,000	135.00	200.00
1,045L3	San Francisco	Burke-Houston			95.00	150.00
1,045L4	San Francisco	White-Mellon			95.00	150.00

Federal Reserve Bank Note/1918/Blue Seal

Face Design:
Portrait of
Ulysses S. Grant

Back Design:
Similar to No. 1,044.

No.	Bank	Government Signatures	Bank Signatures	Printed & Issued	Very Fine	New
1,046	St. Louis	T-B	Atterbery-Wells	4,000	2,200.00	6,000.00

Plates were prepared for all 12 Federal Reserve districts, but St. Louis was the only bank to issue this denomination. 64 notes were outstanding in 1956; 28 have been accounted for by the late William A. Philpott, Jr.

T-B: Teehee-Burke

Federal Reserve Bank Notes/1929/Brown Seal

SMALL SIZE

Face Design:
Portrait of
Ulysses S. Grant.

Back Design

The following bear the signatures of Jones-Woods

No.	Bank	Notes Printed	Very Fine	Extra Fine	New
1,047A	Boston	None	—	—	—
1,047B	New York	636,000	65.00	85.00	145.00
1,047C	Philadelphia	None	—	—	—
1,047D	Cleveland	684,000	65.00	85.00	145.00
1,047E	Richmond	None	—	—	—
1,047F	Atlanta	None	—	—	—
1,047G	Chicago	300,000	67.50	90.00	150.00
1,047H	St. Louis	None	—	—	—
1,047I	Minneapolis	132,000	95.00	150.00	215.00
1,047J	Kansas City	276,000	75.00	115.00	185.00
1,047K	Dallas	168,000	80.00	130.00	200.00
1,047L	San Francisco	576,000	65.00	85.00	145.00

National Bank Notes/1929/Brown Seal

Face Design:
Type I.

Face Design:
Type II has the bank charter number printed a second time near the serial number.

Back Design:
Similar to No. 1,047.

Both types bear the signatures of Jones-Woods.

No.	Rarity*	Type I			Type II		
		Very Fine	Extra Fine	New	Very Fine	Extra Fine	New
	1	70.00	100.00	135.00	75.00	110.00	145.00
	2	75.00	110.00	145.00	80.00	110.00	150.00
	3	80.00	120.00	165.00	85.00	130.00	170.00
	4	85.00	135.00	190.00	95.00	145.00	200.00
1,048	5	100.00	145.00	200.00	110.00	160.00	225.00
	6	130.00	180.00	235.00	140.00	200.00	260.00
	7	150.00	200.00	275.00	160.00	235.00	300.00
	8	275.00	350.00	500.00	325.00	400.00	675.00
	9	None Issued			None Issued		

The total issue for both types was 1,160,812.

*Rarity table on page 41.

Federal Reserve Notes/Green Seal

Face Design

Back Design:
Similar to No. 1,047.

1928 Series, signatures of Tate-Mellon

No.	Bank	Notes Printed	Extra Fine	New
1,049A	Boston	265,200	75.00	135.00
1,049B	New York	1,351,800	75.00	115.00
1,049C	Philadelphia	997,056	75.00	115.00
1,049D	Cleveland	1,161,900	75.00	125.00
1,049E	Richmond	539,400	85.00	130.00
1,049F	Atlanta	538,800	85.00	130.00
1,049G	Chicago	1,348,620	75.00	115.00
1,049H	St. Louis	627,300	90.00	150.00
1,049I	Minneapolis	106,200	100.00	160.00
1,049J	Kansas City	252,600	90.00	150.00
1,049K	Dallas	109,920	100.00	160.00
1,049L	San Francisco	447,600	85.00	135.00

Federal Reserve Notes/Green Seal

Face Design:
Letter replaces
number in Federal
Reserve Seal

1928A Series, signatures of Woods-Mellon

No.	Bank	Notes Printed	Extra Fine	New
1,050A	Boston	1,834,989	75.00	110.00
1,050B	New York	3,392,328	75.00	110.00
1,050C	Philadelphia	3,078,944	75.00	110.00
1,050D	Cleveland	2,453,364	75.00	110.00
1,050E	Richmond	1,516,500	75.00	115.00
1,050F	Atlanta	338,400	85.00	145.00
1,050G	Chicago	5,263,956	75.00	100.00
1,050H	St. Louis	880,500	85.00	125.00
1,050I	Minneapolis	780,240	85.00	125.00
1,050J	Kansas City	791,604	85.00	125.00
1,050K	Dallas	701,496	85.00	125.00
1,050L	San Francisco	1,522,620	75.00	110.00

Federal Reserve Notes/Green Seal

1934 Series, signatures of Julian-Morgenthau

No.	Bank	Notes Printed	Extra Fine	New
1,051A	Boston	2,729,400	70.00	90.00
1,051B	New York	17,894,676	65.00	75.00
1,051C	Philadelphia	5,833,200	65.00	85.00
1,051D	Cleveland	8,817,720	65.00	80.00
1,051E	Richmond	4,826,628	65.00	85.00
1,051F	Atlanta	3,069,348	70.00	90.00
1,051G	Chicago	8,675,940	65.00	80.00
1,051H	St. Louis	1,497,144	75.00	100.00
1,051I	Minneapolis	539,700	75.00	115.00
1,051J	Kansas City	1,133,520	75.00	100.00
1,051K	Dallas	1,194,876	75.00	100.00
1,051L	San Francisco	8,101,200	65.00	80.00

1934A Series, signatures of Julian-Morgenthau

No.	Bank	Notes Printed	Extra Fine	New
1,052A	Boston	406,200	65.00	80.00
1,052B	New York	4,710,648	55.00	75.00
1,052C	Philadelphia	No Record		
1,052D	Cleveland	864,168	60.00	75.00
1,052E	Richmond	2,235,372	60.00	75.00
1,052F	Atlanta	416,100	65.00	80.00
1,052G	Chicago	1,014,600	60.00	75.00
1,052H	St. Louis	361,944	70.00	85.00
1,052I	Minneapolis	93,300	75.00	92.50
1,052J	Kansas City	189,300	70.00	85.00
1,052K	Dallas	266,700	70.00	85.00
1,052L	San Francisco	162,000	60.00	80.00

Federal Reserve Notes/Green Seal

1934B Series, signatures of Julian-Vinson

No.	Bank	Notes Printed	Extra Fine	New
1,053A	Boston	None	—	—
1,053B	New York	None	—	—
1,053C	Philadelphia	509,100	65.00	90.00
1,053D	Cleveland	359,100	80.00	115.00
1,053E	Richmond	596,700	70.00	100.00
1,053F	Atlanta	416,720	75.00	110.00
1,053G	Chicago	306,000	70.00	100.00
1,053H	St. Louis	306,000	70.00	100.00
1,053I	Minneapolis	120,000	70.00	115.00
1,053J	Kansas City	221,340	70.00	100.00
1,053K	Dallas	120,108	70.00	110.00
1,053L	San Francisco	441,000	70.00	100.00

1934C Series, signatures of Julian-Snyder

No.	Bank	Notes Printed	Extra Fine	New
1,054A	Boston	117,600	77.50	115.00
1,054B	New York	1,556,400	65.00	80.00
1,054C	Philadelphia	107,283	65.00	85.00
1,054D	Cleveland	374,400	60.00	75.00
1,054E	Richmond	1,821,960	60.00	75.00
1,054F	Atlanta	107,640	70.00	90.00
1,054G	Chicago	294,432	70.00	90.00
1,054H	St. Louis	535,200	70.00	90.00
1,054I	Minneapolis	118,800	75.00	115.00
1,054J	Kansas City	303,600	70.00	90.00
1,054K	Dallas	429,900	75.00	95.00
1,054L	San Francisco	None	—	—

Federal Reserve Notes/Green Seal

1934D Series, signatures of Clark-Snyder

No.	Bank	Notes Printed	Extra Fine	New
1,055A	Boston	279,600	65.00	85.00
1,055B	New York	898,776	60.00	75.00
1,055C	Philadelphia	699,000	60.00	75.00
1,055D	Cleveland	No Record	—	—
1,055E	Richmond	156,000	75.00	100.00
1,055F	Atlanta	216,000	65.00	90.00
1,055G	Chicago	494,016	60.00	80.00
1,055H	St. Louis	No Record	—	—
1,055I	Minneapolis	No Record	—	—
1,055J	Kansas City	No Record	—	—
1,055K	Dallas	103,200	75.00	110.00
1,055L	San Francisco	No Record	—	—

1950 Series, signatures of Clark-Snyder

No.	Bank	Notes Printed	Extra Fine	New
1,056A	Boston	1,248,000	60,00	80.00
1,056B	New York	10,236,000	—	70.00
1,056C	Philadelphia	2,352,000	—	75.00
1,056D	Cleveland	6,180,000	—	70.00
1,056E	Richmond	5,064,000	—	70.00
1,056F	Atlanta	1,812,000	60.00	80.00
1,056G	Chicago	4,212,000	—	70.00
1,056H	St. Louis	892,000	60.00	85.00
1,056I	Minneapolis	384,000	65.00	90.00
1,056J	Kansas City	696,000	60.00	85.00
1,056K	Dallas	1,100,000	60.00	80.00
1,056L	San Francisco	3,996,000	—	75.00

1950A Series, signatures of Priest-Humphrey

No.	Bank	Notes Printed	Extra Fine	New
1,057A	Boston	720,000		75.00
1,057B	New York	6,480,000		70.00
1,057C	Philadelphia	1,728,000		70.00
1,057D	Cleveland	1,872,000		70.00
1,057E	Richmond	2,016,000		70.00
1,057F	Atlanta	288,000		80.00
1,057G	Chicago	2,016,000		70.00
1,057H	St. Louis	576,000		75.00
1,057I	Minneapolis	No Record		—
1,057J	Kansas City	144,000		85.00
1,057K	Dallas	864,000		75.00
1,057L	San Francisco	576,000		75.00

Federal Reserve Notes/Green Seal

1950B Series, signatures of Priest-Anderson

No.	Bank	Notes Printed	New
1,058A	Boston	864,000	75.00
1,058B	New York	8,352,000	65.00
1,058C	Philadelphia	2,592,000	70.00
1,058D	Cleveland	1,728,000	70.00
1,058E	Richmond	1,584,000	70.00
1,058F	Atlanta	No Record	—
1,058G	Chicago	4,320,000	65.00
1,058H	St. Louis	576,000	77.50
1,058I	Minneapolis	No Record	—
1,058J	Kansas City	1,008,000	75.00
1,058K	Dallas	1,008,000	75.00
1,058L	San Francisco	1,872,000	70.00

1950C Series, signatures of Smith-Dillon

No.	Bank	Notes Printed	New
1,059A	Boston	720,000	70.00
1,059B	New York	5,328,000	62.50
1,059C	Philadelphia	1,296,000	70.00
1,059D	Cleveland	1,296,000	70.00
1,059E	Richmond	1,296,000	70.00
1,059F	Atlanta	No Record	—
1,059G	Chicago	1,728,000	70.00
1,059H	St. Louis	576,000	75.00
1,059I	Minneapolis	144,000	80.00
1,059J	Kansas City	432,000	75.00
1,059K	Dallas	720,000	75.00
1,059L	San Francisco	1,152,000	70.00

1950D Series, signatures of Granahan-Dillon

No.	Bank	Notes Printed	New
1,060A	Boston	1,728,000	60.00
1,060B	New York	7,200,000	60.00
1,060C	Philadelphia	2,736,000	60.00
1,060D	Cleveland	2,880,000	60.00
1,060E	Richmond	2,016,000	60.00
1,060F	Atlanta	576,000	65.00
1,060G	Chicago	4,176,000	65.00
1,060H	St. Louis	1,440,000	65.00
1,060I	Minneapolis	288,000	67.50
1,060J	Kansas City	720,000	65.00
1,060K	Dallas	1,296,000	60.00
1,060L	San Francisco	2,160,000	60.00

1950E Series, signatures of Granahan-Fowler

No.	Bank	Notes Printed	New
1,061B	New York	3,024,000	70.00
1,061G	Chicago	1,008,000	75.00
1,061L	San Francisco	1,296,000	75.00

Federal Reserve Notes/Green Seal

1963A Series, signatures of Granahan-Fowler. 1969 Series, signatures of Elston-Kennedy
"IN GOD WE TRUST" now on back

No.	Bank	Notes Printed	New	No.	Bank	Notes Printed	New
1,062A	Boston	1,536,000	60.00	1,063A	Boston	2,048,000	—
1,062A(☆)	Boston	320,000	75.00	1,063A(☆)	Boston	None Printed	—
1,062B	New York	11,008,000	60.00	1,063B	New York	12,032,000	—
1,062B(☆)	New York	1,408,000	65.00	1,063B(☆)	New York	384,000	65.00
1,062C	Philadelphia	3,328,000	60.00	1,063C	Philadelphia	3,584,000	—
1,062C(☆)	Philadelphia	704,000	65.00	1,063C(☆)	Philadelphia	128,000	70.00
1,062D	Cleveland	3,584,000	60.00	1,063D	Cleveland	3,584,000	—
1,062D(☆)	Cleveland	256,000	75.00	1,063D(☆)	Cleveland	192,000	70.00
1,062E	Richmond	3,072,000	60.00	1,063E	Richmond	2,560,000	—
1,062E(☆)	Richmond	704,000	65.00	1,063E(☆)	Richmond	64,000	75.00
1,062F	Atlanta	768,000	60.00	1,063F	Atlanta	256,000	60.00
1,062F(☆)	Atlanta	384,000	70.00	1,063F(☆)	Atlanta	None Printed	—
1,062G	Chicago	6,912,000	60.00	1,063G	Chicago	9,728,000	—
1,062G(☆)	Chicago	768,000	65.00	1,063G(☆)	Chicago	256,000	70.00
1,062H	St. Louis	512,000	65.00	1,063H	St. Louis	256,000	60.00
1,062H(☆)	St. Louis	128,000	75.00	1,063H(☆)	St. Louis	None Printed	—
1,062I	Minneapolis	512,000	65.00	1,063I	Minneapolis	512,000	60.00
1,062I(☆)	Minneapolis	128,000	75.00	1,063I(☆)	Minneapolis	None Printed	—
1,072J	Kansas City	512,000	65.00	1,063J	Kansas City	1,280,000	—
1,062J(☆)	Kansas City	64,000	85.00	1,063J(☆)	Kansas City	64,000	75.00
1,062K	Dallas	1,536,000	60.00	1,063K	Dallas	1,536,000	—
1,062K(☆)	Dallas	128,000	75.00	1,063K(☆)	Dallas	64,000	75.00
1,062L	San Francisco	4,352,000	60.00	1,063L	San Francisco	6,912,000	—
1,062L(☆)	San Francisco	704,000	65.00	1,063L(☆)	San Francisco	256,000	70.00

Federal Reserve Notes/Green Seal

1969A Series, signatures of Kabis-Connally

No.	Bank	Notes Printed	New
1,064 A	Boston	1,536,000	—
1,064 A(☆)	Boston	128,000	65.00
1,064 B	New York	9,728,000	—
1,064 B(☆)	New York	704,000	60.00
1,064 C	Philadelphia	2,560,000	—
1,064 C(☆)	Philadelphia	None Printed	—
1,064 D	Cleveland	2,816,000	—
1,064 D(☆)	Cleveland	None Printed	—
1,064 E	Richmond	2,304,000	—
1,064 E(☆)	Richmond	64,000	70.00
1,064 F	Atlanta	256,000	60.00
1,064 F(☆)	Atlanta	64,000	70.00
1,064 G	Chicago	3,584,000	—
1,064 G(☆)	Chicago	192,000	70.00
1,064 H	St. Louis	256,000	60.00
1,064 H(☆)	St. Louis	None Printed	—
1,064 I	Minneapolis	512,000	—
1,064 I(☆)	Minneapolis	None Printed	—
1,064 J	Kansas City	256,000	60.00
1,064 J(☆)	Kansas City	None Printed	—
1,064 K	Dallas	1,024,000	—
1,064 K(☆)	Dallas	64,000	75.00
1,064 L	San Francisco	5,120,000	—
1,064 L(☆)	San Francisco	256,000	65.00

1969B Series, signatures of Banuelos-Connally

No.	Bank	Notes Printed
1,065 A	Boston	1,024,000
1,065 B	New York	2,560,000
1,065 C	Philadelphia	2,048,000
1,065 D	Cleveland	None
1,065 E	Richmond	1,536,000
1,065 F	Atlanta	512,000
1,065 G	Chicago	1,124,000
1,065 H	St. Louis	None
1,065 I	Minneapolis	None
1,065 J	Kansas City	None
1,065 K	Dallas	1,024,000
1,065 K(☆)	Dallas	128,000
1,065 L	San Francisco	None

Federal Reserve Notes

1969C Series, signatures of Banuelos-Shultz.   1974 Series, signatures of Neff-Simon.

No.	Bank	Notes Printed
1,066A	Boston	1,792,000
1,066A(☆)	Boston	64,000
1,066B	New York	7,040,000
1,066B(☆)	New York	192,000
1,066C	Philadelphia	3,584,000
1,066C(☆)	Philadelphia	256,000
1,066D	Cleveland	5,120,000
1,066D(☆)	Cleveland	192,000
1,066E	Richmond	2,304,000
1,066E(☆)	Richmond	64,000
1,066F	Atlanta	256,000
1,066F(☆)	Atlanta	64,000
1,066G	Chicago	6,784,000
1,066G(☆)	Chicago	576,000
1,066H	St. Louis	2,688,000
1,066H(☆)	St. Louis	64,000
1,066I	Minneapolis	256,000
1,066I(☆)	Minneapolis	64,000
1,066J	Kansas City	1,280,000
1,066J(☆)	Kansas City	128,000
1,066K	Dallas	3,456,000
1,066K(☆)	Dallas	64,000
1,066L	San Francisco	4,608,000
1,066L(☆)	San Francisco	256,000

Gold Certificate/Gold Seal

Face Design:
Portrait of Ulysses S. Grant.

Back Design:
Similar to No. 1,047.

No.	Date	Signatures	Notes Printed	Very Fine	Extra Fine	New
1,119	1928	Woods-Mellon	5,520,000	75.00	100.00	185.00
1,119(☆)	1928(☆)	Woods-Mellon		165.00	235.00	385.00

United States Notes/Red Seal

LARGE SIZE

Face Design

Back Design

The following bear the signatures of Chittenden-Spinner.

No.	Date		Notes Printed	Very Good	Very Fine	New
1,120	1862*	⎤		850.00	6,000.00	14,000.00
1,120a	1862**		400,000	850.00	6,000.00	16,000.00
1,121	1863**	⎦		850.00	6,000.00	15,000.00

*First obligation, an estimated 130,000. First obligation notes were printed by both the National Bank Note Company and the American National Bank Note Company.
**Second obligation, an estimated 270,000.

United States Notes/1869/Red Seal

Face Design: The portrait of Abraham Lincoln was engraved by Charles Burt. *Reconstruction* was engraved by Louis Delnoce for the sum of $475.

Back Design

No.	Signatures	Notes Issued	Very Good	Very Fine	New
1,122	Allison-Spinner	371,040	1200.00	6750.00	17,500.00

About 8-10 are in existence today.

United States Notes

Face Design:
Similar to No. 1122.

Back Design

No.	Date	Signatures	Seal	Notes Issued	Very Good	Very Fine	New
		Nos. 1,123A–1,125 have a red floral pattern.					
1,123A	1875A*	Allison-New	Red-r	126,000	750.00	1,500.00	3,500.00
1,124	1875	Allison-Wyman	Red-r	40,000	675.00	1,200.00	2,750.00
1,125	1878	Allison-Gilfillan	Red-r	202,000	675.00	1,100.00	2,500.00
		Nos. 1,126–1,136 have a black floral pattern.					
1,126	1880	Bruce-Gilfillan	Brown		275.00	425.00	1,075.00
1,127	1880	Bruce-Wyman	Brown		275.00	425.00	1,075.00
1,128	1880	Rosecrans-Jordan	Lg. Red		275.00	425.00	1,075.00
1,129	1880	Rosecrans-Hyatt	Lg. Red		275.00	425.00	1,075.00
1,130	1880	Rosecrans-Hyatt	Lg. Red-sp	836,000	275.00	365.00	1,125.00
1,131	1880	Rosecrans-Huston	Lg. Red-sp	(printed)	375.00	600.00	1,350.00
1,132	1880	Rosecrans-Huston	Brown		275.00	425.00	1,075.00
1,133	1880	Tillman-Morgan	Sm. Red-sc		235.00	375.00	1,000.00
1,134	1880	Bruce-Roberts	Sm. Red-sc		235.00	375.00	1,000.00
1,135	1880	Lyons-Roberts	Sm. Red-sc		235.00	375.00	1,025.00
1,136	1880	Napier-McClung	Sm. Red-sc		Existence doubtful		

*There are 2 known.
r: with rays sp: with spikes sc: with scallops

Compound Interest Treasury Notes/6%/Act of March 3, 1863

Face Design:
The *Lansdowne portrait of Washington* by Gilbert Stuart was engraved by Owen G. Hanks. The vignette on the right is entitled *Justice and Shield; The Guardian* is on the left.

Back Design:
Redemption figures

No.	Signatures	Notes Printed	Notes Issued	Outstanding	Fine
1,137	Chittenden-Spinner	40,032	39,176		—
		Act of June 30, 1864			
1,138	Chittenden-Spinner	272,480	260,140	316	
1,139	Colby-Spinner	266,800	243,600		4,500.00

The above notes were counterfeited extensively.

Interest-bearing Notes

One-Year Notes—5% (Act of March 3, 1863)

Face Design:
See No. 1,139 for
vignette descriptions.

Back Design

(Illustrations courtesy
of Amon Carter, Jr.)

No.	Date	Signatures	Notes Printed	Outstanding	Known
1,140	March 25, 1864	Chittenden-Spinner	140,400	62	1

Two-Year Notes—6% (Act of March 2, 1861)

No.	Notes Printed	Notes Issued
1,141	—	69,567*

*8,719 from old plates included. Addtional notes were probably issued.

Interest-bearing Notes/Act of March 3, 1863

Two-Year Notes—5%

Face Design:
The vignettes are entitled, *Farmer and Mechanics, The Treasury Building* and *In The Turret*

Back Design

In 1961 this heretofore unknown note was discovered at the Citizens National Bank of Lebanon, Ky., which made these photographs available.

No.	Notes Printed	Notes Issued	Outstanding
1,142	96,800	96,800	19
1,143	144,844	144,800 (with 3 coupons)	80

Interest-bearing Notes/Act of July 17, 1861

Three Year Notes—7-3/10%

No example of Nos. 1,144-1,148 is known, the uniface specimen illustrated which bears Alfred Jones's engraving of General Winfield Scott was printed by the American Bank Note Co. (Courtesy, Mayflower Coin Auctions, Inc.)

No.	Dated		Notes Printed	Notes Issued	Outstanding
1,144	Aug. 19, 1861	(red numerals)		90,000	73
1,145	Oct. 1,1861	(red numerals)		103,075	37
1,146	Oct. 1, 1861	(blue numerals)		1,066	0

Act of June 30, 1864

No.	Dated	Notes Printed	Notes Issued	Outstanding	Known
1,147	Aug. 15, 1864	550,400	566,039	219	
1,148	Mar. 3, 1865	86,552			

Interest-bearing Notes/Act of March 3, 1865

Face Design:
General Winfield
Scott, Supreme
Commander of the
U.S. Army from July
1841 to November
1861. Vain and
pompous, he was
called "Old Fuss and
Feathers." This note
retains three of the
five original coupons.

Back Design

(Illustrations courtesy
of Amon Carter, Jr.)

No.	Dated	Notes Printed	Notes Issued	Outstanding	Known
1,149	June 15, 1865	401,048	338,227	122½	
1,150	July 15, 1865	500,000	472,080	215½	2

National Bank Notes/First Charter Period

Face Design:
W.H. Powell's painting of *The Battle of Lake Erie* was engraved by Louis Delnoce. The engraving of *Union* was executed by James Bannister.

Back Design:
John Trumbull's famous painting of *The Signing of the Declaration of Independence* was engraved by Frederick Girsch.

No.	Date	Signatures	Seal	Very Good	Very Fine	Extra Fine
1,151	Orig*	Chittenden-Spinner	Red-r	2,250.00	4,000.00	5,250.00
1,152	Orig*	Colby-Spinner	Red-r	2,250.00	4,000.00	5,250.00
1,153	Orig*	Allison-Spinner	Red-r	2,250.00	4,000.00	5,250.00
1,154	1875	Allison-New	Red-sc	2,250.00	4,000.00	5,250.00
1,155	1875	Allison-Wyman	Red-sc	2,250.00	4,000.00	5,250.00
1,156	1875	Allison-Gilfillan	Red-sc	2,250.00	4,000.00	5,250.00
1,157	1875	Scofield-Gilfillan	Red-sc	2,250.00	4,000.00	5,250.00
1,158	1875	Bruce-Gilfillan	Red-sc	2,250.00	4,000.00	5,250.00
1,159	1875	Bruce-Wyman	Red-sc	2,250.00	4,000.00	5,250.00
1,160	1875	Rosecrans-Huston	Red-sc	2,250.00	4,000.00	5,250.00
1,161	1875	Rosecrans-Nebeker	Red-sc	—	—	—
1,162	1875	Tillman-Morgan	Red-sc	2,250.00	4,000.00	5,250.00

A total of 16,309 notes are outstanding for all the above, about 55 are in existence.

*The original notes did not have a date printed on the face.
 r: with rays   sc: with scallops

National Bank Notes/1882/Second Charter Period

First Issue—Brown Seal. The face design of this note is similar to No. 1,152 and the back design is similar to No. 288.

No.	Signatures	Very Good	Very Fine	New
1,163	Bruce-Gilfillan	300.00	700.00	1,500.00
1,164	Bruce-Wyman	300.00	700.00	1,500.00
1,165	Bruce-Jordan	350.00	725.00	1,550.00
1,166	Rosecrans-Jordan	300.00	700.00	1,500.00
1,167	Rosecrans-Hyatt	300.00	700.00	1,500.00
1,168	Rosecrans-Huston	300.00	700.00	1,500.00
1,169	Rosecrans-Nebeker	300.00	700.00	1,500.00
1,170	Rosecrans-Morgan	575.00	1,575.00	2,850.00
1,171	Tillman-Morgan	300.00	700.00	1,425.00
1,172	Tillman-Roberts	350.00	725.00	1,550.00
1,173	Bruce-Roberts	300.00	700.00	1,550.00
1,174	Lyons-Roberts	300.00	700.00	1,550.00
1,174a	Vernon-Treat		Possible existence	

Second Charter Period—Second Issue, Blue Seal

Face Design:
Similar to No. 1,152.

Back Design:
Green. The eagle on the left was engraved by Harry L. Chorlton.

No.	Signatures	Very Good	Very Fine	New
1,175	Rosecrans-Huston	300.00	675.00	1,400.00
1,176	Rosecrans-Nebeker	300.00	675.00	1,400.00
1,177	Tillman-Morgan	300.00	675.00	1,400.00
1,178	Tillman-Roberts	325.00	725.00	1,575.00
1,179	Bruce-Roberts	325.00	800.00	1,575.00
1,180	Lyons-Roberts	300.00	700.00	1,400.00
1,181	Vernon-Treat	750.00	1,100.00	1,750.00

National Bank Notes/1882/Second Charter Period

Face Design:
Similar to No. 1,152.

Back Design

(Courtesy of
John Hickman and
Dean Oakes)

Third Issue—Blue Seal

No.	Signatures	Notes Printed	Notes Issued	Notes Known
1,183	Lyons-Roberts	3,100	2,857	1

The Winters National Bank of Dayton, Ohio and The Canal-Commercial National Bank of New Orleans were the only two banks to issue this denomination. The illustrated note was purchased in 1974 for $25,000 and is the only one known to be extant.

National Bank Notes/1902/Third Charter Period

Face Design:
John J. Knox
(1828–1892) held
the office of Comp-
troller of Currency
from 1872 to 1884.
Ostrander Smith was
the designer of this
note and George
F.C. Smillie the en-
graver.

Back Design:
The design is the
same for all three
issues. The second
issue has
"1902–1908."

No.	Signatures	Very Good	Very Fine	New
	First Issue—Red Seal			
1,184	Lyons-Roberts	425.00	850.00	1,350.00
1,185	Lyons-Treat	425.00	850.00	1,400.00
1,186	Vernon-Treat	425.00	850.00	1,400.00
	Second Issue—Blue Seal			
1,187	Lyons-Roberts	225.00	400.00	600.00
1,188	Lyons-Treat	225.00	400.00	600.00
1,189	Vernon-Treat	225.00	400.00	600.00
1,190	Vernon-McClung	225.00	400.00	600.00
1,191	Napier-McClung	225.00	400.00	600.00
1,192	Napier-Thompson	300.00	525.00	800.00
1,193	Napier-Burke	275.00	425.00	675.00
1,194	Parker-Burke	275.00	425.00	675.00
1,195	Teehee-Burke	300.00	600.00	800.00

In 1956, 220 notes were outstanding for 1,184–1,186.

National Bank Notes

No.	Signatures	Very Good	Very Fine	New
	Third Issue—Blue Seal			
1,196	Lyons-Roberts	145.00	350.00	700.00
1,197	Lyons-Treat	145.00	350.00	700.00
1,198	Vernon-Treat	145.00	350.00	700.00
1,198	Vernon-McClung	145.00	350.00	700.00
1,199	Napier-McClung	145.00	350.0C	700.00
1,201	Napier-Thompson	225.00	700.00	1,300.00
1,202	Parker-Burke	150.00	350.00	750.00
1,203	Teehee-Burke	145.00	350.00	700.00
1,204	Elliott-Burke	145.00	350.00	700.00
1,205	Elliott-White	145.00	350.00	700.00
1,206	Speelman-White	145.00	350.00	700.00
1,206a	Woods-White		2 Known	

(Courtesy of Vince Bulman.)

National Gold Bank Notes/Red Seal

The face design of this note is similar to No. 1,152, and the back is similar to No. 343. The following bear the signatures of Allison-Spinner with the exception of No. 1,208, which has the signatures of Bruce-Gilfillan.

No.	Date	Issuing Bank	City	Notes Issued	Good	Very Good
1,207	1870	First National Gold Bank	San Francisco	2,000	3,000.00	4,500.00
1,208	1875	First National Gold Bank	San Francisco	620	3,000.00	5,000.00
1,208a	1875	Same as above, unique on white paper				
1,209	1873	First National Gold Bank	Santa Barbara	200	1 Known	
1,210	1874	First National Gold Bank	Petaluma*	400	2 Known	
1,211	1875	Union National Gold Bank	Oakland	100	Unknown	
1,211a	1872	National Gold Bank and Trust Company	San Francisco	2,856	Unknown	
1,211b	1872	National Gold Bank of D. O. Mills and Company	Sacramento	604	—	
1,211c	1873	First National Gold Bank	Stockton	867	Unknown	
1,211d	1874	Farmers National Gold Bank	San Jose	400	Unknown	

A total of 84 notes are outstanding.

*1973 private sale, $10,500 in fine condition.

Silver Certificates

Face Design:
The portrait of fifth
President, James
Monroe was
engraved by L.
Delnoce from a
portrait by Vanderlyn.

Back Design

The following notes have red seals and bear the signatures of Scofield-Gilfillan.

No.	Date	Countersigned by	Payable at	Notes Issued	Very Good	Very Fine
1,212*	1878	W. G. White	New York ⎤		Unique	
1,212a	1878	J. C. Hopper	New York	5,000**	Unknown	
1,212b	1878	T. Hillhouse	New York ⎦		Unknown	
1,213	1878	R. M. Anthony***	San Francisco	2,400	Unique	
1,214	1878	A. U. Wyman***	Washington, D.C.	4,000	Unknown	
1,214a†	1878	A. U. Wyman	Washington, D.C.	24,000	4,000.00	7,000.00

*This note was No. 1,214 in the first edition of this catalog.
**8,000 notes were printed and it is believed 6,800 bore these autographed countersignatures.
The remaining 1,200 could have had the engraved countersignature of T. Hillhouse. See
Numismatic News, May 24, 1975 for Part II of Walter Breen's continuing series on the *1878 Silver
Certificates.*
***Autographed countersignatures.
†This note was No. 1,212 in the first edition of this catalog

Silver Certificates

Face Design:
Portrait of James
Monroe, engraved
by Louis Delnoce.

Back Design:
Similar to No. 1,212.

No.	Date	Signatures	Seal	Notes Issued	Very Good	Very Fine	New
1,215	1880	Scofield-Gilfillan	Brown-r	16,000	—	—	—
1,216	1880	Bruce-Gilfillan	Brown-r	40,000	1,250.00	3,000.00	7,000.00
1,217	1880	Bruce-Wyman	Brown-r	80,000	1,250.00	3,000.00	7,000.00

The following note has neither the *C* nor the *100*.

No.	Date	Signatures	Seal	Notes Issued	Very Good	Very Fine	New
1,218	1880	Rosecrans-Huston	Brown-sp	100,000	1,200.00	3,000.00	8,000.00

The seal is now at lower right.

No.	Date	Signatures	Seal	Notes Issued	Very Good	Very Fine	New
1,219	1880	Rosecrans-Nebeker	Sm. Red	40,000	1,250.00	3,000.00	9,000.00

r: with rays   sp: with spikes

Face Design:
The seal is now at
right center.
Engraved by
D.M. Cooper,
W.H. Dougal,
J.R. Hill,
E.E. Myers,
W.G. Phillips, and
G.U. Rose, Jr.

Back Design
Engraved by
D.M. Cooper,
W.H. Dougal,
E.M. Hall,
W.F. Lutz, and
G.U. Rose, Jr.

No.	Date	Signatures	Seal	Notes Printed	Very Good	Very Fine	New
1,220	1891	Rosecrans-Nebeker	Sm. Red	504,000	500.00	3,750.00	6,000.00
1,221	1891	Tillman-Morgan*	Sm. Red		500.00	3,750.00	9,000.00

*In 1897 there was an attempt to recall the entire issue of 260,000 notes due to superb
counterfeits made by William M. Jacobs.

Gold Certificates/Act of March 3, 1863

Face Design
(First Issue): The
vignette entitled *E
Pluribus Unum* was
also used for
No. 827a. See No.
1,435a for the
complete *Altar of
Liberty,* only the head
appears here.

Back Design

(Photographs
courtesy The Coin
and Currency
Institute, Inc.)

Face Design:
Thomas H. Benton
(1782-1858), whose
portrait appears on
the second and third
issue, served in the
Senate and the House
of Representatives.
Benton favored
Western development
and spoke out
against slavery. (This
uniface note is
illustrated through the
courtesy of the
Division of
Numismatics, The
Smithsonian
Institution.)

The following notes are countersigned and dated by hand. Nos. 1,222 and 1,224 bear the engraved signatures of Colby-Spinner, No. 1,225 bears those of Allison-New.

No.	Issue	Payable at	Date	Notes Printed	Notes Issued	Outstanding
1,222	First	Washington	1863	118,000	116,449	44
1,223	The note previously listed here does not exist.					
1,224	Second	New York	1871	50,000	48,000	27
1,225	Third	New York	1875	56,894	35,984	8

Gold Certificates/1882

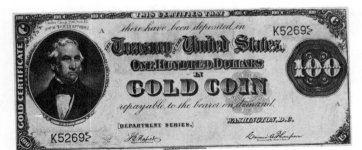

Face Design:
Portrait of Thomas H.
Benton.

Back Design:
The eagle was
engraved by J.
Ourdan.

No. ·	Signatures	Seal	Notes Issued	Very Good	Very Fine	New
		Nos. 1,226 and 1,227 are payable at New York.				
1,226	Bruce-Gilfillan*	Brown	9,000		Unknown	
1,227	Bruce-Gilfillan**	Brown	71,000		Unique	
1,228	Bruce-Gilfillan	Brown	80,000	650.00	1,500.00	4,000.00
1,229	Bruce-Wyman	Brown	40,000	650.00	1,500.00	4,000.00
1,230	Rosecrans-Hyatt	Lg. Red	56,000	750.00	1,650.00	4,250.00
1,231	Rosecrans-Huston	Lg. Brown	44,000	—	—	—
1,232	Lyons-Roberts	Sm. Red	1,160,000	150.00	325.00	750.00
1,233	Lyons-Treat	Sm. Red	296,000	165.00	375.00	825.00
1,234	Vernon-Treat	Sm. Red	56,800	165.00	375.00	850.00
1,235	Vernon-McClung	Sm. Red		150.00	325.00	750.00
1,236	Napier-McClung	Sm. Red-r		150.00	325.00	750.00
1,237	Napier-Thompson	Sm. Red	196,000	375.00	600.00	1,000.00
1,238	Napier-Burke	Sm. Red	320,000	165.00	375.00	850.00
1,239	Parker-Burke	Sm. Red		165.00	375.00	850.00
1,240	Teehee-Burke	Sm. Red	744,000	140.00	300.00	700.00
1,241 (☆)	Speelman-White***	Sm. Red	2,444,000†	135.00	200.00	500.00

   *Autographed countersignature of Thomas C. Acton
  **Printed countersignature of Thomas C. Acton.
***This note is dated 1922.
 †Printed.
  r: with rays

Treasury Notes

Face Design:
David G. Farragut (1801–1870) was the first man to hold the rank of admiral in the U.S. Navy. Although he was born in Tennessee, he served in the Union Navy during the Civil War. His portrait was engraved by Charles Schlecht.

Back Design Engraved by W.A. Copenhaver, W.H. Dougal, G.U. Rose, Jr., and J.A. Rueff.

No.	Date	Signatures	Seal	Notes Printed	Very Good	Very Fine	New
1,242	1890	Rosecrans-Huston	Brown	120,000*	1,500.00	7,000.00	15,000.00

Face Design:
The seal is now red and smaller.

Back Design:
Engraved by D.M. Cooper, W.H. Dougal, E.M. Hall, and E.E. Myers.

| 1,243 | 1891 | Rosecrans-Nebeker | Red | 80,000** | 6,500.00 | 12,500.00 | — |

*298 notes are outstanding, about 25 are in existence, 10-12 are known.
**60,000 notes were issued, 6 are known.

Federal Reserve Notes/1914/Red Seal

Face Design:
Portrait of Benjamin
Franklin.

Back Design:
The original
engraving was
prepared by George
F.C. Smillie.

The following bear the signatures of Burke-McAdoo.

No.	Bank	Very Good	Very Fine	New
1,244A	Boston	150.00	275.00	525.00
1,244B	New York	150.00	275.00	525.00
1,244C	Philadelphia	150.00	275.00	525.00
1,244D	Cleveland	150.00	275.00	525.00
1,244E	Richmond	150.00	275.00	525.00
1,244F	Atlanta	150.00	275.00	525.00
1,244G	Chicago	150.00	275.00	525.00
1,244H	St. Louis	150.00	275.00	525.00
1,244I	Minneapolis	150.00	275.00	525.00
1,244J	Kansas City	150.00	275.00	525.00
1,244K	Dallas	150.00	275.00	525.00
1,244L	San Francisco	150.00	275.00	525.00

The first day of issue for the above was November 16, 1914.
A total of 119 notes are outstanding.

Federal Reserve Notes/1914/Blue Seal

No.	Bank	Signatures	Notes Printed	Notes Issued	Very Fine	New
1,245A1	Boston	Burke-McAdoo			115.00	225.00
1,245A2	Boston	Burke-Glass	728,000	728,000	135.00	275.00
1,245A3	Boston	Burke-Houston			115.00	225.00
1,245A4	Boston	White-Mellon			115.00	225.00
1,245B1	New York	Burke-McAdoo			115.00	225.00
1,245B2	New York	Burke-Glass	3,084,000	3,084,000	135.00	275.00
1,245B3	New York	Burke-Houston			115.00	225.00
1,245B4	New York	White-Mellon			115.00	225.00
1,245C1	Philadelphia	Burke-McAdoo			115.00	225.00
1,245C2	Philadelphia	Burke-Glass	666,000	636,000	135.00	275.00
1,245C3	Philadelphia	Burke-Houston			115.00	225.00
1,245C4	Philadelphia	White-Mellon			115.00	225.00
1,245D1	Cleveland	Burke-McAdoo			115.00	225.00
1,245D2	Cleveland	Burke-Glass	668,000	668,000	135.00	275.00
1,245D3	Cleveland	Burke-Houston			115.00	225.00
1,245D4	Cleveland	White-Mellon			115.00	225.00
1,245E1	Richmond	Burke-McAdoo			115.00	225.00
1,245E2	Richmond	Burke-Glass	504,000	416,000	135.00	275.00
1,245E3	Richmond	Burke-Houston			115.00	225.00
1,245E4	Richmond	White-Mellon			115.00	225.00
1,245F1(☆)	Atlanta	Burke-McAdoo			115.00	225.00
1,245F2	Atlanta	Burke-Glass	540,000	476,000	135.00	275.00
1,245F3	Atlanta	Burke-Houston			115.00	225.00
1,245F4	Atlanta	White-Mellon			115.00	225.00
1,245G1	Chicago	Burke-McAdoo			115.00	225.00
1,245G2	Chicago	Burke-Glass	888,000	888,000	135.00	275.00
1,245G3	Chicago	Burke-Houston			115.00	225.00
1,245G4	Chicago	White-Mellon			115.00	225.00
1,245H1	St. Louis	Burke-McAdoo			115.00	225.00
1,245H2	St. Louis	Burke-Glass	188,000	188,000	135.00	275.00
1,245H3	St. Louis	Burke-Houston			115.00	225.00
1,245H4	St. Louis	White-Mellon			115.00	225.00

Federal Reserve Notes 1914/Blue Seal

No.	Bank	Signatures	Notes Printed	Notes Issued	Very Fine	New
1,245I1	Minneapolis	Burke-McAdoo			115.00	225.00
1,245I2	Minneapolis	Burke-Glass	124,000	120,000	135.00	300.00
1,245I3	Minneapolis	Burke-Houston			115.00	225.00
1,245I4	Minneapolis	White-Mellon			115.00	225.00
1,245J1 (☆)	Kansas City	Burke-McAdoo			115.00	225.00
1,245J2	Kansas City	Burke-Glass	256,000	256,000	135.00	300.00
1,245J3	Kansas City	Burke-Houston			115.00	225.00
1,245J4	Kansas City	White-Mellon			115.00	225.00
1,245K1	Dallas	Burke-McAdoo			115.00	225.00
1,245K2	Dallas	Burke-Glass	140,000	124,000	135.00	300.00
1,245J3	Dallas	Burke-Houston			115.00	225.00
1,245J4	Dallas	White-Mellon			115.00	225.00
1,245L1	San Francisco	Burke-McAdoo			115.00	225.00
1,245L2	San Francisco	Burke-Glass	1,064,000	1,064,000	135.00	285.00
1,245L3	San Francisco	Burke-Houston			115.00	225.00
1,245L4	San Francisco	White-Mellon			115.00	225.00

United States Note/Red Seal

SMALL SIZE

Face Design:
Portrait of Benjamin
Franklin.

Back Design:
Independence Hall.

No.	Date	Signatures	Notes Printed	New
1,246	1966	Granahan-Fowler	768,000	145.00
1,246(☆)	1966(☆)	Granahan-Fowler	128,000	160.00
1,247	1966A	Elston-Kennedy	512,000	130.00

Federal Reserve Bank Notes/1929/Brown Seal

Face Design:
Portrait of
Benjamin Franklin.

Back Design

The following bear the signatures of Jones-Woods.

No.	Bank	Notes Printed	Very Fine	Extra Fine	New
1,248A	Boston	None	—	—	—
1,248B	New York	480,000	—	120.00	175.00
1,248C	Philadelphia	None	—	—	—
1,248D	Cleveland	276,000	—	135.00	200.00
1,248E	Richmond	192,000	120.00	170.00	235.00
1,248F	Atlanta	None	—	—	—
1,248G	Chicago	384,000	—	125.00	190.00
1,248H	St. Louis	None	—	—	—
1,248I	Minneapolis	144,000	120.00	170.00	235.00
1,248J	Kansas City	96,000	130.00	185.00	265.00
1,248K	Dallas	36,000	135.00	190.00	300.00
1,248L	San Francisco	None	—	—	—

National Bank Notes/1929/Brown Seal

Face Design:
Type I.

Face Design:
Type II has the bank charter number printed a second time near the serial number.

Back Design:
Similar to No. 1,248.

Both types bear the signatures of Jones-Woods.

No.	Rarity*	Type I			Type II		
		Very Fine	Extra Fine	New	Very Fine	Extra Fine	New
	1	130.00	165.00	200.00	140.00	175.00	215.00
	2	140.00	175.00	210.00	150.00	185.00	225.00
	3	150.00	185.00	220.00	160.00	195.00	245.00
	4	160.00	195.00	230.00	170.00	215.00	275.00
1,249	5	175.00	210.00	250.00	185.00	250.00	350.00
	6	190.00	240.00	300.00	205.00	275.00	500.00
	7	225.00	300.00	400.00	235.00	325.00	—
	8	275.00	350.00	500.00	—	—	—
	9		None Issued				

The total issue for both types was 456,915.

*Rarity table is on page 41.

Federal Reserve Notes/Green Seal

Face Design

Back Design:
Similar to No. 1,248.

1928 Series, signatures of Woods-Mellon

No.	Bank	Notes Printed	Extra Fine	New
1,250A	Boston	376,000	145.00	200.00
1,250B	New York	755,400	145.00	190.00
1,250C	Philadelphia	389,100	145.00	190.00
1,250D	Cleveland	542,400	145.00	190.00
1,250E	Richmond	364,416	160.00	210.00
1,250F	Atlanta	357,000	160.00	210.00
1,250G	Chicago	783,300	135.00	185.00
1,250H	St. Louis	187,200	160.00	215.00
1,250I	Minneapolis	102,000	175.00	220.00
1,250J	Kansas City	234,612	165.00	200.00
1,250K	Dallas	80,140	175.00	225.00
1,250L	San Francisco	486,000	150.00	190.00

Federal Reserve Notes/Green Seal

Face Design:
Number replaces
letter in Federal
Reserve Seal.

Back Design:
Similar to No. 1,248.

1928A Series, signatures of Woods-Mellon

No.	Bank	Notes Printed	Extra Fine	New
1,251A	Boston	980,400	140.00	185.00
1,251B	New York	2,938,176	140.00	175.00
1,251C	Philadelphia	1,496,844	140.00	180.00
1,251D	Cleveland	992,436	140.00	180.00
1,251E	Richmond	621,364	145.00	185.00
1,251F	Atlanta	371,400	150.00	190.00
1,251G	Chicago	4,010,424	140.00	175.00
1,251H	St. Louis	749,544	160.00	190.00
1,251I	Minneapolis	503,040	160.00	200.00
1,251J	Kansas City	681,804	160.00	190.00
1,251K	Dallas	594,456	160.00	200.00
1,251L	San Francisco	1,228,032	140.00	180.00

Federal Reserve Notes/Green Seal

1934 Series, signatures of Julian-Morgenthau

No.	Bank	Notes Printed	Extra Fine	New
1,252A	Boston	3,710,000	145.00	175.00
1,252B	New York	3,086,000	130.00	165.00
1,252C	Philadelphia	2,776,800	145.00	175.00
1,252D	Cleveland	3,447,108	145.00	175.00
1,252E	Richmond	4,317,600	145.00	175.00
1,252F	Atlanta	3,264,420	145.00	175.00
1,252G	Chicago	7,075,000	130.00	165.00
1,252H	St. Louis	2,106,192	145.00	175.00
1,252I	Minneapolis	852,600	160.00	185.00
1,252J	Kansas City	1,932,900	145.00	175.00
1,252K	Dallas	1,506,516	145.00	175.00
1,252L	San Francisco	6,521,940	140.00	170.00

1934A Series, signatures of Julian-Morgenthau

No.	Bank	Notes Printed	Extra Fine	New
1,253A	Boston	102,000	145.00	185.00
1,253B	New York	15,278,892	130.00	160.00
1,253C	Philadelphia	588,000	145.00	175.00
1,253D	Cleveland	645,300	145.00	175.00
1,253E	Richmond	770,100	145.00	175.00
1,253F	Atlanta	589,896	145.00	175.00
1,253G	Chicago	3,328,800	130.00	160.00
1,253H	St. Louis	434,208	145.00	175.00
1,253I	Minneapolis	153,000	160.00	185.00
1,253J	Kansas City	455,100	145.00	175.00
1,253K	Dallas	226,164	145.00	180.00
1,253L	San Francisco	1,130,400	140.00	175.00

Federal Reserve Notes/Green Seal

1934B Series, signatures of Julian-Vinson

No.	Bank	Notes Printed	Extra Fine	New
1,254A	Boston	41,400	165.00	210.00
1,254B	New York	None	—	—
1,254C	Philadelphia	39,600	165.00	215.00
1,254D	Cleveland	61,200	165.00	210.00
1,254E	Richmond	977,400	140.00	175.00
1,254F	Atlanta	645,000	140.00	175.00
1,254G	Chicago	396,000	165.00	200.00
1,254H	St. Louis	676,200	140.00	175.00
1,254I	Minneapolis	377,000	140.00	175.00
1,254J	Kansas City	364,500	165.00	210.00
1,254K	Dallas	392,700	150.00	185.00
1,254L	San Francisco	None	—	—

1934C Series, signatures of Julian-Snyder

No.	Bank	Notes Printed	Extra Fine	New
1,255A	Boston	13,800	175.00	225.00
1,255B	New York	1,556,400	125.00	150.00
1,255C	Philadelphia	13,200	175.00	225.00
1,255D	Cleveland	1,473,200	140.00	175.00
1,255E	Richmond	No Record	—	—
1,255F	Atlanta	493,900	125.00	160.00
1,255G	Chicago	612,000	125.00	160.00
1,255H	St. Louis	957,000	125.00	160.00
1,255I	Minneapolis	392,904	130.00	165.00
1,255J	Kansas City	401,100	130.00	165.00
1,255K	Dallas	280,700	130.00	165.00
1,255L	San Francisco	432,600	130.00	165.00

Federal Reserve Notes/Green Seal

1934 D Series, signatures of Clark-Snyder

No.	Bank	Notes Printed	Extra Fine	New
1,256A	Boston	No Record	—	—
1,256B	New York	156	Rare	
1,256C	Philadelphia	308,400	140.00	175.00
1,256D	Cleveland	No Record	—	—
1,256E	Richmond	No Record	—	—
1,256F	Atlanta	260,400	140.00	175.00
1,256G	Chicago	78,000	140.00	175.00
1,256H	St. Louis	166,800	140.00	175.00
1,256I	Minneapolis	No Record	—	—
1,256J	Kansas City	No Record	—	—
1,256K	Dallas	66,000	140.00	180.00
1,256L	San Francisco	No Record	—	—

1950 Series, signatures of Clark-Snyder

No.	Bank	Notes Printed	Extra Fine	New
1,257A	Boston	768,000	115.00	160.00
1,257B	New York	3,908,000	—	135.00
1,257C	Philadelphia	1,332,000	—	145.00
1,257D	Cleveland	1,632,000	—	145.00
1,257E	Richmond	4,076,000	—	135.00
1,257F	Atlanta	1,824,000	—	145.00
1,257G	Chicago	4,428,000	—	130.00
1,257H	St. Louis	1,284,000	—	145.00
1,257I	Minneapolis	564,000	115.00	165.00
1,257J	Kansas City	864,000	115.00	160.00
1,257K	Dallas	1,216,000	—	145.00
1,257L	San Francisco	2,524,000	—	140.00

Federal Reserve Notes/Green Seal

1950A Series, signatures of Priest-Humphrey

No.	Bank	Notes Printed	New
1,258A	Boston	1,008,000	135.00
1,258B	New York	2,880,000	125.00
1,258C	Philadelphia	576,000	145.00
1,258D	Cleveland	288,000	150.00
1,258E	Richmond	2,160,000	125.00
1,258F	Atlanta	288,000	150.00
1,258G	Chicago	864,000	140.00
1,258H	St. Louis	432,000	145.00
1,258I	Minneapolis	144,000	160.00
1,258J	Kansas City	288,000	150.00
1,258K	Dallas	432,000	145.00
1,258L	San Francisco	720,000	140.00

1950B Series, signatures of Priest-Anderson

No.	Bank	Notes Printed	New
1,259A	Boston	720,000	140.00
1,259B	New York	6,636,000	125.00
1,259C	Philadelphia	720,000	140.00
1,259D	Cleveland	432,000	140.00
1,259E	Richmond	1,008,000	130.00
1,259F	Atlanta	576,000	140.00
1,259G	Chicago	2,592,000	125.00
1,259H	St. Louis	1,152,000	130.00
1,259I	Minneapolis	288,000	150.00
1,259J	Kansas City	720,000	140.00
1,259K	Dallas	1,728,000	125.00
1,259L	San Francisco	2,880,000	125.00

Federal Reserve Notes/Green Seal

1950C Series, signatures of Smith-Dillon

No.	Bank	Notes Printed	New
1,260A	Boston	864,000	130.00
1,260B	New York	2,448,000	125.00
1,260C	Philadelphia	576,000	135.00
1,260D	Cleveland	576,000	135.00
1,260E	Richmond	1,440,000	125.00
1,260F	Atlanta	1,296,000	125.00
1,260G	Chicago	1,584,000	125.00
1,260H	St. Louis	720,000	135.00
1,260I	Minneapolis	288,000	150.00
1,260J	Kansas City	432,000	140.00
1,260K	Dallas	720,000	135.00
1,260L	San Francisco	2,160,000	125.00

1950D Series, signatures of Granahan-Dillon

No.	Bank	Notes Printed	New
1,261A	Boston	1,872,000	125.00
1,261B	New York	7,632,000	120.00
1,261C	Philadelphia	1,872,000	125.00
1,261D	Cleveland	1,584,000	125.00
1,261E	Richmond	2,880,000	125.00
1,261F	Atlanta	1,872,000	125.00
1,261G	Chicago	4,608,000	120.00
1,261H	St. Louis	1,440,000	125.00
1,261I	Minneapolis	432,000	130.00
1,261J	Kansas City	864,000	130.00
1,261K	Dallas	1,728,000	125.00
1,261L	San Francisco	3,312,000	120.00

1950E Series, signatures of Granahan-Fowler

No.	Bank	Notes Printed	New
1,262B	New York	3,024,000	120.00
1,262G	Chicago	576,000	135.00
1,262L	San Francisco	2,736,000	125.00

1963A Series, signatures of Granahan-Fowler. "IN GOD WE TRUST" now on back

No.	Bank	Notes Printed	New
1,263A	Boston	1,536,000	115.00
1,263A(☆)	Boston	128,000	125.00
1,263B	New York	12,544,000	115.00
1,263B(☆)	New York	1,536,000	—
1,263C	Philadelphia	1,792,000	115.00
1,263C(☆)	Philadelphia	192,000	—
1,263D	Cleveland	2,304,000	115.00
1,263D(☆)	Cleveland	192,000	115.00
1,263E	Richmond	2,816,000	115.00
1,263E(☆)	Richmond	192,000	115.00
1,263F	Atlanta	1,280,000	115.00
1,263F(☆)	Atlanta	128,000	125.00
1,263G	Chicago	4,352,000	115.00
1,263G(☆)	Chicago	.512,000	—
1,263H	St. Louis	1,536,000	115.00
1,263H(☆)	St. Louis	256,000	—
1,263I	Minneapolis	512,000	120.00
1,263I(☆)	Minneapolis	128,000	125.00
1,263J	Kansas City	1,024,000	115.00
1,263J(☆)	Kansas City	128,000	125.00
1,263K	Dallas	1,536,000	115.00
1,263K(☆)	Dallas	192,000	115.00
1,263L	San Francisco	6,400,000	115.00
1,263L(☆)	San Francisco	832,000	—

Federal Reserve Notes/Green Seal

1969 Series, signatures of Elston-Kennedy				1969A Series, signatures of Kabis-Connally			
No.	**Bank**	**Notes Printed**	**New**	**No.**	**Bank**	**Notes Printed**	**New**
1,264A	Boston	2,048,000	—	1,265A	Boston	1,280,000	
1,264A(☆)	Boston	128,000	115.00	1,265A(☆)	Boston	320,000	
1,264B	New York	11,520,000	—	1,265B	New York	11,264,000	
1,264B(☆)	New York	128,000	115.00	1,265B(☆)	New York	640,000	
1,264C	Philadelphia	2,560,000	—	1,265C	Philadelphia	2,048,000	
1,264C(☆)	Philadelphia	128,000	115.00	1,265C(☆)	Philadelphia	448,000	
1,264D	Cleveland	768,000	115.00	1,265D	Cleveland	1,280,000	
1,264D(☆)	Cleveland	64,000	125.00	1,265D(☆)	Cleveland	192,000	
1,264E	Richmond	2,560,000	—	1,265E	Richmond	2,304,000	
1,264E(☆)	Richmond	192,000	115.00	1,265E(☆)	Richmond	192,000	
1,264F	Atlanta	2,304,000	—	1,265F	Atlanta	2,304,000	
1,264F(☆)	Atlanta	128,000	115.00	1,265F(☆)	Atlanta	640,000	
1,264G	Chicago	5,888,000	—	1,265G	Chicago	5,376,000	
1,264G(☆)	Chicago	256,000	—	1,265G(☆)	Chicago	320,000	
1,264H	St. Louis	1,280,000	—	1,265H	St. Louis	1,024,000	
1,264H(☆)	St. Louis	64,000	125.00	1,265H(☆)	St. Louis	664,000	
1,264I	Minneapolis	512,000	115.00	1,265I	Minneapolis	1,024,000	
1,264I(☆)	Minneapolis	64,000	125.00	1,265I(☆)	Minneapolis	None Printed	
1,264J	Kansas City	1,792,000	—	1,265J	Kansas City	512,000	
1,264J(☆)	Kansas City	384,000	—	1,265J(☆)	Kansas City	None Printed	
1,264K	Dallas	2,048,000	—	1,265K	Dallas	3,328,000	
1,264K(☆)	Dallas	128,000	115.00	1,265K(☆)	Dallas	128,000	
1,264L	San Francisco	7,168,000	—	1,265L	San Francisco	4,352,000	
1,264L(☆)	San Francisco	320,000	—	1,265L(☆)	San Francisco	576,000	

Federal Reserve Notes/Green Seal

1969C Series, signatures of Banuelos-Shultz.   1974 Series, signatures of Neff-Simon.

No.	Bank	Notes Printed	New
1,267A	Boston	2,048,000	
1,267A(☆)	Boston	64,000	
1,267B	New York	15,616,000	
1,267B(☆)	New York	256,000	
1,267C	Philadelphia	2,816,000	
1,267C(☆)	Philadelphia	64,000	
1,267D	Cleveland	3,456,000	
1,267D(☆)	Cleveland	64,000	
1,267E	Richmond	7,296,000	
1,267E(☆)	Richmond	128,000	
1,267F	Atlanta	2,432,000	
1,267F(☆)	Atlanta	64,000	
1,267G	Chicago	6,016,000	
1,267G(☆)	Chicago	320,000	
1,267H	St. Louis	5,376,000	
1,267H(☆)	St. Louis	64,000	
1,267I	Minneapolis	512,000	
1,267I(☆)	Minneapolis	64,000	
1,267J	Kansas City	4,736,000	
1,267J(☆)	Kansas City	192,000	
1,267K	Dallas	2,944,000	
1,267K(☆)	Dallas	64,000	
1,267L	San Francisco	10,240,000	
1,267L(☆)	San Francisco	512,000	

Gold Certificate/Gold Seal

Face Design:
Portrait of Benjamin
Franklin. The
engravers of this note
were J. Eissler, E.M.
Hall, and F.
Lamasure.

Back Design:
Similar to No. 1,248.

No.	Date	Signatures	Notes Printed	Very Fine	Extra Fine	New
1,319	1928	Woods-Mellon	3,240,000	135.00	175.00	275.00
1,319(☆)	1928(☆)	Woods-Mellon		300.00	400.00	725.00
1,319A	1928A	Woods-Mills	120,000		Not Issued	

United States Notes/Red Seal

Face Design:
Albert Gallatin was elected to the United States Senate from Pennsylvania in 1793, 13 years after he arrived in America from Geneva, Switzerland, where he was born in 1761. Three Presidents appointed Gallatin to three different offices. President Jefferson made him Secretary of the Treasury in 1801, Madison sent Gallatin to France as Minister in 1816, and Adams appointed Gallatin Minister to England in 1826. Following his political career, Gallatin became president of the National Bank of New York, 1832-39.

Back Design

No.	Date	Signatures	Obligation	Notes Issued
1,320	1862	Chittenden-Spinner	First	
1,320a	1862	Chittenden-Spinner	Second	117,972*
1,321	1863	Chittenden-Spinner	Second	

*451 notes were outstanding according to records of 1889. Nos. 1,320-1,321 are extremely rare.

United States Note

Back Design

Face Design:
Charles Burt
engraved the portrait
of John Quincy
Adams, our sixth
president. Adams
was born in Quincy,
Massachusetts, on
July 11, 1767. Adams
was appointed
Minister to Holland in
1794, Berlin in 1797,
Russia in 1809, and
Great Britain in 1815.
The year following the
end of his
Presidency, Adams
was elected to
Congress. He died in
1848 holding
Congressional office.
Before his death,
Adams assembled a
nice collection of
coins. The female
figure on the left,
entitled *Justice,* was
engraved by S.A.
Schoff.

No.	Date	Signatures	Seal	Notes Issued	Outstanding in 1889
1,322	1869	Allison-Spinner	Lg. Red	87,980	499

These notes were withdrawn due to deceptive counterfeits.

United States Notes

Face Design: Joseph King Mansfield, a West Point graduate, was born in New Haven, Connecticut, in 1803. Early in the Civil War Mansfield was made a Brigadier General and was killed at the Battle of Antietam. The female figure, entitled *Victory* and the portrait were engraved by Charles Burt.

Back Design

No.	Date	Signatures	Seal	Notes Issued
1,323	1874	Allison-Spinner	Sm. Red-r	56,000
1,324	1875	Allison-New	Sm. Red-r	56,800
1,325	1875	Allison-Wyman	Sm. Red-r	
1,326	1878	Allison-Gilfillan	Sm. Red-r	24,000
1,327	1880	Scofield-Gilfillan	Lg. Brown	
1,328	1880	Bruce-Wyman	Lg. Brown	
1,329	1880	Rosecrans-Jordan	Lg. Red	
1,330	1880	Rosecrans-Hyatt	Lg. Red	
1,331	1880	Rosecrans-Huston	Lg. Red-sp	108,000 (printed)
1,332	1880	Rosecrans-Nebeker	Lg. Brown	
1,333	1880	Tillman-Morgan	Sm. Red-sc	
1,334	1880	Bruce-Roberts	Sm. Red-sc	
1,335	1880*	Lyons-Roberts	Sm. Red-sc	
1,336	1880	Napier-McClung	Sm. Red-sc	

*In 1975, advertised at $18,000 in extra fine condition.
  r: with rays   sp: with spikes   sc: with scallops

Compound Interest Treasury Notes/6%

Face Design:
This note bears
vignettes of *The
Standard Bearer* and
the ship *New
Ironsides.*

Back Design:
This recently
uncovered proof
design answers to the
description recorded
by earlier
researchers.

Act of March 3, 1863

No.	Signatures	Notes Printed	Notes Issued	Outstanding
1,337	Chittenden-Spinner	21,388	16,468	1
1,338	Colby-Spinner	20,000	None	—

Act of June 30, 1864

No.	Signatures	Notes Printed	Notes Issued	Outstanding
1,339	Chittenden-Spinner	84,612	76,000	22
1,340	Colby-Spinner	78,000		

Interest-bearing Notes

One-Year Notes—5% (Act of March 3, 1863)

No. 1,340a This note has the same design as No. 1,339.

Two-Year Notes—6% (Act of March 2, 1861)

Face Design:
This proof note, printed by the National Bank Note Co. bears J. P. Ourdan's engraving of General Winfield Scott.

Back Design:
Unknown

No.	Notes Issued	Outstanding
1,340b	48,448*	Unknown

Two-Year Notes—5% (Act of March 3, 1863)

Face Design:
Liberty & Union was engraved by Charles Burt and *The Eagle's Nest* which was also used on the 1882, $5,000 gold certificates is the work of Louis Delnoce. Only the upper fragment of a specimen is known. The vignettes were reconstructed, the remaining portions suggest what the note probably looked like.

Back Design: Unknown

No.	Notes Issued	Outstanding
1,341	Without coupons, printed but not issued	—
1,342	With 3 coupons, 80,604	3

---

*4,291 from old plates included. Additional notes were probably issued.

Interest-bearing Notes

Three-Year Notes—7-3/10% (Act of July 17, 1861)
These notes bear the portrait of George Washington.

No.	Dated	Numerals	Notes Issued	Outstanding
1,343	Aug. 19, 1861	Red	24,200	6
1,344	Oct. 1, 1861	Red	46,391	8
1,345	Oct. 1, 1861	Blue	1,117	0

Act of June 30, 1864

Face Design:
Mortar Firing,
Alexander Hamilton
and George
Washington.

Back Design

(Photographs
courtesy The Coin
and Currency
Institute, Inc.)

No.	Dated	Notes Printed	Notes Issued	Outstanding
1,346	Aug. 15, 1864	154,250	171,668	17
1,347	Mar. 3, 1865	45,887		

Act of March 3, 1865

1,348	June 15, 1865	181,813	175,682	28
1,349	July 15, 1865	115,000	108,654	12

National Bank Note/First Charter Period/Red Seal

Face Design:
J.D. Smillie's
Civilization is seen on
the left, and the
*Arrival of the Sirius,
1838* is on the right.

Back Design:
*The Surrender of
General Burgoyne to
General Gates at
Saratoga,* a painting
by John Trumbull,
was engraved by
Frederick Girsch.
This painting hangs in
the Capitol in
Washington, D.C.

No.	Date	Signatures	Notes Issued	Outstanding	Known
1,350	Original*	Colby-Spinner ⎤			
1,351	1875	Colby-Spinner ⎟	23,924	173	3
1,351a	1875	Allison-New ⎦			

*Original notes did not have the series printed on the face.

National Gold Bank Notes/Red Seal

Face Design:
Similar to No. 1,350.

Back Design:
Similar to No. 343.

The following notes bear the signatures of Allison-Spinner.

No.	Date	Issuing Bank	City	Notes Issued	Notes Outstanding
1,351b	1875	First National Gold Bank	San Francisco	300	
1,351c	1872	National Gold Bank and Trust Company	San Francisco	250	4
1,351d	1872	National Gold Bank of D.O. Mills and Company	Sacramento	60	

Silver Certificates

Face Design:
Bostonian Charles
Sumner was born on
January 6, 1811, and
graduated from
Harvard Law School
in 1834. In 1852 he
was elected to the
United States Senate
by a margin of one
vote. Sumner was an
opponent of slavery.
His portrait was
engraved by Charles
Burt.

Back Design

Nos. 1,360-1,362 bear the printed signatures of Scofield-Gilfillan and handwritten countersignatures. All have large red seals.

No.	Date	Countersigned By	Payable At	Notes Issued	Known
1,352	1878*		New York	400	0
1,353	1878	R.M. Anthony	San Francisco	4,900	0
1,354	1878	A.U. Wyman	Washington, D.C.	4,000	0

No.	Date	Signatures	Seal	Notes Issued	Known
1,355	1880	Scofield-Gilfillan	Brown	Doubtful	0
1,356	1880	Bruce-Gilfillan	Brown	16,000	3
1,357	1880	Bruce-Wyman	Brown	8,000	1

*Autographed countersignatures of W.G. White, J.C. Hopper, or T. Hillhouse.

Gold Certificates/Act of March 3, 1863

Nos. 1,358, 1,359, and 1,361 are countersigned and dated by hand and are payable at New York.

No.	Issue	Date	Signatures	Notes Printed	Notes Issued	Outstanding
1,358	First*	1863	Colby-Spinner	18,000	15,000	0
1,359	Second	1870	Allison-Spinner	40,000	36,000	11
1,360	The note previously listed here does not exist.					
1,361	Third	1875	Allison-New	11,628	11,628	0

No. 1,358 is similar to No. 827a. 1,359 and 1,361 bear the portrait of Abraham Lincoln.

* As this book went to press, a photo of this note's recently uncovered back design became available. It appears on page 50.

Face Design: Portrait of Abraham Lincoln, engraved by Charles Burt.

Back Design: Eagle with Flag, was engraved for the Baldwin Bank Note Co.

No.	Date	Signatures	Notes Issued
1,362	1882*	Bruce-Gilfillan	20,000
1,363	1882	Bruce-Gilfillan	8,000
1,364	1882	Bruce-Wyman	20,000
1,365	1882	Rosecrans-Hyatt	16,000
1,366	1882	Lyons-Roberts	108,000
1,367	1882	Parker-Burke	
1,368	1882	Teehee-Burke	
1,369	1922	Speelman-White	84,000 (printed)

* This note bears the handwritten countersignature of Thomas C. Acton and is payable at New York. I have seen proof impressions with the signatures of Napier-McClung.

Federal Reserve Notes/1918/Blue Seal

Face Design:
Portrait of John
Marshall.

Back Design:
*DeSoto Discovering
the Mississippi in
1541*, a painting by
W.H. Powell, was
engraved by
Frederick Girsch.

No.	Bank	Signatures	Notes Printed	Notes Issued
1,370A2	Boston	Burke-Glass ⎤	17,600	13,600
1,370B2	New York	Burke-Glass ⎦	125,600	125,600
1,370B4	New York	White-Mellon		
1,370C	Philadelphia		24,000	6,000
1,370D2	Cleveland	Burke-Glass	15,600	15,600
1,370E	Richmond		23,200	4,000
1,370F	Atlanta		34,400	26,800
1,370G1	Chicago	Burke-McAdoo ⎤	38,000	30,000
1,370G2	Chicago	Burke-Glass ⎦		
1,370H	St. Louis		14,400	6,800
1,370I	Minneapolis		7,200	4,000
1,370J2	Kansas City	Burke-Glass	16,000	7,200
1,370K	Dallas		6,000	4,400
1,370L2	San Francisco	Burke-Glass	24,000	20,400

Although the figures above include all signatures combinations, only those that have been observed thus far are listed.

Federal Reserve Notes/Green Seal

Face Design:
William McKinley.

Back Design

1928 Series, signatures of Woods-Mellon			1934 Series, signatures of Julian-Morgenthau		
No.	Bank	Notes Printed	No.	Bank	Notes Printed
1,372A	Boston	69,120	1,373A	Boston	56,628
1,372B	New York	299,400	1,373B	New York	288,000
1,372C	Philadelphia	135,120	1,373C	Philadelphia	31,200
1,372D	Cleveland	166,440	1,373D	Cleveland	39,000
1,372E	Richmond	84,720	1,373E	Richmond	40,800
1,372F	Atlanta	69,360	1,373F	Atlanta	46,200
1,372G	Chicago	573,600	1,373G	Chicago	212,400
1,372H	St. Louis	66,180	1,373H	St. Louis	24,000
1,372I	Minneapolis	34,680	1,373I	Minneapolis	24,000
1,372J	Kansas City	510,720	1,373J	Kansas City	40,800
1,372K	Dallas	70,560	1,373K	Dallas	31,200
1,372L	San Francisco	64,080	1,373L	San Francisco	83,400

Federal Reserve Notes/Green Seal

1934A Series, signatures of Julian-Morgenthau

No.	Bank	Notes Printed	No.	Bank	Notes Printed
1,374A	Boston	None	1,374G	Chicago	214,800
1,374B	New York	276,000	1,374H	St. Louis	57,600
1,374C	Philadelphia	45,300	1,374I	Minneapolis	14,400
1,374D	Cleveland	28,800	1,374J	Kansas City	55,200
1,374E	Richmond	36,000	1,374K	Dallas	34,800
1,374F	Atlanta	None	1,374L	San Francisco	93,000

1934B Series, signatures of Julian-Vinson

No.	Bank	Notes Printed
1374F-1	Atlanta	2,472

1934C Series, signatures of Julian-Snyder

No.	Bank	Notes Printed
1374A-1	Boston	1,440
1374B-1	New York	204

Gold Certificate

1,375

1928 Series, signatures of Woods-Mellon. This note is the same as No. 1,373 with the exception of the seal and the obligation. 420,000 notes were printed.

United States Notes/Red Seal

LARGE SIZE

Face Design:
Robert Morris, U.S.
Senator and
Superintendent of
Finance. The
engraving is by
Charles Schlecht.

Back Design**

No.	Date	Signatures	Notes Printed	Outstanding in 1889
1,376	1862*	Chittenden-Spinner ⎤		
1,377	1862**	Chittenden-Spinner ⎟	155,928	201
1,378***	1863**	Chittenden-Spinner ⎦		

*First obligation, an estimated 12,000.
**Second obligation.
***2 known

United States Notes/Red Seal

Face Design:
DeWitt Clinton
graduated from
Columbia College in
1786, 17 years after
his birth in Little
Britain, New York. He
was elected to the
United States Senate,
became Mayor of
New York City, and
served three terms as
Governor of New
York. His portrait was
engraved by Charles
Burt. On the left,
Columbus
contemplates the
Earth.

Back Design

No.	Date	Signatures	Notes Printed	Notes Issued
1,379	1869	Allison-Spinner	87,100	79,709

United States Notes

Face Design:
Similar to No. 1,379.

Back Design

No.	Date	Signatures	Seal	Notes Printed	Notes Issued
1,380	1878	Allison-Gilfillan	Sm Red-r		24,000
1,381	1880	Bruce-Wyman	Lg Brown ⌐		12,000**
1,382	1880	Rosecrans-Jordan	Lg Red		21,148**
1,383	1880	Rosecrans-Hyatt	Lg Red		6,852**
1,384	1880	Rosecrans-Huston	Lg Red-sp		8,000**
1,385	1880	Rosecrans-Nebeker	Lg Brown ⌐		18,380**
1,386	1880	Tillman-Morgan	Sm Red-sc	188,000	
1,387	1880	Tillman-Roberts	Sm Red-sc		
1,388	1880	Bruce-Roberts	Sm Red-sc		
1,389	1880	Lyons-Roberts*	Sm Red-sc		
1,390	1880	Vernon-Treat	Sm Red-sc		
1,391	1880	Napier-McClung	Sm Red-sc ⌐		

*At least 4 notes are known.
**Estimated figure.
r: with rays; sp: with spikes; sc: with scallops

Compound Interest Treasury Notes/6%

Act of June 30, 1864

No.	Signatures	Notes Printed	Notes Issued	Outstanding
1,392	Chittenden-Spinner	24,000	20,000	
1,393	Colby-Spinner	39,200	37,400	4

Interest-Bearing Notes

One-Year Note—5% (Act of March 3, 1863)

Face Design: *Justice* on the left, eagle with shield in the center, and *Liberty* on the right. All of these notes were probably redeemed.

Back Design: Unknown.

No.
1,393a

Two-Year Notes—6% (Act of March 2, 1861)

No.	Notes Issued
1,393b	27,547*

*3,068 from old plates included. Additional notes were probably issued.

Two-Year Notes—5% (Act of March 3, 1863)

Face Design: The *Naval Engagement between the Guerriere and the Constitution* and the *Discovery of the Mississippi by DeSoto* appear on this unknown note.

No.	Notes Issued	Outstanding
1,394	Without coupons, printed not issued	—
1,395	With 3 coupons, 89,308	19

Some of the notes with three coupons were printed by the Continental Bank Note Company.

Interest-Bearing Notes

Three-Year Notes—7 3/10% (Act of July 17, 1861)

Face Design:
Portrait of Salmon P.
Chase.

Back Design

No.	Dated	Notes Printed	Notes Issued	Outstanding
1,396	Aug. 19, 1861*		22,922	3
1,397	Oct. 1, 1861*		37,998	3
1,398	Oct. 1, 1861**		1,380	0
	Act of June 30, 1864			
1,399	Aug. 15, 1864	114,540	118,528	5
1,400	Mar. 3, 1865	43,460		

*Red numerals
**Blue numerals

Interest-bearing Notes

Face Design:
Seated figure of
Justice. The note
illustrated here is the
only one known; it
was made available
by Amon Carter, Jr.

Back Design

Act of March 3, 1865

No.	Dated	Notes Printed	Notes Issued	Outstanding
1,401	June 15, 1865	189,200	179,965	3
1,402	July 15, 1865	81,000	71,879	8

National Bank Note/First Charter Period/Red Seal

Face Design: John Trumbull's painting of *General Scott's Entrance Into Mexico* was engraved by Alfred Jones and James Smillie. The United States Capitol was engraved by James Smillie.

Back Design: *Washington Resigning his Commission,* another mural by John Trumbull, was engraved by Frederick Girsch and Louis Delnoce.

No.	Date	Signatures	Notes Issued	Outstanding
1,403	Orig*	Chittenden-Spinner	7,379	21
1,404	1875	Allison-Wyman		

*Original notes did not have the series date printed on the face.

Silver Certificates

Face Design: William L. Marcy was born on December 12, 1786, in Southbridge, Massachusetts. Following his graduation from Brown University, Marcy held numerous political positions, the most notable being Secretary of State under Franklin Pierce.

Back Design

Nos. 1,405-1,407 bear the signatures of Scofield-Gilfillan.

No.	Date	Countersigned By	Payable At	Seal	Notes Issued
1,405	1878	T. Hillhouse (?)	New York	Red	90
1,406	1878	R.M. Anthony*	San Francisco	Red	10,400
1,407	1878	A.U. Wyman**	Washington, D.C.	Red	2,000
1,407a	1878	A.U. Wyman	Washington, D.C.	Red	2,000

No.	Date	Signatures	Seal	Notes Printed
1,408	1880	Scofield-Gilfillan	Brown ⎤	
1,409	1880	Bruce-Gilfillan	Brown ⎟ 16,000
1,410	1880	Bruce-Wyman***	Brown ⎦	

*A portion of this issue could have autographed countersignatures.

**Autographed countersignatures. This figure is based on conjecture, see *Numismatic News,* May 24, 1975 for Part II of Walter Breen's continuing series on the 1878 Silver Certificates.

***3 notes are known

Silver Certificate/Red Seal

Face Design:
A smaller portrait of
William L. Marcy was
retained for this note.
Engraved by D.M.
Cooper, J. Kennedy,
S.B. Many, W.
Ponickau, G.U. Rose,
Jr. and G.F.C. Smillie.

Back Design:
Engraved by D.M.
Cooper, E. M. Hall, W.
F. Lutz, R. Ponickau,
and G. U. Rose, Jr.
(This unique note was
made available by
Amon Carter, Jr.)

No.	Date	Signatures	Notes Printed	Notes Issued	Notes Known
1,411	1891	Tillman-Morgan	8,000	5,600	1

A total of nine notes are outstanding for nos. 1,405-1,411.

Gold Certificates/Act of March 3, 1863

Nos. 1,412, 1,414, and 1,415 are countersigned and dated by hand and are payable at New York.

No.	Issue	Date	Signatures	Notes Printed	Notes Issued	Outstanding
1,412	First	1863	Colby-Spinner	117,000	60,000	7
1,413	Second	1870	Allison-Spinner	50,000	47,500	16
1,414	The note previously listed here does not exist.					
1,415	Third	1875	Allison-New	14,371	14,371	0

Back Design:
No. 1412

This note is a proof impression. No. 1,412 is similar to No. 827a. 1,413 and 1,415 bear the portrait of Alexander Hamilton.

Gold Certificates

Face Design:
Portrait of Alexander
Hamilton. The space
on the left of this proof
impression is
reserved for the
countersignature.

Back Design

No.	Date	Signatures	Notes Issued
1,416	1882*	Bruce-Gilfillan	12,000
1,417	1882	Bruce-Gilfillan	8,000
1,418	1882	Bruce-Wyman	20,000
1,419	1882	Rosecrans-Hyatt	16,000
1,419a	1882	Rosecrans-Huston	8,000
1,420	1882	Rosecrans-Nebeker	8,000
1,421	1882	Lyons-Roberts	96,000
1,422	1882	Lyons-Treat	16,000

*This note is countersigned by Thomas C. Acton and is payable at New York.

Gold Certificates

Face Design:
Portrait of Alexander
Hamilton.

Back Design: The
Great Seal of the
United States. The
engravers of this
design were E. M.
Hall, R. Ponickau,
G. U. Rose, Jr., and
R. H. Warren.

No.	Date	Signatures	Notes Printed
1,423	1907	Vernon-Treat	
1,423a	1907	Vernon-McClung*	
1,423b	1907	Napier-McClung	228,000
1,423c	1907	Parker-Burke	
1,423d	1907	Teehee-Burke	
1,423e	1907	Napier-Burke	
1,424	1922	Speelman-White	80,000

*Rumored to exist.

Treasury Notes

Face Design:
George Gordon
Meade, born in Cadiz
on December 31,
1815, was the fourth
person of foreign
birth to appear on our
currency. He
advanced in rank to
Major General in 1864
after serving and
being wounded in the
Civil War. His portrait
was engraved by
Charles Burt.

Back Design:
Engraved by W. H.
Dougal, E. M. Hall, G.
U. Rose, Jr., and D.
M. Russel.

No.	Date	Signatures	Seal	Notes Issued	Notes Known
					3
1,425	1890	Rosecrans-Huston	Brown ⎤	28,000	
1,426	1890	Rosecrans-Nebeker	Red ⎦		
1,427	1891	Tillman-Morgan	Red ⎤	32,000	1
1,428	1891	Rosecrans-Nebeker	Red ⎦		1

Back Design for 1891
series; the face
design is similar to
No. 1,425. Engraved
by D. M. Cooper, W.
H. Dougal, E. M. Hall,
A. L. Helm, and G. U.
Rose, Jr.

Federal Reserve Notes/1918/Blue Seal

Face Design:
Portrait of Alexander
Hamilton.

Back Design:
The eagle vignette
was engraved by
M.W. Baldwin.

1918 Series, various signatures

No.	Bank	Signatures	Notes Printed	Notes Issued
1,429A2	Boston	Burke-Glass	39,600	20,800
1,429B2	New York	Burke-Glass	124,800	124,800
1,429B3	New York	Burke-Houston		
1,429C2	Philadelphia	Burke-Glass	16,400	12,800
1,429D2	Cleveland	Burke-Glass	8,800	8,800
1,429E2	Richmond	Burke-Glass	17,600	8,400
1,429F2	Atlanta	Burke-Glass	43,200	43,200
1,429F4	Atlanta	White-Mellon		
1,429G2	Chicago	Burke-Glass	23,600	19,600
1,429H2	St. Louis	Burke-Glass	8,400	4,400*
1,429I2	Minneapolis	Burke-Glass	7,600	2,800
1,429J2	Kansas City	Burke-Glass	15,200	4,400
1,429K2	Dallas	Burke-Glass	6,000	4,400
1,429L2	San Francisco	Burke-Glass	22,400	22,000

Although the figures above include all signature combinations, only those that have been
observed thus far are listed.

*This figure might prove to be incomplete.

Federal Reserve Notes/Green Seal

SMALL SIZE

Face Design:
Portrait of Grover
Cleveland.

Back Design

1928 Series, signatures of Woods-Mellon

No.	Bank	Notes Printed	No.	Bank	Notes Printed
1,430A	Boston	58,320	1,430G	Chicago	355,800
1,430B	New York	139,200	1,430H	St. Louis	60,000
1,430C	Philadelphia	96,708	1,430I	Minneapolis	26,640
1,430D	Cleveland	79,680	1,430J	Kansas City	62,172
1,430E	Richmond	66,840	1,430K	Dallas	42,960
1,430	Atlanta	47,400	1,430L	San Francisco	67,920

Federal Reserve Notes/Green Seal

1934 Series, signatures of Julian-Morgenthau			1934 A Series, signatures of Julian-Morgenthau		
No.	**Bank**	**Notes Printed**	**No.**	**Bank**	**Notes Printed**
1,431 A	Boston	46,200	1,432 A	Boston	30,000
1,431 B	New York	332,784	1,432 B	New York	174,348
1,431 C	Philadelphia	33,000	1,432 C	Philadelphia	78,000
1,431 D	Cleveland	35,400	1,432 D	Cleveland	28,800
1,431 E	Richmond	19,560	1,432 E	Richmond	16,800
1,431 F	Atlanta	67,800	1,432 F	Atlanta	80,964
1,431 G	Chicago	167,040	1,432 G	Chicago	134,400
1,413 H	St. Louis	22,440	1,432 H	St. Louis	39,600
1,431 I	Minneapolis	12,000	1,432 I	Minneapolis	4,800
1,431 J	Kansas City	51,840	1,432 J	Kansas City	21,600
1,431 K	Dallas	46,800	1,432 K	Dallas	No Record
1,431 L	San Francisco	90,600	1,432 L	San Francisco	36,600

1934 C Series, signatures of Julian-Snyder

No.	Bank	Notes Printed
1,432 aA	Boston	1,200
1,432 aB	New York	168

Gold Certificate

The face and back design are similar to No. 1,430 with the exception of the seal and obligation. The engravers were O. Benzing, J. Eissler, and W.B. Wells.

No.	Date	Signatures	Notes Printed
1,433	1928	Woods-Mellon	288,000
1,434	1934	Julian-Morgenthau	84,000

United States Notes/Brown Seal

Face Design:
Portrait of James
Madison, engraved
by A. Sealey. The
note illustrated is a
specimen; it was
made available for
illustration by Amon
Carter, Jr.

Back Design:
The central vignette
was engraved by
William Chorlton.

No.	Date	Signatures	Notes Issued
1,435	1878	Scofield-Gilfillan	4,000

All notes have been redeemed.

Interest-bearing Notes

One-Year Notes—5% (Act of March 3, 1863)

The face design of this note bears a vignette entitled *Altar of Liberty.*

Face Design: The two figures are entitled *Justice* and *America. America* was engraved by Louis Delnoce. (Photograph courtesy The Coin and Currency Institute, Inc.)

Three-Year Notes—7-3/10% (Act of July 17, 1861)

No.	Dated	Notes Printed	Notes Issued
1,436	Aug. 19, 1861*		1,089
1,437	Oct. 1, 1861*		1,871
	Act of June 30, 1864		
1,438	Aug. 15, 1864	6,145	4,166
1,439	Mar. 3, 1865	1,020	
	Act of March 3, 1865		
1,440	June 15, 1865	4,430	4,045
1,441	July 15, 1865	2,800	1,684

All the notes above have been redeemed.

*Red numerals

Currency Certificates of Deposit/Act of June 8, 1872

Face Design: London, England, was the birthplace of E.D. Baker. Five years after his birth on February 24, 1811, he came to America. Baker studied and practiced law in Springfield, Illinois, served as state senator in 1840, and was elected to Congress in 1844. During the early days of the Civil War, Baker was mortally wounded while commanding a Union brigade. Baker's portrait was engraved by Charles Burt. The illustration above is that of a proof impression.

No.	Date	Signatures	Seal	Notes Printed
1,441a	1872	Allison-Spinner	Red	8,000
1,441b	1875	Various	Red	10,002*

*Two additional sheets of three subjects each were prepared in 1889—one each for the Chinese and Japanese government.

Gold Certificates/Act of March 3, 1863

Nos. 1,422-1,445 are countersigned and dated by hand and payable at New York.

No.	Issue	Date	Signatures	Notes Printed	Notes Issued	Outstanding
1,442	First*	1863	Colby-Spinner	94,000	64,600	0
1,443	Second	1870	Allison-Spinner	40,000	21,000	3
1,444	The note previously listed here does not exist.					
1,445	Third	1875	Allison-New	5,977	5,977	0

No. 1,442 is similar to No. 827a; 1,443-1,445 bear the portrait of James Madison.

*As this book went to press, a photo of this note's recently uncovered back design became availale. It appears on page 50.

Face Design:
The proof impression illustrated bears the portrait of James Madison and the signatures of Napier-Thompson. The signatures of Lyons-Treat and Parker-Burke also have been found on proof impressions.

Back Design:
The Eagle's Nest

No.	Date	Signatures	Notes Issued	Outstanding
1,446	1882*	Bruce-Gilfillan	4,000	
1,447	1882	Bruce-Gilfillan	500	
1,448	1882	Bruce-Wyman	3,500	
1,449	1882	Rosecrans-Hyatt	4,000	
1,450	1882	Rosecrans-Nebeker	4,000	
1,451	1882	Lyons-Roberts	16,000	10
1,452	1882	Vernon-Treat	4,000	
1,452a	1882	Vernon-McClung		
1,452b	1882	Napier-McClung		
1,453	1882	Teehee-Burke		

*This note bears the autographed countersignatures of Thomas C. Acton and is payable at New York.

Gold Certificates

Face Design:
The proof impression illustrated bears the portrait of James Madison and the signatures of Napier-McClung. The signatures of Rosecrans-Hyatt and Rosecrans-Nebeker also have been seen on proof impressions.

Back Design:
Similar to the preceding note.

No.	Date	Payable to Order in	Notes Issued
1,454	1888	Baltimore	512
1,455	1888	Chicago	974
1,456	1888	New York	6,388
1,457	1888	Philadelphia	1,600
1,458	1888	St. Louis	48
1,459	1888	San Francisco	1,736
1,460	1888	Washington, D.C.	75

All the above notes have been redeemed or destroyed.

Federal Reserve Note/1918/Green Seal

Face Design:
Portrait of James
Madison. The note
illustrated is a proof
impression.

Back Design:
*Washington
Resigning his
Commission,* a
painting by John
Trumbull, was
engraved by Louis
Delnoce and
Frederick Girsch.

No.	Bank	Notes Printed	Notes Issued
1,461A	Boston	2,800	800
1,461B	New York	5,200	1,600
1,461C	Philadelphia	2,000	None
1,461D	Cleveland	800	400
1,461E	Richmond	1,600	400
1,461F	Atlanta	400	None
1,461G	Chicago	2,800	800*
1,461H	St. Louis	1,200	400*
1,461I	Minneapolis	None	None
1,461J	Kansas City	None	None
1,461K	Dallas	1,200	None
1,461L	San Francisco	3,600	2,800

Although 13 notes are still outstanding, the one illustrated above is the only note observed thus far.

*These figures might prove to be incomplete.

Federal Reserve Notes

Face Design:
Portrait of James
Madison.

Back Design

1928 Series, signatures of Woods-Mellon			1934 Series, signatures of Julian-Morgenthau		
No.	**Bank**	**Notes Printed**	**No.**	**Bank**	**Notes Printed**
1,462A	Boston ·	1,320	1,463A	Boston	9,480
1,462B	New York	2,640	*1,463B*	New York	11,520
1,462C	Philadelphia	No record	1,463C	Philadelphia	3,000
1,462D	Cleveland	3,000	1,463D	Cleveland	1,680
1,462E	Richmond	3,984	1,463E	Richmond	2,400
1,462F	Atlanta	1,440	1,463F	Atlanta	3,600
1,462G	Chicago	3,480	1,463G	Chicago	6,600
1,462H	St. Louis	No record	1,463H	St. Louis	2,400
1,462I	Minneapolis	No record	1,463I	Minneapolis	No record
1,462J	Kansas City	720	1,463J	Kansas City	2,400
1,462K	Dallas	360	1,463K	Dallas	2,400
1,462L	San Francisco	51,300	1,463L	San Francisco	6,000

1934A Series, signatures of Julian-Morgenthau			1934B Series, signatures of Julian-Vinson		
No.	**Bank**	**Notes Printed**	**No.**	**Bank**	**Notes Printed**
1,463aH	St. Louis	1,440	1,463bA	Boston	1,200
			1,463bB	New York	12

Gold Certificate

The face and back design are similar to No. 1,463 with the exception of the seal and obligation.

No.	Date	Signatures	Notes Printed
1,464	1928	Woods-Mellon	24,000

United States Notes/Brown Seal

LARGE SIZE

Face Design:
The Portrait of
Andrew Jackson was
engraved by A.
Sealey from a
painting by Thomas
Sully. The illustration
is of a proof
impression; all notes
of the regular issue
have been redeemed.

Back Design

No.	Date	Signatures	Notes Issued
1,465	1878	Scofield-Gilfillan	4,000

All notes have been redeemed.

Gold Certificates/Act of March 3, 1863

Nos. 1,466, 1,467, and 1,469 are countersigned and dated by hand and are payable at New York. All have been redeemed.

No.	Issue	Date	Signature	Notes Printed	Notes Issued
1,466	First*	1863	Colby-Spinner	2,500	2,500
1,467	Second	1870	Allison-Spinner	20,000	20,000
1,468	The note previously listed here does not exist.				
1,469	Third	1875	Allison-New	8,933	8,933

No. 1,466 is similar to No. 827a; 1,467 and 1,469 bear the portrait of Andrew Jackson.

*As this book went to press, a photo of this note's recently uncovered back design became available. It appears on page 50.

Face Design:
The note illustrated, which bears the portrait of Andrew Jackson, is a proof impression. The signatures of Lyons-Treat, Vernon-McClung, Napier-Burke, and Parker-Burke also appear on proof impressions.

Back Design:
The Eagle of the Capitol.

No.	Date	Signatures	Notes Issued	Outstanding
1,470	1882*	Bruce-Gilfillan	8,000	
1,471	1882	Bruce-Gilfillan	500	
1,472	1882	Bruce-Wyman	4,000	
1,473	1882	Rosecrans-Hyatt	4,000	
1,474	1882	Rosecrans-Nebeker	4,000	8
1,475	1882	Lyons-Roberts	7,000	
1,476	1882	Vernon-Treat	4,000	
1,477	1882	Teehee-Burke		

*This note bears the autographed countersignatures of Thomas C. Acton and is payable at New York.

Gold Certificates

Face Design:
The note illustrated, which bears the portrait of Andrew Jackson, is a proof impression. The signatures of Napier-McClung also appear on proof impressions. Regular issues with signatures of Rosecrans-Hyatt and Rosecrans-Nebeker have been recorded.

No.	Date	Payable to Order in	Notes Issued
1,478	1888	Baltimore	523
1,479	1888	Chicago	952
1,480	1888	New York	6,952
1,481	1888	Philadelphia	2,665
1,482	1888	San Francisco	17,000
1,483	1888	St. Louis	320
1,484	1888	Washington, D.C.	150

Nos. 1,478-1,484 have all been redeemed.

Gold Certificates

Face Design:
On the left side of this note is a cancellation, "Payable to the Treasurer of the U.S. or a Federal Reserve Bank." Proof impressions were made with the signatures of Vernon-McClung, Napier-McClung, Napier-Burke and Parker-Burke. Regular issues with signatures of Lyons-Roberts, Lyons-Treat, Vernon-Treat and Teehee-Burke have been recorded.

No.	Date	Payable to Order in	Notes Issued
1,485	1900	Baltimore	17,265
1,485a	1900	Boston	9,803
1,486	1900	Chicago	9,916
1,487	1900	Cincinnati	2,790
1,488	1900	New Orleans	986
1,489	1900	New York	73,701
1,490	1900	Philadelphia	67,397
1,491	1900	St. Louis	7,097
1,492	1900	San Francisco	12,714
1,492a	1900	Washington, D.C.	75,881

Notes from the above, still outstanding came from the December 13,1935 fire at the Post Office at 12th and Pennsylvania Avenue in Washington, D.C. In a fruitless attempt to keep the fire from gutting the building, waste paper was thrown out of the windows. As part of this waste, these canceled notes were carried by the wind, into the hands of passers-by. These notes are not redeemable.

Currency Certificates of Deposit/Act of June 8, 1872

Face Design: Stephen A. Douglas, born on April 23, 1813, rose from a cabinet maker's apprentice to become one of our great statesmen. From the age of 21, when he was elected to Congress, Douglas devoted his life to public service. He was the Democratic nominee for President in 1860, receiving 12 electoral votes. Douglas died on June 3, 1861. Charles Burt engraved the portrait on this note. The illustration above is that of a proof impression.

No.	Date	Signatures	Seal	Notes Printed
1,492b	1872	Allison-Spinner	Red	20,000
1,492c	1875	Various	Red	114,198*

*Two additional sheets of 3 subjects each were prepared in 1889—one each for the Chinese and Japanese governments.

Federal Reserve Notes/1918/Green Seal

Face Design:
Portrait of Salmon
P. Chase

Back Design

No.	Bank	Notes Printed	Notes Issued
1,493A	Boston	2,000	800
1,493B	New York	5,600	1,600
1,493C	Philadelphia	2,400	None
1,493D	Cleveland	800	400
1,493E	Richmond	800	400
1,493F	Atlanta	400	None
1,493G	Chicago	1,200	None
1,493H	St. Louis	1,200	400*
1,493I	Minneapolis	None	None
1,493J	Kansas City	None	None
1,493K	Dallas	1,200	None
1,493L	San Francisco	2,800	2,000

Although 10 notes are still outstanding, the one illustrated above is the only note observed thus far.

*This figure might prove to be incomplete.

Federal Reserve Notes/Green Seal

SMALL SIZE

Face Design:
Portrait of Salmon
P. Chase.

Back Design

1928 Series, signatures of Woods-Mellon

No.	Bank	Notes Printed
1,494A	Boston	1,320
1,494B	New York	4,680
1,494C	Philadelphia	No record
1,494D	Cleveland	960
1,494E	Richmond	3,024
1,494F	Atlanta	1,440
1,494G	Chicago	1,800
1,494H	St. Louis	480
1,494I	Minneapolis	480
1,494J	Kansas City	480
1,494K	Dallas	360
1,494L	San Francisco	1,824

1934 Series, signatures of Julian-Morgenthau

No.	Bank	Notes Printed
1,495A	Boston	9,720
1,495B	New York	11,520
1,495C	Philadelphia	6,000
1,495D	Cleveland	1,480
1,495E	Richmond	1,200
1,495F	Atlanta	2,400
1,495G	Chicago	3,840
1,495H	St. Louis	2,040
1,495I	Minneapolis	No record
1,495J	Kansas City	1,200
1,495K	Dallas	1,200
1,495L	San Francisco	3,600

1934A Series, signatures of Julian-Morgenthau

No.	Bank	Notes Printed
1,495aG	Chicago	1,560

1934B Series, signatures of Julian-Vinson

No.	Bank	Notes Printed
1,495bB	New York	24

Gold Certificates

The face and back design are similar to No. 1,495 with the exception of the seal and obligation.

No.	Date	Signatures	Notes Printed
1,496	1928	Woods-Mellon	48,000
1,497	1934	Julian-Morgenthau	36,000

ONE HUNDRED THOUSAND DOLLARS

Gold Certificate

Face Design:
Portrait of Woodrow Wilson, our twenty-eighth President. This design was engraved by O. Benzing and W. B. Wells.

Back Design:
The engraver was F. Pauling.

No.	Date	Signatures	Notes Issued
1,498	1934	Julian-Morgenthau	42,000

This is the highest denomination note ever printed by the Bureau of Engraving and Printing. It was not meant for general circulation but was to be used in transactions between Federal Reserve banks.

UNISSUED AND REJECTED DESIGNS

At one time, a limited number of patterns, essais, and trial pieces were struck before a new coin design was accepted. The recipients of the pieces usually were government officials who would give an opinion or vote on these proposed designs. Many of these pieces have found their way into the numismatic marketplace.

Paper money designs, other than those accepted, rarely left the Bureau of Engraving and Printing. The syngraphist is therefore left to wonder what unissued and rejected designs looked like. With the exception of Nos. 1,499b, f, s, and possibly r, all the illustrations in this section are being presented for the first time in any publication. Except for 1,499b and n, both paintings, all designs illustrated in this section are proof impressions or die proofs. The handwritten number that appears on most of these impressions is the currency die number. As you view these illustrations, I hope you feel only half the excitement that came over me when I first discovered these unissued and rejected designs.

1,499   In February 1928 engravers E.M. Hall and R. Ponickau began work on this $1 silver certificate. Work on this design never progressed to the point where plates were manufactured.

1,499a   The $1 United States note Nos. 6-27 in this catalog had another design. Engraving work by E.M. Hall commenced on this rejected design in March 1917.

1,499b   This painting by W.H. Low was his design for the $2 educational note. If you turn to No. 186 you will see the accepted design for this issue.

1,499c   This much discussed design finally surfaced in 1974. Nos. 1 and 153a had their respective denomination highlighted on the face design so it was a surprise to see a change in design on the $3 note. See the author's article in *COINage*, October, 1974.

1,499d   E.M. Hall began engraving the vignette *Harvesting* in January 1914 for this back, originally intended to grace a national currency note. Marcus W. Baldwin engraved the male and female figures, and E.E. Meyers, H.L. Chorlton, and F. Lamasure were responsible for the remaining portions of the design.

It was later decided that this design would serve better as the back for the 1915 Federal Reserve bank note. Eventually, the *Harvesting* scene was coupled with the vignette *Manufacture* to make up the back for the $10 Federal Reserve bank notes and Federal Reserve notes.

1,499e   These uniface national bank note designs were prepared by the Continental Bank Note Co. See *The Essay-Proof Journal,* Vol. 32, No. 1, 1975 for the author's article on this subject. The issued design is seen on page 133 in this catalog.

1,499f   The vignette of *Agriculture and Forestry* was designed by Walter Shirlaw and engraved by Charles Schlecht. The lettering and portions of the border were designed by Thomas F. Morris and engraved by George U. Rose, Jr. This note was to be part of the Educational Series, see pp. 57, 79 & 101.

1,499g   This note also was originally prepared as a back for a national currency note and then as a back for a Federal Reserve bank note. The male figures were engraved by Marcus W. Baldwin; the scene of *Manufacture* is the work of H. L. Chorlton. E.M. Hall, O. Benzing, and F. Lamasure engraved the remaining portions of this die proof.

1,499h   A letter dated December 22, 1900, to W.M. Meridith, Director of the Bureau of Engraving and Printing, from Ellis H. Roberts, Treasurer, suggests that "the new $10 plate" be used for a United States note rather than a silver certificate.

The two portraits, Commander William Bainbridge on the left and Stephen Decatur on the right, were engraved by G.F.C. Smillie. The battleship *Massachusetts* was engraved by Marcus W. Baldwin. The work began on January 8, 1900. The remaining portions of this design were engraved by E.M. Hall, G.U. Rose, and R. Ponickau; their work began on November 3, 1900. See No. 483 for the adaptation of this basic design.

1,499i   I have been unable to uncover any information pertaining to this cancelled die. The engraving work on this back appears to be the work of E.M. Hall and/or E.M. Weeks.

1,499j   Engraving work for this gold certificate was begun on April 10, 1924, by E.M. Hall and J. Eissler. The same design was issued earlier with the portrait of Washington. (See nos. 834-842.) The written notation on this proof refers to small size $1,000 notes with the portrait of Cleveland.

1,499k   This uniface specimen is actually an interest-bearing note with an overprint. Although never adopted, such a note would have filled an obvious gap in the nation's currency system since neither legal tender nor interest-bearing notes could be accepted as payment toward duties.

1,499l   This beautiful note bears a vignette entitled *The Return of Peace* engraved by Charles Smith and a portrait of Ulysses S. Grant engraved by Charles Burt. Both engravers began their work in 1869. The accepted design for this issue is illustrated as No. 928.

1,499m   No $50 treasury notes of the 1890 series were issued. An example of the face design could not be located, however the back design is illustrated here. The design was completed on Nov. 29, 1890 by the following engravers: D. M. Cooper, W. A. Coppenhaver, E. M. Hall, E. E. Myers, and G. U. Rose, Jr.

1,499n   E. H. Blashfield's painting, his design for the $50 educational note, hangs in the Bureau of Engraving and Printing. This denomination was not issued as part of the educational series, however. The design was adopted for the $2 denomination illustrated as No. 186.

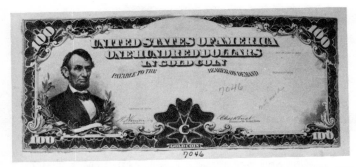

1,499o   In 1908 George H. Blake wrote, "At present writing these certificates ($50 and $100) have not been placed in circulation." Plates were never made for these 1908 gold certificates, and therefore neither was placed in circulation. The $50 note is still unknown, though I was fortunate enough to uncover the $100 denomination. E. M. Hall, G. U. Rose, Jr., R. Ponickau, and E. E. Meyers began the engraving work on January 31, 1908 and completed the task on October 28, 1908.

1,499p   Although records indicate this reverse as being intended for Series 1907, I feel certain it was to be the back for No. 1,499 . The same four engravers with the assistance of F. Pauling also commenced work on this back in January 1908.

1,499q   Even though this back was left in an unfinished state, I find it extremely attractive. Engraving work was begun in July 1923 by E. M. Hall and E. M. Weeks. This design was undoubtedly intended for a United States note or silver certificate.

1,499r   This unissued denomination follows the same design pattern as the issued denominations; the portrait is placed on the left. For the Federal Reserve notes the portraits were placed in the center.

1,499s In 1972 *Paper Money* printed an account of this newly discovered treasury note by William T. Anton, Jr., and Morey Perlmutter. In 1893, 16,000 notes, unsealed, were delivered to the Treasury Department; however, there is no record of issue. The specimen illustrated in *Paper Money* bears the signatures of Bruce-Roberts. We can now include one more signature combination that appears on this illustrated proof impression.

In August 1892 engraving work commenced on this note, and before its completion six different engraving artists were involved: John R. Hill, W. Adolph, D.M. Cooper, E.M. Hall, W.H. Dougal, and G.U. Rose, Jr.

1,499t This illustrated specimen which is printed in black on india paper and mounted on cardboard, was intended for the backs of Nos. 1539-1541.

FRACTIONAL CURRENCY

As the Civil War got under way, the value of essential metals began to rise rapidly. The intrinsic value of coinage soon exceeded the face value of the coins. The coins in circulation began to disappear, either into the hoarder's chest or into the melting pot. Commerce was handicapped because ordinary, daily transactions were impeded by the lack of change. Change for a sale often was taken in merchandise. Merchants were forced to issue tokens and notes of value in denominations less than one dollar, and these would be redeemed only by the issuing firm. All privately issued "wild cat" bank notes were discounted with the hope of putting some of the coins back into circulation.

On July 17, 1862, at the suggestion of Salmon P. Chase, President Lincoln signed into law a bill authorizing the acceptance of stamps as currency. Post office supplies of regular stamps were exhausted before special, ungummed stamps could be prepared. Almost immediately the Treasury Department had a sticky problem on its hands—the redemption of millions of soiled, mutilated stamps.

The Treasury Department began to issue notes that resembled postage stamps, but these had no legal backing since the law of July 17 applied only to genuine postage stamps. This defect in the law was corrected by the Act of March 3, 1863, which clearly stated that the government would issue fractional currency notes. Four private bank note companies, at the request of the federal government, printed notes of 3, 5, 10, 15, 25, and 50 cents.

There were five issues of fractional currency in these denominations. As the normal metal coinage slowly returned to circulation, Acts of Congress of January 14, 1875, and April 17, 1876, allowed for coin redemption of all these notes.

A total of $368,720,000 in these small notes was issued between 1862 and 1876; $2,000,000 worth are still unredeemed and presumably in the hands of collectors.

Issue	Dates	Denominations
First*	August 21, 1862 to May 27, 1863	5, 10, 25, and 50 cents
Second	October 10, 1863 to February 23, 1867	5, 10, 25, and 50 cents
Third	December 5, 1864 to August 16, 1869	3, 5, 10, 25, and 50 cents
Fourth	July 14, 1869 to February 16, 1875	10, 15, 25, and 50 cents
Fifth	February 26, 1874 to February 15, 1876	10, 25, and 50 cents

*This issue is often referred to as postage currency due to the postage stamp facsimiles that were used to adorn these notes.

Three-Cent Notes/Third Issue

Face: Portrait of
George Washington.

Back: Green.

No.	Description	Notes Issued	Fine	Extra Fine	New
1,500	Portrait has light background	20,064,130*	15.00	27.50	50.00
1,501	Portrait has dark background		20.00	35.00	70.00

*20,175,000 notes were printed.

Five-Cent Notes/First Issue

Face: Brown, portrait of Thomas Jefferson on a 5¢ stamp of 1861 (Scott 75).

Back: Five on black.

No.	Description	Notes Issued	Fine	Extra Fine	New
1,502	Perforated edges, monogram ABNCO on back		15.00	32.50	70.00
1,503	Perforated edges, without monogram	44,857,780	17.50	40.00	90.00
1,504*	Straight edges, monogram ABNCO on back		9.00	20.00	42.50
1,505	Straight edges, without monogram		20.00	45.00	95.00

*Lot 406 of the Julian S. Marks collection (1971) was a cancelled cover with this note as postage.

Five-Cent Notes/Second Issue

Face: The portrait of George Washington was engraved by James Duthie.

Back: Brown designed by George W. Casilear.

No.	Description	Notes Issued	Fine	Extra Fine	New
1,506	Value in bronze on back		10.00	22.50	47.50
1,507	Surcharge "18 63" on back	55,250,097	10.00	22.50	47.50
1,508	Surcharge "S" and "18 63" on back		15.00	35.00	65.00
1,509	Surcharge "R1" and "18 63" on back	296,425	20.00	45.00	100.00

Five-Cent Notes/Third Issue

Face: Portrait of Spencer M. Clark,* Superintendent of the National Currency Bureau under Lincoln. Clark was responsible for designing the seal, a variation of which is still used on our nation's securities.

Face: Placement of letter "a"

Back: Green or red.

No.	Description	Notes Printed	Fine	Extra Fine	New
1,510	Green back		10.00	22.50	50.00
1,511	Letter *A* on face, green back	13,400,000	12.50	27.50	60.00
1,512	Red back		17.50	40.00	80.00
1,513	Letter *A* on face, red back		20.00	45.00	100.00

*When this note appeared, Congress passed a law (14 Stat. 25) forbidding the portrait of a living person to appear on notes or other obligations. Clark seemed to be the only one criticized for the use of his likeness, while the portraits of Lincoln, Chase, and Spinner were ignored.

Ten-Cent Notes/First Issue

Face: Portrait of George Washington facing to the left on a stamp of 1861 (Scott 68). The original painting was by Gilbert Stuart.

Back: Green.

No.	Description	Notes Issued	Fine	Extra Fine	New
1,514	Perforated edges, monogram ABNCO on back		15.00	32.50	70.00
1,515*	Perforated edges, without monogram	41,153,780	20.00	40.00	85.00
1,516	Plain edges, monogram ABNCO on back		9.00	20.00	45.00
1,517	Plain edges, without monogram		22.50	55.00	105.00

*Back illustration is no. 1,515.

Ten-Cent Notes/Second Issue

Face: The portrait of George Washington was engraved by James Duthie.

Back: Green.

No.	Description	Notes Issued	Fine	Extra Fine	New
1,518	Value only on back		10.00	22.50	45.00
1,519	Surcharge "18 63" on back		10.00	22.50	45.00
1,520	Surcharge "S" and "18 63" on back	61,808,393	12.50	25.00	50.00
1,521	Surcharge "1" and "18 63" on back		22.50	45.00	90.00
1,522	Surcharge "O" and "63" on back		—	650.00	1,200.00
1,523	Surcharge "T1" and "18 63" on back	427,450	22.50	45.00	90.00

Ten-Cent Notes/Third Issue

Face: Portrait of George Washington.

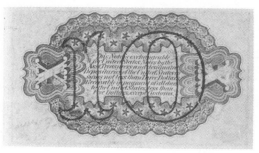

Face: Placement of "1"

Back: Green or red.

Ten-Cent Notes/Third Issue

No.	Description	Notes Issued	Fine	Extra Fine	New
1,524	Printed signatures of Colby-Spinner, green back		9.00	20.00	35.00
1,525	As above with "1" near left margin on face		11.00	22.50	42.50
1,526	Printed signatures of Colby-Spinner, red back		13.50	30.00	60.00
1,527	As above with "1" near left margin on face	169,761,345*	16.00	35.00	75.00
1,528	Autographed signatures of Colby-Spinner, red back		22.50	47.50	90.00
1528a	Autographed signatures of Colby-Spinner, green back			3 Known	
1,529	Autographed signatures of Jeffries-Spinner, red back		30.00	65.00	125.00

There is a noticeable lack of reference to any denomination whatsoever: however, these pieces circulated as ten-*cent* notes.

*18,000 have red backs.

Ten-Cent Notes/Fourth Issue

Face Design: The Model for the bust of Liberty is said to be Mary Hull, designed by Charles Burt and engraved by Frederick Girsch.

Back Design: Green, printed by the National Bank Note Company.

No.	Description	Notes Issued	Fine	Extra Fine	New
1,530	Large red seal on watermarked paper with light fibers		7.50	15.00	30.00
1,531	Large red seal, pink fibers in paper	179,097,600	7.50	15.00	32.50
1,532	Large red seal, pink fibers with blue ends		8.50	17.50	35.00
1,533	Large brown seal		125.00	225.00	425.00
1,534	Small red seal, pink fibers with blue ends	170,312,600	7.50	15.00	32.50

Large seal 40 mm, small seal 38 mm.

Ten-Cent Notes/Fifth Issue

Face Design: The portrait of William Meredith, Secretary of the Treasury 1849–1850, was designed by Thomas Knollwood.

Back Design

No.	Description	Notes Issued	Fine	Extra Fine	New
1,535	Long key in green seal ⎤		10.00	22.50	50.00
1,536	Long key in red seal	199,899,000	6.50	12.50	27.50
1,537	Short key in red seal ⎦		6.50	12.50	27.50

Fifteen-Cent Notes/Fourth Issue

Face Design: The bust of Columbia was designed by Douglas C. Romerson and engraved by Frederick Girsch. The National Bank Note Co. prepared the plates.

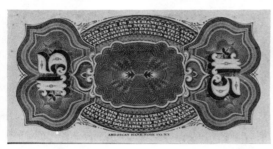

Back Design: Green, plates prepared by the American Bank Note Co.

No.	Description	Notes Issued	Fine	Extra Fine	New
1,539	Large red seal on watermarked paper with pink fibers		17.50	40.00	75.00
1,540	Large red seal on unwatermarked paper with pink fibers		17.50	40.00	75.00
1,541	Large red seal on paper with blue fibers and blue ends	27,240,040	17.50	40.00	85.00
1,541a	Large brown seal on paper with blue fibers and blue ends		150.00	250.00	400.00
1,542	Small red seal on paper with blue fibers and blue ends	8,121,400	17.50	40.00	75.00

1,542a This is an essai for Nos. 1,539–1,542. As you can see, a smaller head was chosen for the accepted design.

Twenty-Five-Cent Notes/First Issue

Face Design: A portrait of Thomas Jefferson is on five 5¢ stamps of 1861 (Scott 75).

Back Design: Black.

No.	Description	Notes Issued	Fine	Extra Fine	New
1,548	Perforated edges with monogram ABNCO on back		25.00	55.00	110.00
1,549	Perforated edges without monogram	20,902,768	27.50	65.00	135.00
1,550	Plain edges with monogram ABNCO on back		16.50	35.00	70.00
1,551	Plain edges without monogram		37.50	90.00	180.00

Twenty-Five-Cent Notes/Second Issue

Face Design:
The portrait of
Washington was
engraved by James
Duthie.

Back Design:
Purple, designed by
George W. Casilear.

No.	Description	Notes Issued	Fine	Extra Fine	New
1,552	Value only on back		12.50	25.00	52.50
1,552a	Surcharge "18 63" on back		15.00	30.00	60.00
1,553	Surcharge "A" and "18 63" on back	29,299,585	12.50	25.00	52.50
1,554	Surcharge "1" and "18 63" on back		17.50	35.00	70.00
1,554a	Surcharge "2" and "18 63" on back		17.50	35.00	70.00
1,555	Surcharge "S" and "18 63" on back		12.50	27.50	52.50
1,556	Surcharge "T-1" and "18 63" on back, fiber paper		25.00	55.00	100.00
1,557	Surcharge "T-2" and "18 63", fiber paper		22.50	50.00	95.00
1,558	Surcharge "S-2" and "18 63", fiber paper	1,173,780		Rare	

Twenty-Five-Cent Notes/Third Issue

Face Design: Joseph Ourdan engraved the portrait of William Pitt Fessenden, Secretary of the Treasury, in 1864. This issue did not comply with the law (14 Stat. 25) since Fessenden was alive at the time and therefore should not have had his likeness on U.S. currency.

Back Design: Green or red.

No.	Description	Notes Issued	Fine	Extra Fine	New
1,559	Red back	⎤	17.50	35.00	75.00
1,560	Same as above, with *a* in lower left corner of face	16,000	20.00	37.50	90.00
1,561	Same as above, with larger *a*	⎤	20.00	37.50	90.00
1,562	Solid surcharge on fiber paper, green back with M 2 6 5 surcharge on back (1561)**		275.00	450.00	900.00
1,563	Same as above, with *a* in lower left corner of face (1562)**		375.00	650.00	1,200.00
1,564*	Outline surcharges on fiber paper, green back with M 2 6 5 surcharge on back	124,566,755	27.50	50.00	100.00
1,565	Same as above, with *a* in lower left corner of face		32.50	60.00	125.00
1,566	Outline surcharge on plain paper, green back without M 2 6 5		10.00	22.50	50.00
1,567	Same as above, with *a* in lower left corner of face		12.50	25.00	55.00
1,567a	Same as above, with larger *a*	⎦	12.50	25.00	55.00

*It is believed that the 7,107 notes issued on March 22, 1865, accounted for this variety.
**Numbers in parentheses refer to original numbers in the first edition of this catalog.

Twenty-Five-Cent Notes/Fourth Issue

Face Design: Washington, Treasury Seal in center. Printed by National Bank Note Co., designed by Douglas C. Romerson, and engraved by Frederick Girsch.

Back Design: Green; printed by American Bank Note Co.

No.	Description	Notes Issued	Fine	Extra Fine	New
1,568	Large red seal on watermarked paper		8.50	20.00	40.00
1,569	Large red seal, plain white paper with pink fibers		7.50	15.00	35.00
1,570	Large red seal, pink fibers with blue ends	235,689,024	8.50	20.00	45.00
1,571*	Smaller red seal, violet fibers with blue ends		8.50	20.00	45.00
1,572	Large brown seal, violet fibers with blue ends		150.00	250.00	475.00

Large seal 40 mm, small seal 38 mm.

*32,516,256 of these notes were issued.

Twenty-Five-Cent Notes/Fifth Issue

Face Design:
Robert Walker, Sec-
retary of the Trea-
sury, 1845–1849.

Back Design:
Green.

No.	Description	Notes Issued	Fine	Extra Fine	New
1,573	Long narrow key in Treasury Seal	144,368,000	7.00	15.00	32.50
1,574	Short key in Treasury Seal		7.00	15.00	30.00

On occasion the ink from the red seal bled through and gave the face a pink color.

Fifty-Cent Notes/First Issue

Face Design:
Portrait of George
Washington on five
10¢ stamps.

Back Design:
Black.

No.	Description	Notes Issued	Fine	Extra Fine	New
1,575	Perforated edges with monogram ABNCO on back		25.00	55.00	110.00
1,575a	Same as above except 14 perforations per 20 mm instead of 12 perforations			12 Known	
1,576	Perforated edges without monogram	17,263,344	27.50	75.00	150.00
1,577	Plain edges with monogram ABNCO on back		15.00	35.00	75.00
1,578	Plain edges without monogram		40.00	90.00	170.00

Fifty-Cent-Notes/Second Issue

Face Design: The portrait of George Washington was engraved by James Duthie.

Back Design: Red

No.	Description	Notes Issued	Fine	Extra Fine	New
1,579	No surcharges on back		Legitimacy Doubtful		
1,580	Surcharge "18 63"	11,844,464	17.50	40.00	80.00
1,581	Surcharge "A" and "18 63" on back		15.00	30.00	65.00
1,582	Surcharge "1" and "18 63" on back		12.50	25.00	50.00
1,583	Surcharge "O-1" and "18 63" on back of fiber paper		35.00	65.00	125.00
1,584	Surcharge "R-2" and "18 63" on back of fiber paper	1,246,000	37.50	75.00	140.00
1,585	Surcharge "T-1" and "18 63" on back of fiber paper		22.50	50.00	95.00

Fifty-Cent Notes/Third Issue

Face Design:
Justice seated with
scales.

Back Design:
Green or red.

The following come with and without the surcharge "A-2-6-5," and all have red backs.

No.	Description	Fine	Extra Fine	New
1,586	No design figures on face, without "A-2-6-5" surcharge	20.00	45.00	80.00
1,586a	As above, with "A-2-6-5" surcharge	15.00	35.00	65.00
1,587	*1* and *a* on face, without "A-2-6-5" surcharge	45.00	100.00	200.00
1,587a	As above, with "A-2-6-5" surcharge	35.00	85.00	160.00
1,588	*1* only on face, without "A-2-6-5" surcharge	25.00	55.00	110.00
1,588a	As above, with "A-2-6-5" surcharge	17.50	35.00	70.00
1,589	*a* only on face, without "A-2-6-5" surcharge	30.00	65.00	120.00
1,589a	As above with "A-2-6-5" surcharge	20.00	45.00	80.00

The following bear autographed signatures of Colby-Spinner and have red backs.

No.	Description	Fine	Extra Fine	New
1,590	No surcharges or design figures	25.00	50.00	95.00
1,591	Surcharges "A-2-6-5" on back	30.00	65.00	125.00
1,592	Surcharge "S-2-6-4" on back of fiber paper	160.00	275.00	425.00

The following have printed signatures on fiber paper, surcharges "S-2-6-4," and have red backs.

No.	Description	Fine	Extra Fine	New
1,593	No design figures on face, fiber paper	275.00	400.00	700.00
1,594	*1* and *a* on face		Unknown	
1,595	*1* only on face Winthrop Sale 1975		525.00	
1,596	*a* only on face Rothert Sale 1973		525.00	

The following do not have the surcharge; all have green backs.

No.	Description	Fine	Extra Fine	New
1,597	No design figures on face	12.50	30.00	60.00
1,598	*1* and *a* on face	27.50	60.00	125.00
1,599	*1* only on face	15.00	35.00	70.00
1,600	*a* only on face	20.00	40.00	80.00

Fifty-Cent Notes/Third Issue

The following have the surcharge "A-2-6-5" in two varieties; one is more widely spaced than the other.

No.	Description	Fine	Extra Fine	New
1,601	No design figures on face, narrow "A-2-6-5"	15.00	30.00	55.00
1,601a	As above, widely spaced "A-2-6-5"	25.00	45.00	80.00
1,602	*1* and *a* on face, narrow "A-2-6-5"	30.00	65.00	135.00
1,602a	As above, widely spaced "A-2-6-5"	52.50	100.00	275.00
1,603	*1* only on face, narrow "A-2-6-5"	17.50	35.00	65.00
1,603a	As above, widely spaced "A-2-6-5"	32.50	60.00	125.00
1,604	*a* only on face, narrow "A-2-6-5"	20.00	40.00	75.00
1,604a	As above, widely spaced "A-2-6-5"	35.00	65.00	150.00

The following have the surcharge "A-2-6-5" on fiber paper; all have green backs.

No.	Description	Fine	Extra Fine	New
1,605	No design figures on face	37.50	75.00	150.00
1,606	*1* and *a* on face	72.50	140.00	325.00
1,607	*1* only on face	45.00	85.00	185.00
1,608	*a* only on face	50.00	90.00	200.00

Based on reconstructed figures, 9,737,135 notes were issued for Nos. 1,586-1,608, which are part of the third issue total of 73,471,853.

Fifty-Cent Notes/Third Issue

Face Design:
Bust of F.E. Spinner,
Treasurer of the
United States,
1861-1875.

Back Design:
Green or red.

Face Design:
Placement of "1"
and "a".

The following are surcharged "A-2-6-5" on red backs.

No.	Description	Fine	Extra Fine	New
1,609	No design figures on face	17.50	40.00	80.00
1,610	*1* and *a* on face	35.00	80.00	180.00
1,611	*1* only on face	20.00	45.00	95.00
1,612	*a* only on face	22.50	50.00	110.00
1,613	Autographed signatures of Colby-Spinner	27.50	55.00	100.00
1,614	Autographed signatures of Allison-Spinner	37.50	75.00	150.00
1,615*	Autographed signatures of Allison-New	700.00	1,250.00	2,300.00

Fifty-Cent Notes/Third Issue

The following come with and without the "A-2-6-5" surcharge; all have green backs.

No.	Description	Fine	Extra Fine	New
1,616	No design on face, without "A-2-6-5" surcharge	10.00	25.00	50.00
1,616a	As above, with "A-2-6-5" surcharge	25.00	45.00	80.00
1,617	*1* and *a* on face, without "A-2-6-5" surcharge	22.50	50.00	95.00
1,617a	As above, with "A-2-6-5" surcharge	50.00	100.00	175.00
1,618	*1* only on face, without "A-2-6-5" surcharge	12.50	30.00	60.00
1,618a	As above, with "A-2-6-5" surcharge	30.00⸱	55.00	100.00
1,619	*a* only on face, without "A-2-6-5" surcharge	15.00	35.00	65.00
1,619a	As above, with "A-2-6-5" surcharge	35.00	60.00	110.00

Based on reconstructed figures, 52,866,690 notes were issued for Nos. 1,609-1,619, which are part of the third issue total of 73,471,853.

"One sheet remained unsigned during Spinner's term through error being signed by Allison some time in 1869 or later, and still later (1875 or '76) by John C. New."—"New Look at Old Notes,"* by Walter Breen, *Numismatic News,* August 15, 1971, p. 28.

Fifty-Cent Notes/Third Issue

Revised back design is green; the face is similar to that of the preceding note.

No.	Description	Fine	Extra Fine	New
1,620	No design figure on face	12.50	27.50	55.00
1,621	*1* and *a* on face	27.50	60.00	120.00
1,622	*1* only on face	17.50	35.00	70.00
1,623	*a* only on face	20.00	40.00	80.00

Based on reconstructed figures, 10,868,028 notes were issued for Nos. 1,620-1,623, which are part of the third issue total of 73,471,853.

Fifty-Cent Notes/Fourth Issue

Face Design:
The bust of Abraham
Lincoln was designed
by Charles Burt.

Back Design:
Green; printed by the
National Bank Note
Co.

No.	Description	Fine	Extra Fine	New
1,624	Watermarked paper, large seal	30.00	65.00	125.00
1,625	Paper with pink fibers, large seal	35.00	70.00	140.00

Nos. 1,624 and 1,625 were recalled due to the abundance of counterfeits.

Fifty-Cent Notes/Fourth Issue

Face Design:
George W. Casilear
is the probable
designer of this note,
which bears a bust
of E.M. Stanton,
Lincoln's Secretary
of War.

Back Design:
Green; printed by
the American Bank
Note Co.

No.	Description		Fine	Extra Fine	New
1,626	Red seal, paper has violet fibers with blue ends.		15.00	37.50	75.00
1,627	The note previously listed here does not exist.	86,048,000			
1,628	Small brown seal, paper has violet fibers and blue ends.		150.00	275.00	450.00

Face Design:
George W. Casilear
is the probable
designer of this note
bearing the bust of
Samuel Dexter,
Secretary of War and
the Treasury
1800-1802.

Back Design:
Green; printed by
the National Bank
Note Co.

1,629	Green seal, paper has violet fibers and blue ends	49,599,200	15.00	37.50	75.00

Fifty-Cent Notes/Fifth Issue

Face Design: The bust of W.H. Crawford, Secretary of War and the Treasury 1815–1825.

Back Design: Green.

No.	Description	Notes Issued	Fine	Extra Fine	New
1,631	Pink paper with silk fibers	13,160,000	12.50	30.00	60.00
1,632	White paper, violet fibers with blue ends		12.50	30.00	60.00

Fractional Currency Shield

Before the release of the fourth and fifth issues of fractional currency, the Treasury Department prepared shields of 39 uniface specimens, comprising 20 faces and 19 backs. For the purpose of comparing notes thought to be counterfeit, these shields were sold unframed to banks and merchants for $4.50. The demand for the shields did not meet the expectations of the Treasury Department. In 1869 the remaining shields were dismantled, and the specimens were sold to collectors. Some shields supposedly were destroyed.

1,633	Shield with grey background	Rare
1,634	Shield with pink background	Very rare
1,635	Shield with green background	Extremely rare
1,636	Shield with lavender background	Possibly unique

Fractional Currency Proof and Specimen Notes

President Andrew Johnson selected members of the cabinet and certain legislators as the recipients of the first proof and specimen notes. Soon thereafter these uniface notes, printed with both wide and narrow margins, were sold to the public. Some specimen notes were also used to make up fractional currency shields.

Most specimen and proof notes were printed from adopted designs. Only wide-margin examples and types not adopted will be illustrated. The numbering system will be the same used for regular fractional currency notes, but an *S* will be added to designate a specimen or proof.

CSA Watermark. On April 27, 1862, Union vessels seized the *Bermuda,* a ship returning from England with a cargo destined for the Confederate coast. Part of the cargo included bank-note paper prepared for the Confederate States of America. This watermarked paper was later purchased by the United States Treasury Department and used for proof and specimen fractional currency. Three separate purchases were made by the Treasury Department, with the average price a little more than $2 per ream. The third purchase included 35 reams of foolscap at $6 per ream. Throughout this section *Pieces Issued* include face, back, wide, and narrow margin pieces.

Proofs and Specimens/Three-Cent Notes

No.	Description	Pieces Issued	Narrow Margin	Wide Margin
1,500S	Face, portrait has light background	7,000	75.00	Ex. Rare
1,501S	Face, portrait has dark background	7,000	40.00	90.00
	Back for each of the above	7,000	30.00	60.00

Proofs and Specimens/Five-Cent Notes

1,505S	Face, plain edges	5,445	40.00	85.00
	Back for the above	5,445	40.00	85.00
1,506S	Face	3,058*	30.00	75.00
	Back for the above, no surcharge	3,058*	30.00	75.00
1,510S	Back, green	10,500	30.00	75.00
1,512S	Back, red	10,500	30.00	75.00
	Face for the two notes above	10,500	30.00	75.00

*This figure reflects the number of wide margin pairs issued as of October 31, 1867; additional pairs probably were issued later.

Proofs and Specimens/Ten-Cent Notes

No.	Description	Pieces Issued	Narrow Margin	Wide Margin
1,517S	Face, plain edges	33,780	45.00	90.00
	Back for the above		45.00	90.00
1,518S	Face		30.00	75.00
	Back for the above, without corner surcharges		30.00	75.00
1,524S	Back, green		30.00	65.00
1,526S	Face with printed signatures of Colby and Spinner		35.00	75.00
1,528S	Face with autographed signatures of Colby and Spinner (specimen not printed on reverse)	54,250	50.00	100.00
1,529S	Face with autographed signatures of Jeffries and Spinner		85.00	Rare
	Red back for the two notes above		30.00	65.00

Proofs and Specimens/Fifteen-Cent Notes

Face Design: Portraits of Sherman and Grant.

No.	Description	Pieces Issued	Narrow Margin	Wide Margin
1,543S	Face with printed signatures of Colby and Spinner		125.00	225.00
	Back for the note above, green		45.00	110.00
1,544S	Face with autographed signatures of Colby and Spinner		500.00	Ex. Rare
1,545S	Face with autographed signatures of Jeffries and Spinner	9,016*	175.00	300.00
1,546S	Face with autographed signatures of Allison and Spinner		200.00	350.00
1,547S	Face with no signatures		925.00**	Unknown
	Back for the four notes above		45.00	90.00

All the notes above exist as specimens only.

*3,513 were outstanding in 1884.
**Rothert sale 1973.

Proofs and Specimens/Twenty-Five Cent Notes

No.	Description	Pieces Issued	Narrow Margin	Wide Margin
1,551S	Face with plain edges	15,672	50.00	100.00
	Back for the above note		50.00	100.00
1,552S	Face		40.00	80.00
	Back without a surcharge		40.00	80.00
1,559S	Back without a surcharge, red	8,600	40.00	80.00
1,563S	Back without a surcharge, green	8,600	40.00	80.00
	Face for the two notes above	8,600	45.00	85.00

Proofs and Specimens/Fifty-Cent Notes

No.	Description	Pieces Issued	Narrow Margin	Wide Margin
1,578S	Face with plain edges	10,872	60.00	120.00
	Back for the note above	10,872	60.00	120.00
1,579S	Face	6,385	45.00	85.00
	Back for the note above without corner surcharges	6,385	45.00	85.00

Proofs and Specimen/Fifty-Cent Notes

No.	Description	Narrow Margin	Wide Margin
1,586S	Face with printed signatures of Colby and Spinner	45.00	90.00
1,590S	Face with autographed signatures of Colby and Spinner	60.00	110.00
1,592S	Face with autographed signatures of Jeffries and Spinner (Only specimens are known for this note.)	150.00	950.00*
	Back for the three notes above without a surcharge, red	40.00	70.00
1,593S	Back without a surcharge, green	40.00	70.00

*Herman sale, 1974

Proofs and Specimens/Fifty-Cent Notes

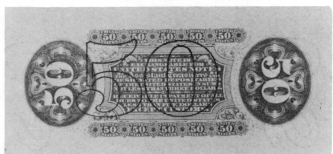

No.	Description	Narrow Margin	Wide Margin
1,609S	Face with printed signatures of Colby and Spinner	45.00	90.00
1,613S	Face with autographed signatures of Colby and Spinner	45.00	110.00
1,614S	Autographed signatures of Allison and Spinner	Ex. Rare*	
1,615S	Face with autographed signatures of Jeffries and Spinner, *not Allison and New.* (Only specimens are known for this note.)	150.00	Ex. Rare
	Back for the preceding three notes without a surcharge, red.	40.00	70.00
1,616S	Back without a surcharge, green	40.00	70.00
1,620S .	Back without a surcharge, green, new design	Ex. Rare**	
	Face for the above note is the same as 1,609		

Specimens of the fourth and fifth issues were printed but not sold to the public. A few of these specimens were presented to VIP's and are very rare.

For nos. 1586S-1620S, 50,584 pieces were printed.

*Herman Sale 1974 $1,100.00 wide margin
**Herman sale 1974 $550.00 wide margin

No.	Entire Back Inverted	Back Surcharge Inverted	Back Engraving Inverted	Other
1,500	Observed			
1,502	Reported			
1,503	Observed			
1,504	Observed			
1,505	Observed			
1,506	Reported	Observed	Reported	Face has back of 1580, Reported
1,506				Face has back of 1583, Observed
1,507	Reported	Observed		
1,510	Observed			
1,511	Reported			
1,515	Observed			
1,516	Observed			
1,517	Observed			

No.	Entire Back Inverted	Back Surcharge Inverted	Back Engraving Inverted	Other
1,518	Reported	Reported	Reported	
1,519		Observed		
1,520	Reported	Observed	Observed	
1,521		Observed		
1,523		Reported		
1,524		Reported		Face and back surcharge inverted, Reported
1,524				Face engraving inverted, Reported
1,524S				Back has denomination surcharge inverted to the engraving. Observed
1,525				Face and back surcharge inverted, Observed
1,549	Reported			
1,550	Observed			
1,551	Reported			
1,552		Observed		Back has surcharge of 1552 and engraving of 1579, Reported
1,552a		Reported		
1,554a		Reported		
1,555		Reported	Reported	"S" of back surcharge inverted, remaining part of surcharge normal, Observed
1,556		Reported		
1,557		Reported		
1,559		Reported		
1,565			Observed	
1,566	Reported	Observed	Reported	
1,567			Observed	
1,575	Reported			
1,576	Observed			
1,577	Observed			
1,578	Reported			
1,579S				Back has denomination surcharge inverted to the engraving, Observed

No.	Entire Back Inverted	Back Surcharge Inverted	Back Engraving Inverted	Other
1,580	Reported		Reported	
1,581		Observed	Reported	
1,582	Observed	Observed	Observed	
1,584	Reported			
1,585		Observed		
1,592			Observed	
1,601		Reported		
1,602		Reported		
1,603		Observed		
1,603a		Observed		
1,604		Reported		
1,605		Reported	Reported	
1,606	Reported	Reported		
1,608		Observed		
1,616	Reported			
1,616S				Back has denomination surcharge inverted to the engraving, Reported
1,616a		Observed	Reported	
1,617		Observed	Observed	
1,620		Observed		
1,623		Observed		

ENCASED POSTAGE STAMPS

Stamp collecting and syngraphics are two great hobbies, and it's a rare event when the two come together. This happened in the first part of the Civil War when postage stamps were used as small change. (Metal coinage had disappeared due to the rise in metal prices.)

A stamp can be a messy item to deal with as it passes from one damp hand to another. Mr. J. Gault solved the problem by patenting a small stamp case, consisting of a brass disc with a mica window. In 1862 the Scovill Button Works in Waterbury, Connecticut, began a massive production of Mr. Gault's stamp cases, and encased postage soon became the nation's medium of small change. Not only did the cases keep the stamp intact, but the brass backings soon became an interesting source of Americana because of the names and advertisements of the merchants of the period.

The stamps of 1861 were issued in the denominations of 1, 2, 3, 5, 10, 12, 24, 30, and 90 cents. The public accepted the postage currency in its windowed discs even though the beleaguered federal government never issued enough of the postage stamps to satisfy the needs of the economy.

These encased postage stamps are of special interest to collectors, be they stamp collectors, coin collectors, or collectors of paper money. Do encased postage stamps belong to the field of numismatics, philately, or syngraphics? They belong to all three and are unique in collecting history.

The prices listed are for pieces in Very Fine condition. The mica covering is expected to be clear, without any cracks or breaks.

One-Cent Stamps/Portrait of Benjamin Franklin

No.	Issuer	Value
1,637	Aerated Bread Co., N.Y.	185.00
1,638	Ayer's Cathartic Pills, Lowell, Massachusetts	60.00
1,639	"Take Ayer's Pills"	65.00
1,640	Ayer's Sarsaparilla, "Ayer's" (small)	70.00
1,641	Same as above except "Ayer's" (medium size)	80.00
1,642	Bailey & Co., Philadelphia	200.00
1,643	Bates, Joseph L., Boston "Fancy Goods"	125.00
1,644	Same as above but "Fancygoods" as one word	100.00
1,645	Brown's Bronchial Troches	120.00
1,646	Buhl, F & C., Detroit	275.00
1,647	Burnett's Cocoaine Kalliston	75.00
1,648	Burnett's Cooking Extracts	65.00
1,649	Claflin, A.M., Hopkinton, R.I.	475.00

No.	Issuer	Value
1,650	Dougan, N.Y.	325.00
1,651	Drake's Plantation Bitters	65.00
1,652	Ellis, McAlpin & Co., Cincinnati	425.00
1,653	Evans, C.G.	200.00
1,654	Gage Brothers & Drake, Chicago	150.00
1,655	Gault, J., in plain frame	60.00
1,656	Gault, J., in ribbed frame	150.00
1,657	Hopkins, L.C. & Co., Cincinnati	425.00
1,658	Hunt & Nash, Irving House, N.Y.	250.00
1,659	Kirkpatrick & Gault, N.Y.	200.00
1,660	Lord and Taylor, N.Y.	325.00
1,661	Mendum's Family Wine Emporium, N.Y.	125.00
1,662	Miles, B.F., Peoria	575.00
1,663	Norris, John W., Chicago	215.00
1,664	North American Life Insurance Co., N.Y. Straight inscription	165.00
1,665	Same as above except inscription is curved	150.00
1,666	Pearce, Tolle & Holton, Cincinnati	500.00
1,667	Schapker & Bussing, Evansville, Indiana	325.00
1,668	Shillito, John & Co., Cincinnati	200.00
1,669	Steinfield, S., N.Y.	150.00
1,670	Taylor, N.G. & Co., Philadelphia	200.00
1,671	Weir & Larminie, Montreal, Canada	425.00
1,672	White the Hatter, N.Y.	225.00

Two-Cent Stamps/Portrait of Andrew Jackson

No.	Issuer	Value
1,673	Gault, J. (not a regular issue)	1,300.00

Three-Cent Stamps/Portrait of George Washington

No.	Issuer	Value
1,674	Ayer's Cathartic Pills, Lowell, Mass.	65.00
1,675	Same as above except with longer arrows	75.00
1,676	"Take Ayer's Pills"	65.00
1,677	Ayer's Sarsaparilla, in plain frame	65.00
1,678	Same as above except "Ayer's" medium size	60.00
1,679	Same as above except "Ayer's" large size	100.00
1,680	Ayer's Sarsaparilla, medium size, in ribbed frame	200.00
1,681	Bailey & Co., Philadelphia	200.00

No.	Issuer	Value
1,682	Bates, Joseph L., Boston "Fancy Goods"	225.00
1,683	Same as above except "Fancygoods" as one word	200.00
1,684	Browns' Bronchial Troches	75.00
1,685	Buhl, F. & Co., Detroit	350.00
1,686	Burnett's Cocoaine Kalliston	90.00

No.	Issuer	Value
1,687	Burnett's Cooking Extracts	75.00
1,688	Claflin, A.M., Hopkinton, R.I.	400.00
1,689	Dougan, N.Y.	250.00
1,690	Drake's Plantation Bitters	65.00
1,691	Ellis, McAlpin & Co., Cincinnati	400.00
1,692	Evans, C.G.	300.00
1,693	Gage Brothers & Drake, Chicago	175.00
1,694	Gault, J. in plain frame	65.00
1,695	Gault, J. in ribbed frame	200.00
1,696	Hopkins, L.C. & Co., Cincinnati	300.00
1,697	Hunt & Nash, Irving House, N.Y.	200.00
1,698	Same as above except in ribbed frame	400.00
1,699	Kirkpatrick & Gault, N.Y.	300.00
1,700	Lord & Taylor, New York	325.00
1,701	Mendum's Family Wine Emporium, N.Y.	275.00
1,702	Norris, John W., Chicago	500.00
1,703	North American Life Insurance Co., N.Y.	100.00
1,704	Same as above except curved inscription	150.00
1,705	Pearce, Tolle & Holton, Cincinnati	250.00
1,706	Schapker & Bussing, Evansville, Indiana	475.00
1,707	Shillito, John & Co., Cincinnati	150.00
1,708	Taylor, N.G. & Co., Philadelphia	225.00
1,709	Weir & Larminie, Montreal, Canada	500.00
1,710	White the Hatter, N.Y.	250.00

Five-Cent Stamps/Portrait of Thomas Jefferson

No.	Issuer	Value
1,711	Ayer's Cathartic Pills, Lowell, Mass.	75.00
1,712	Same as above except longer arrows	85.00
1,713	"Take Ayer's Pills," in plain frame	75.00
1,714	"Take Ayer's Pills," in ribbed frame	200.00
1,715	Ayer's Sarsaparilla, "Ayer's" in medium letters	65.00
1,716	Same as above except in large letters	100.00
1,717	Bailey & Co., Philadelphia	275.00
1,718	Bates, Joseph L., Boston in plain frame	225.00
1,719	Bates, Joseph L., Boston in ribbed frame	250.00
1,720	Same as above except "Fancygoods" as one word	300.00
1,721	Brown's Bronchial Troches	90.00
1,722	Buhl, F. & C., Detroit	200.00
1,723	Burnett's Cocoaine Kallison	100.00
1,724	Burnett's Cooking Extracts	75.00
1,725	Claflin, A.M., Hopkinton, R.I.	400.00
1,726	Cook, H.A., Evansville, Indiana	300.00
1,727	Dougan, N.Y.	300.00
1,728	Drake's Plantation Bitters in plain frame	85.00
1,729	Drakes Plantation Bitters in ribbed frame	200.00
1,730	Ellis, McAlpin & Co., Cincinnati	250.00
1,731	Evans, C.G.	500.00
1,732	Gage Brothers — Drake, Chicago	100.00
1,733	Gault, J., in plain frame	75.00
1,734	Gault, J., in ribbed frame	175.00
1,735	Hopkins, L.C. & Co., Cincinnati	325.00
1,736	Hunt & Nash, Irving House, N.Y., in plain frame	200.00
1,737	Same as above except in ribbed frame	250.00
1,738	Kirkpatrick & Gault, N.Y.	100.00
1,739	Lord & Taylor, N.Y.	285.00
1,740	Mendum's Family Wine Emporium, N.Y.	125.00
1,741	Miles, B.F., Peoria	400.00
1,742	Norris, John W., Chicago	285.00
1,743	North American Life Insurance Co., N.Y.	200.00
1,743a	Same as above in ribbed frame	375.00
1,744	Pearce, Tolle & Holton, Cincinnati	425.00
1,745	Sands Ale	300.00
1,746	Schapker & Bussing, Evansville, Ind.	225.00

No.	Issuer	Value
1,747	Shillito, John & Co., Cincinnati	200.00
1,748	Steinfield, S., N.Y.	225.00
1,749	Taylor, N.G. & Co., Philadelphia	375.00
1,750	Weir & Larminie, Montreal, Canada	475.00
1,751	White the Hatter, N.Y.	500.00

Nine-Cent (three 3¢) Stamps/Portrait of George Washington

No.	Issuer	Value
1,752	Feuchtwanger back	250.00

Ten-Cent Stamps/Portrait of George Washington

No.	Issuer	Value
1,753	Ayer's Cathartic Pills, Lowell, Mass., with short arrow	175.00
1,754	Same as above except with long arrows	275.00
1,755	"Take Ayer's Pills"	200.00
1,756	Ayer's Sarsaparilla, in plain frame	85.00
1,757	As above, "Ayer's" in small letters	100.00
1,758	As above, "Ayer's" in large letters	100.00
1,759	As above, "Ayer's" in medium letters, ribbed frame	165.00
1,760	Bailey & Co., Philadelphia	225.00
1,761	Bates, Joseph L., Boston in plain frame	125.00
1,762	Bates, Joseph L., Boston in ribbed frame	185.00
1,763	Same as above except "Fancygoods" as one word in ribbed frame	250.00
1,764	Brown's Bronchial Troches	115.00
1,765	Buhl, F. & Co., Detroit	265.00
1,766	Burnett's Cocoaine Kalliston	115.oo
1,767	Burnett's Cooking Extracts, in plain frame	100.00
1,768	Burnett's Cooking Extracts in ribbed frame	285.00
1,769	Cook, H.A., Evansville, Indiana	350.00
1,770	Claflin, A.M., Hopkinton, R.I.	400.00
1,771	Dougan, N.Y.	325.00
1,772	Drake's Plantation Bitters, in plain frame	100.00
1,773	Same as above in ribbed frame	275.00
1,774	Ellis, McAlpin & Co., Cincinnati	285.00

No.	Issuer	Value
1,775	Evans, C.G.	500.00
1,776	Gage Brothers & Drake, Chicago, in plain frame	100.00
1,777	Same as above in ribbed frame	250.00
1,778	Gault, J. in plain frame	75.00
1,779	Same as above in ribbed frame	150.00
1,780	Hopkins, L.C. & Co., Cincinnati	525.00
1,781	Hunt & Nash, Irving House, N.Y., in plain frame	125.00
1,782	Same as above in ribbed frame	250.00
1,783	Kirkpatrick & Gault, New York	100.00
1,784	Lord & Taylor, New York	400.00
1,785	Mendum's Family Wine Emporium, N.Y., in plain frame	150.00
1,786	Same as above in ribbed frame	335.00
1,787	Norris, John W., Chicago	425.00
1,788	North American Life Insurance Co., N.Y., in plain frame	225.00
1,789	Same as above with curved inscription	300.00
1,790	North American Life Insurance Co., N.Y., in ribbed frame and curved inscription	400.00
1,791	Pearce, Tolle & Holton, Cincinnati	475.00
1,792	Sands Ale	500.00
1,793	Schapker & Bussing, Evansville, Indiana	250.00
1,794	Shillito, John & Co., Cincinnati	250.00
1,795	Steinfeld, S., N.Y.	250.00
1,796	Taylor, N. & Co., Philadelphia	425.00
1,797	Weir & Larminie, Montreal, Canada	300.00
1,798	White the Hatter, N.Y.	325.00

Twelve-Cent Stamps/Portrait of George Washington

No.	Issuer	Value
1,799	Ayer's Cathartic Pills, Lowell, Mass.	250.00
1,800	Same as above, with long arrows	275.00
1,801	"Take Ayer's Pills"	225.00
1,802	Ayer's Sarsaparilla, "Ayer's" in medium letters	200.00
1,803	Same as above except "Ayer's" in small letters	250.00
1,804	Bailey & Co., Philadelphia	400.00
1,805	Bates, Joseph L., Boston	300.00
1,806	Brown's Bronchial Troches	250.00

No.	Issuer	Value
1,807	Buhl, F. & Co., Detroit	400.00
1,808	Burnett's Cocoaine Kalliston	300.00
1,809	Burnett's Cooking Extracts	250.00
1,810	Claflin, A.M., Hopkinton, R.I.	475.00
1,811	Drake's Plantation Bitters	225.00
1,812	Ellis, McAlpin & Co., Cincinnati	400.00
1,813	Gage Brothers & Drake, Chicago	275.00
1,814	Gault, J., in plain frame	150.00
1,815	Same as above in ribbed frame	325.00
1,816	Hunt & Nash, Irving House, N.Y., in plain frame	200.00
1,817	Same as above in ribbed frame	350.00
1,818	Kirkpatrick & Gault, N.Y.	200.00
1,819	Lord & Taylor, N.Y.	450.00
1,820	Mendum's Family Wine Emporium, N.Y.	300.00
1,821	North American Insurance Co., N.Y.	475.00
1,822	Pearce, Tolle & Holton, Cincinnati	465.00
1,823	Sands Ale	650.00
1,824	Schapker & Bussing, Evansville, Indiana	525.00
1,825	Shillito, John & Co., Cincinnati	500.00
1,826	Steinfeld, S., N.Y.	500.00
1,827	Taylor, N.G. & Co., Philadelphia	600.00

Twenty-Four-Cent Stamps/Portrait of George Washington

No.	Issuer	Value
1,828	Ayer's Cathartic Pills, Lowell, Mass.	525.00
1,829	Ayer's Sarsaparilla	400.00
1,830	Brown's Bronchial Troches	400.00
1,831	Buhl. F. & Co., Detroit	400.00
1,832	Burnett's Cocoaine Kalliston	400.00
1,833	Burnett's Cooking Extracts	400.00
1,834	Drake's Plantation Bitters	425.00
1,835	Ellis, McAlpin & Co., Cincinnati	425.00
1,836	Gault, J., in plain frame	400.00
1,837	Same as above in ribbed frame	425.00
1,838	Hunt & Nash, Irving House, N.Y., in plain frame	385.00
1,839	Same as above in ribbed frame	500.00
1,840	Kirkpatrick & Gault, N.Y.	385.00
1,841	Lord & Taylor, N.Y.	550.00
1,842	Pearce, Tolle & Holton, Cincinnati	600.00

Thirty-Cent Stamps/Portrait of Benjamin Franklin

No.	Issuer	Value
1,843	Ayer's Cathartic Pills	—
1,844	Ayer's Sarsaparilla	400.00
1,845	Brown's Bronchial Troches	400.00
1,846	Brunett's Cocoaine Kalliston	525.00
1,847	Burnett's Cooking Extracts	525.00
1,848	Drake's Plantation Bitters	450.00
1,849	Gault, J., in plain frame	325.00
1,850	Gault, J., in ribbed frame	425.00
1,851	Hunt & Nash, Irving House, N.Y.	450.00
1,852	Kirkpatrick & Gault, N.Y.	450.00
1,853	Lord & Taylor, N.Y.	500.00
1,854	Sands Ale	650.00

Ninety-Cent Stamps/Portrait of George Washington

No.	Issuer	Value
1,855	Ayer's Sarsaparilla	—
1,856	"Take Ayer's Pills"	—
1,857	Burnett's Cocoaine Kalliston	1,650.00
1,858	Drake's Plantation Bitters	1,650.00
1,859	Gault, J.	1,650.00
1,860	Kirkpatrick & Gault, N.Y.	1,650.00
1,861	Lord & Taylor, N.Y.	1,750.00

UNCUT SHEETS

Our current Federal Reserve notes are printed on 32-subject sheets; for the most part our early, large-size notes were printed on 4-subject sheets.

Since 1840 the preferred method of manufacturing United States currency has been by intaglio plates. With the exception of fractional currency, the first notes were printed from 4-subject plates; some interest-bearing notes were printed from 3-subject plates. In 1918, 8-subject plates were put into use. Prior to 1898 only single-plate hand presses were in use, which yielded one sheet per impression. Later, larger steam presses handled up to four plates simultaneously.

The reduction in size of our paper money in 1928 and the need for more circulating money brought printing improvements to the Bureau of Engraving and Printing. One such improvement in productivity involved the use of presses that would accommodate larger engraved plates that print sheets comprised of more subjects.

As for the notes produced by the older methods, some of the most interesting were the national bank notes. Large-size national bank notes usually were printed on sheets of 4 subjects, although some plates were prepared with only 2 subjects. For the printing of some $500 and $1,000 national bank notes, 1-subject plates were used. Surviving sheets represent only a small fraction of known subject combinations: eight sheets of the first charter period, each sheet comprised of three $1 subjects and one $2 subject; ten sheets of brown backs consisting of three $10 subjects and one $20 subject; about ten sheets of brown backs with four $5 subjects and one sheet of three $10 subjects and one $20 subject, both with dated backs. There are dozens of third-charter sheets, the vast majority being sheets of four $5 subjects with blue seals. Combinations such as $50-50-50-100 and $10-10-20-50 were made, but none have been preserved. Thus it is not always possible to tell the combination of the sheet from which any given national bank note was clipped.

Uncut fractional currency sheets were shipped to post offices and banks and sold directly to the public. National bank notes also were shipped uncut to the issuing banks and occasionally were saved as souvenirs. Others sheets—with very few exceptions—were separated and trimmed into single notes at the Bureau; the exceptions were a few sheets of 1896 silver certificates, several $1, $2, and $5 silver certificates of 1899, and two sheets of $5 United States notes of 1907, all of which appear to have been presented uncut to VIPs. A.A. Grinnell also had a pair of uncut Chicago 1915 Federal Reserve bank note sheets in denominations of $10 and $20. To date no others have been reported. Even some of the presentation sheets were separated, as were their small-sized counterparts of 1928-1934.

Small-size notes, first printed in sheets of 12 on August 6, 1928, were sold in sheet form to the general public beginning in 1935. The 1928-1934 uncut issues were presentation items; from six to a few dozen were made. When the 18-subject sheets of $1 notes were introduced in 1952, followed by higher denominations in May 1953, a few hundred sheets of each were distributed uncut, after which time the Treasury discontinued the practice. No 32-subject sheets have been issued to the general public, though presentation to VIPs cannot be ruled out. It is probable that many 18-subject sheets were subsequently separated, since they are rarer than the 12-subject sheets.

Small-size national bank notes, like their big brothers, were shipped uncut to the 6,994 issuing banks in panels of 6. They had been printed in 12-subject sheets, as were all other small-sized notes, series 1928 through 1953. The national bank notes were printed minus the bank information and then were stored and over-printed by logotypes as orders arrived from individual banks. At present over 850 such sheets have been recorded, the vast majority with serial number 1 (Type I) or 1-6 (Type II). Over half are $5 notes. Of the rest, $10 notes outnumber $20s by 3 to 1; the $50 and $100 sheets are exceedingly rare.

Uncut sheets usually are collected by states. Texas, Michigan, and New York are the most common. The rarities are Delaware, Washington, D.C., Arizona, Idaho, and Wyoming. No sheets are known for Alaska or Hawaii.

RECORDED UNCUT SHEETS

United States Notes/Sheets of Four

No.	Denomination	Series	Signatures	Value
263	$5	1880	Lyons-Roberts	—
271	$5	1907	Elliott-White	600.00

No. 57 $1 Series 1899

Silver Certificates/Sheets of Four

No. 45 $1, series 1896.

No. 185 $2, series 1896.
(From Donlon, April 30, 1976 Sale.)

No.	Denomination	Series	Signatures	Value
45	$1	1896	Tillman-Morgan	—
46	$1	1896	Bruce-Roberts	—
48	$1	1899	Lyons-Roberts	650.00
54	$1	1899	Parker-Burke	550.00
57	$1	1899	Elliot-White	550.00
185	$2	1896	Tillman-Morgan	Unique
187	$2	1899	Lyons-Roberts	750.00
193	$2	1899	Parker-Burke	750.00
196	$2	1899	Speelman-White	650.00
371	$5	1899	Speelman-White	650.00
358	$5	1896	Tillman-Morgan	—

Treasury or Coin Notes/Sheets of Four

No.	Denomination	Series	Signatures	Value
62	$1	1890	Rosecrans-Huston	Unique

This sheet was sold to the Chief Engraver, George W. Casilear, who made the following inscription on the bottom margin. "This sheet of four $1.00 Treasury Notes, being the designer, as a courtesy and my request, were delivered to me through the Treasurer of the United States, by paying $4.00 without separation, Geor. W. Casilear, Chief Engraver."

National Bank Notes/First Charter Period/Sheets of Four

No.	Denomination	Series	Signatures	Value
29 & 171	$1(3), $2(1)	1865	Colby-Spinner	—
33 & 175	$1(3), $2(1)	1865	Allison-Wyman	—
34 & 176	$1(3), $2(1)	1865	Allison-Gilfillan	2,500.00
282	$5	1875	Bruce-Gilfillan	—
501 & 732	$10(3), $20(1)	1875	Allison-New	—

National Bank Notes/Second Charter Period/Sheets of Four

			First Issue	
No.	**Denomination**	**Series**	**Signatures**	**Value**
288	$5	1882	Bruce-Wyman	800.00
291	$5	1882	Rosecrans-Hyatt	800.00
292	$5	1882	Rosecrans-Huston	800.00
293	$5	1882	Rosecrans-Nebeker	800.00
298	$5	1882	Lyons-Roberts	800.00
512 & 744	$10(3), $20(1)	1882	Rosecrans-Jordan	—
514 & 746	$10(3), $20(1)	1882	Rosecrans-Huston	—
515 & 747	$10(3), $20(1)	1882	Rosecrans-Nebeker	—
520 & 752	$10(3), $20(1)	1882	Lyons-Roberts	—

National Bank Notes/Second Charter Period/Sheets of Four

No.	Denomination	Series	Signatures	Value
			Second Issue	
303	$5	1882	Tillman-Morgan	800.00
526 & 758	$10(3), $20(1)	1882	Tillman-Morgan	—
527 & 758	$10(3), $20(1)	1882	Tillman-Morgan	—
			Third Issue	
311	$5	1882	Lyons-Roberts	—

National Bank Notes/Third Charter Period/Sheets of Four

			First Issue	
316	$5	1902	Lyons-Roberts	300.00
317	$5	1902	Lyons-Treat	300.00
318	$5	1902	Vernon-Treat	300.00
			Second Issue	
319	$5	1902	Lyons-Roberts	250.00
321	$5	1902	Vernon-Treat	250.00
322	$5	1902	Vernon-McClung	250.00
			Third Issue	
328	$5	1902	Lyons-Roberts	300.00
331	$5	1902	Vernon-McClung	300.00
333	$5	1902	Napier-Thompson	425.00
335	$5	1902	Parker-Burke	275.00
336	$5	1902	Teehee-Burke	275.00
337	$5	1902	Elliot-Burke	275.00
338	$5	1902	Elliot-White	275.00
339	$5	1902	Speelman-White	275.00
341	$5	1902	Woods-Tate	300.00

National Bank Notes/Third Charter Period/Sheets of Four

Third Issue, Series 1902—Sheets of $10(3), $20(1)

No.	Signatures	Value
552 & 785	Lyons-Roberts	475.00
554 & 787	Vernon-Treat	475.00
555 & 788	Vernon-McClung	475.00
556 & 789	Napier-McClung	500.00
558 & 791	Napier-Burke	550.00
559 & 792	Parker-Burke	550.00
560 & 793	Teehee-Burke	625.00
561 & 794	Elliot-Burke	500.00
563 & 796	Speelman-White	500.00·
565 & 798	Woods-Tate	700.00

Federal Reserve Bank Notes/Series 1915/Sheets of Four

No.	Denomination	Signatures
620G1	$10 .	Teehee-Burke
850G	$20	Teehee-Burke

These two sheets were offered in the Grinnell sale and are considered to be unique.

United States Notes/One Dollar/Sheets of Twelve

No.	Series	Signatures	Sheets Delivered	Value	Known
69	1928	Woods-Woodin	11	Rare	8

United States Notes/Two Dollars

Sheets of Twelve

No.	Series	Signatures	Sheets Delivered	Value	Known
204	1928	Tate-Mellon	No record	—	3
204A	1928A	Woods-Mellon	No record	—	0
204B	1928B	Woods-Mills	No record	—	0
204C	1928C	Julian-Morgenthau	25	600.00	12
204D	1928D	Julian-Morgenthau	50	600.00	9
204E	1928E	Julian-Vinson	50	750.00	20
204F	1928F	Julian-Snyder	100	525.00	20
204G	1928G	Clark-Snyder	100	450.00	20

Sheets of Eighteen

205	1953	Priest-Humphrey	100		16

United States Notes/Five Dollars

Sheets of Twelve

No.	Series	Signatures	Sheets Delivered	Value	Known
383	1928	Woods-Mellon	5	1,750.00	1
383A	1928A	Woods-Mills	No record	—	0
383B	1928B	Julian-Morgenthau	No record	—	0
383C	1928C	Julian-Morgenthau	No record	—	0
383D	1928D	Julian-Vinson	No record	1,750.00	13
383E	1928E	Julian-Snyder	100	1,200.00	14
383F	1928F	Clark-Snyder	No record	—	0

Sheets of Eighteen

No.	Series	Signatures	Sheets Delivered	Value	Known
384	1953	Priest-Humphrey	100	1,500.00	13

Silver Certificates/One Dollar

Sheets of Twelve

No.	Series	Signatures	Sheet Delivered	Value	Known
70	1928	Tate-Mellon	No record	1,500.00	11
71	1928A	Woods-Mellon	No record	—	0
72	1928B	Woods-Mills	6	Rare	0
73	1928C	Woods-Woodin	11	Rare	7
74	1928D	Julian-Woodin	60	—	20
75	1928E	Julian-Morgenthau	25	Rare	7
76	1934	Julian-Morgenthau	25	1,750.00	9
77	1935	Julian-Morgenthau	100	550.00	21
78	1935A	Julian-Morgenthau	100	1,000.00	17

Silver Certificates/One Dollar

No.	Series	Signatures	Sheet Delivered	Value
79	1935A (Hawaii)	Julian-Morgenthau	25	2,000.00
80	1935A (N. Africa)	Julian-Morgenthau	25	2,500.00
83	1935B	Julian-Vinson	100	1,250.00
84	1935C	Julian-Snyder	100	1,000.00
85	1935D	Clark-Snyder	300	850.00

Silver Certificates/One Dollar

Sheets of Eighteen

No.	Series	Signatures	Sheets Delivered	Value
86	1935D	Clark-Snyder	102	1,250.00
87	1935E	Priest-Humphrey	400	1,000.00

Silver Certificates/Five Dollars

(From Donlon, April 30, 1976 Sale.)

Sheets of Twelve

No.	Series	Signatures	Sheets Delivered	Value	Known
386	1934	Julian-Morgenthau	25	2,500.00	12
386A	1934A	Julian-Morgenthau	No record	—	0
386B	1934B	Julian-Vinson	No record	2,500.00	10
386C	1934C	Julian-Snyder	100	1,500.00	10
386D	1934D	Clark-Snyder	100	1,250.00	19

Sheets of Eighteen

388	1953	Priest-Humphrey	100	2,000.00	20

Silver Certificates/Ten Dollars

Sheets of Twelve

No.	Series	Signatures	Sheets Delivered	Value	Known
621	1933	Julian-Woodin	1	—	0
621A	1933A	Julian-Morgenthau	1	—	0
622	1934	Julian-Morgenthau	10	Rare	7

Sheets of Eighteen

| 625 | 1953 | Priest-Humphrey | 100 | 2,000.00 | 9 |

Federal Reserve Notes/1928 Series

Sheets of Twelve
The following statistics are from the records at the Bureau of Engraving and Printing.

Bank	Denomination	Signatures	Sheets Delivered
Boston	$ 5	Tate-Mellon	10
		Tate-Mellon	10
	20	Tate-Mellon	10
	50	No record	10

New York	5	Tate-Mellon	12
	10	Tate-Mellon	12
	20*	Woods-Mellon	12
	50	No record	1

*A sheet bearing the signatures of Tate-Mellon was offered in the Grinnell sale.

Federal Reserve Notes/1928 Series

Bank	Denomination	Signatures	Sheets Delivered
Philadelphia	5	Tate or Woods-Mellon	5
	10	Tate or Woods-Mellon	5
	20*	Woods-Mellon	5
	50	Woods-Mellon	5
Cleveland	5	Tate or Woods-Mellon	2
	10	Tate or Woods-Mellon	2
	20	Woods-Mellon	2
	50	Woods-Mellon	2
Richmond	5	Tate or Woods-Mellon	1
	10	Tate or Woods-Mellon	1
	20	Tate or Woods-Mellon	1
	50	Tate or Woods-Mellon	1
Chicago	5*	No record	
	10*	No record	
	20*	No record	
Minneapolis	5**	No record	5
	10*	Woods-Mellon	5
	20*	No record	
Kansas City	5	Tate or Woods-Mellon	5
	10*	Woods-Mellon	5
	20*	Woods-Mellon	5
Dallas	5*	Woods-Mellon	5
	10*	Woods-Mellon	5
San Francisco	5	Tate-Mellon	2
	10	Tate-Mellon	2
	50	Woods-Mellon	2

*A sheet bearing the signatures of Tate-Mellon was offered in the Grinnell sale.
**A sheet (1928B) bearing the signatures of Woods-Mellon was offered in the Grinnell sale.

National Currency/Series 1929/Sheets of Six*

Denomination	Rarity 1&2	Rarity 3&4	Rarity 5	Rarity 6	Rarity 7	Rarity 8
$ 5	350.00	350.00	400.00	500.00	600.00	1150.00
10	375.00	425.00	450.00	550.00	650.00	1200.00
20	425.00	500.00	550.00	600.00	700.00	1325.00
50	1000.00	1150.00	1275.00	1375.00	1425.00	1600.00
100	1350.00	1500.00	1650.00	1850.00	2250.00	2750.00

The valuations above are for Type I notes; Type II notes command a much higher premium, in some instances twice the amount. See page 41 for rarity table.

*All small-size national currency and Federal Reserve bank notes were printed in sheets of twelve. They were cut and delivered to the issuing bank in sheets of six.

Federal Reserve Bank Notes/Series 1929/Sheets of Twelve

Bank	Denomination	Signatures	Known
New York	10	Jones-Woods	2
Philadelphia	20	Jones-Woods	1
Chicago	20	Jones-Woods	1
Minneapolis	20	Jones-Woods	1

NOTES OF SPECIAL INTEREST

There are many avenues to follow in assembling a collection of paper money. One can collect all the signature combinations within a particular series or all denominations for a series. Some collectors prefer to collect notes by denomination; others might assemble notes representing the work of a particular engraver or designer. These are only a few of the ways in which one can satisfy a syngraphic interest.

A fascinating path to follow is that of seeking out unusual notes. On the following pages you will see a few illustrations of notes that any collector would consider to be of special interest.

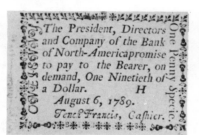

When this note circulated in the American Colonies, the Spanish Milled Dollar, exchangable at 7 shillings 6 pence, or 90 pence, was the standard unit of currency.

The Bank of North America was the only national bank to receive the privilege of deleting the word "national" from its title. The Bank of North America was chartered by the Continental Congress on December 31, 1781. The man most responsible for the charter was Alexander Hamilton, the first Secretary of the Treasury. For some unknown reason the bank's charter was allowed to expire in 1811. A second Bank of North America was later formed and became nationalized on December 4, 1864. The members of the Congress at that time thought it fitting that the only bank to be chartered by the Continental Congress should retain its original title.

The Bank of North America was liquidated on February 28, 1923, and therefore issued large-sized notes only. All are scarce and of great historical interest.

Forbidden Titles

National bank notes that used the title "United States," "Federal," or "Reserve" were discouraged by the passage of the Federal Reserve Act of 1913. These forbidden titles were then outlawed altogether by an Act of Congress on May 24, 1926. Between 1863 and 1926, 33 banks were chartered using "United States" in their titles. Of these banks 19 issued notes; 6 banks used "Federal," and 4 used "Federal Reserve" in their titles. All notes bearing such forbidden titles are extremely desirable and very scarce.

Racketeer Note
The National Bank of the Republic of New York had 1,000 as its charter number. The first notes isssued by this bank under its second charter were sought by swindlers, who tried to pass them to illiterates as $1,000 bills.

A $5 note of historic interest from the city of the Alamo.

A note that brings to mind the days of the stagecoach.

At first glance this note seems to bear the names of two states. It was issued by the community of California in the state of Missouri.

A national bank note with an extremely long title.

A national bank note issued by a community with a three-letter name.

Jackson's Disappearing Fingers

Excluding his portrait on broken bank notes, Andrew Jackson made his first appearance on U.S. paper money on a $5 United States note, series 1869. This portrait was engraved by Alfred Sealey.

Going ... A $10 note of series 1923 also has a portrait of Jackson, somewhat modified. The oval in which the portrait is framed is smaller as well. Jackson's left hand is much closer to the rim of this smaller oval.

Going ... Prior to the printing of the $20 notes, series 1950E, in 1957, wet paper had been used on flatbed presses. A certain amount of shrinkage took place as the mill-wet paper dried after being impressed with the plates, which were somewhat larger than the plates currently in use. To allow for this shrinkage, a new engraving of a larger portrait was prepared.

Gone. In order to retain the necessary size of Jackson's portrait on bills made from intaglio presses, a redesign was necessary. The most obvious change is the missing finger.

Tombstone, Arizona, the town too tough to die, was the scene for the gunfight at the O.K. Corral where Wyatt Earp and "Doc" Holiday fought the Clantons. (Photograph courtesy of Hickman & Oakes.)

See the following numbers in this catalog for additional notes of special interest, such as low or interesting serial numbers and interesting bank titles: Nos. 1, 47, 68C1, 171, 203, 483, 512, 545, 590, 605, 987, 1,042, and 1,248.

ERROR AND FREAK NOTES

Inspectors at the Bureau of Engraving and Printing are constantly on the alert for errors, and since most of the printing is now performed automatically by COPE, the chances for error should be slight. Nevertheless, errors do slip through occasionally, and it is a delight for a collector to find such a prize.

No two errors are exactly alike, and so the degree of error will determine the price of a particular note. The values for the different types of errors illustrated in this section do not include the face value or the collectors' value. Due to the nature of the error, certain notes would probably never circulate and therefore would only be found in new condition. Errors of this type will only be priced in one condition.

One spurious error deserves mention here. People often show me bills with blue or yellow backs (the seals and serial numbers on the face are not always affected). These doctored notes are not errors. The inks prepared at the Bureau are constantly checked during each preparation, and no one who knows paper money has ever seen an off-color note produced at the Bureau. How then did these bills change color? As we all remember from our first art class in grammar school, green is made up of blue and yellow. The alkali found in certain detergents or peroxide will alter the green ink, usually to yellow. The green ink will turn to blue if exposed to certain acids or acidic fumes.

The question the proud owner of one of these abominations usually has in reserve is, "How come the face of the bill did not change color as well?" The answer is that except for the seal and serial number, the face of our paper money is printed with black ink, not green. The first demand notes of 1861 were labelled "greenbacks," and it is still the backs that are green.

Two For One

This error is a classic. These notes received normal face and back printings as well as normal overprints, but the COPE cutting blades caught the sheet out of alignment. (Photograph courtesy of Harry E. Jones.)

New
750.00

Off-Center Notes

Faulty alignment during the cutting operation produced these errors. Notes are always cut and trimmed with the face showing; nevertheless, the $1 note illustrated above was improperly trimmed.

Very Fine	Extra Fine	New
12.50	17.50	30.00

Improperly Trimmed Notes

These notes were improperly trimmed, one having been folded prior to the trimming operation. The $20 note was folded in such a way that a portion of the face printing appears on the underside of the corner tab.

New
35.00

This 1969B Federal Reserve note received normal initial printings. The second photo illustrates the corner unfolded.

Very Fine	Extra Fine	New
100.00	135.00	225.00

Mismatched Serial Numbers

The prefix letters of the serial numbers do not match; they are not even close. A serious malfunction of the number cylinder caused this error.

Very Fine	Extra Fine	New
25.00	30.00	50.00

This note is a prize—a replacement note with mismatched serial numbers.

Very Fine	Extra Fine	New
85.00	100.00	135.00

Rarely does a note of such a high denomination with an error escape the eyes of the inspectors. (Remember, the face value is not included in the prices listed in this section.)

Very Fine	Extra Fine	New
25.00	35.00	100.00

An inspector wrote the correct number in pencil on this note; somehow the note entered circulation.

Very Fine	Extra Fine	New
25.00	35.00	50.00

Partially Missing Serial Numbers

This set of notes first came to my attention in an article by Lee Worthley with assistance from Peter Huntoon. The article appeared in *Paper Money,* the official publication of the Society of Paper Money Collectors. The check letter A4 indicates the error was recorded in the same position on five sheets.

Higher serial numbers are always printed first in order to allow the finished sheets to be ejected in numerical order. Some foreign matter forced the 8 to move with the 3; you can see the 7 trying to appear. The dirt or foreign matter became dislodged after a short time, and the error corrected itself on the second note from the top.

Value for the complete set, $1,500.00

Ink Smudge and Insufficient Ink

Either a portion of the plate lacked sufficient ink or a floating piece of debris caused this smudge. Both of the above notes were found in a pack of new notes, and when placed next to each other they show the complete error. (The price below is for a single note.)

Very Fine	Extra Fine	New
7.50	10.00	15.00

The plate for this 1969 Federal Reserve note was insufficiently inked, and the result was this ghostlike image of George Washington.

Extra Fine	New
20.00	40.00

Misaligned Overprint

The sheet from which this note came was accidentally given half a turn before the bank charter number was added.

Very Fine	Extra Fine	New
40.00	50.00	100.00

The two notes above have the overprint out of line. This was caused by improper alignment of the sheet as it was fed into the press for the overprint.

Very Fine	Extra Fine	New
15.00	20.00	30.00 .

Double Printing
During the first printing plate 145 was used, after which the sheet was accidentally fed into the press again. This time plate 126 was used.

The reverse of this note received two printings also; plates 1490 and 1499 were used.

Very Fine	Extra Fine	New
135.00	175.00	225.00

Yes, you are seeing double. This note went through the complete overprinting process twice.

Very Fine	Extra Fine	New
300.00	375.00	500.00

Missing Overprint

All three notes lack the overprinting of seals and serial numbers. The $10 note bearing a reject sticker and lacking both signatures was produced after 1938, when the signature portions of the overprint were no longer engraved on the plate.

Very Fine	Extra Fine	New
75.00	100.00	175.00

Inverted Overprint

The sheets from which these notes came were fed into the press after they were inadvertently rotated 180 degrees. High denomination errors such as the one above seldom escape the Bureau. An unprecedented number of series 1974 and 1976 notes received an inverted overprint; current prices on these are extremely speculative.

Very Fine	Extra Fine	New
125.00	150.00	200.00

Offset Print

The press must have been started without paper in position. The impression roller touched the engraved plate, and the sheet that followed received the full face impression in retrograde on the back. When this happens each impression to follow will print less of the offset. After a few impressions the offset will disappear completely.

Very Fine	Extra Fine	New
85.00	110.00	150.00

The above note had only a portion of the opposite side offset onto the side illustrated.

Very Fine	Extra Fine	New
50.00	75.00	100.00

Back Printing on Face

A sheet was fed into the press as it was being inked up, accounting for the lightness and the low placement of the back impression (on the face). Then the sheet was accidentally turned over and around. The sheet received the normal back printing followed by a normal face printing *over* the first weak back impression. (Photograph courtesy of Peter Huntoon.)

New
400.00

Paper Fold

All the notes above with folds in the paper went undetected during the printing of the face. The two $10 notes have two folds and cost proportionately more.

Very Fine	Extra Fine	New
20.00	35.00	50.00

Paper Fold

The sheet from which this 1969B $1 note came was folded when it was fed into the press for the overprint of seals and serial numbers. The second and third photographs show the face and back unfolded. (This note illustrated through the courtesy of Mrs. Lois Stancoff.)

New

300.00

Paper Fold
Here is another unusual error that obviously received both face and back printings as intended. Before the overprinting of seals and serial numbers, the sheet was folded and remained in that position through the cutting operation. (Courtesy of Harry E. Jones.)

New
300.00

Paper Fold

As was the case with the preceding note, this note received normal face and back printings but was folded before the overprinting operation. The first illustration shows the position of the face during the overprinting; the second and third photographs show the back with and without the fold. (Courtesy of Harry E. Jones.)

New
250.00

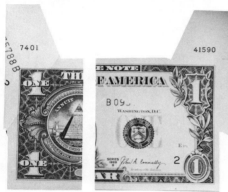

Paper Fold With Faulty Overprint

These photographs of the same note in different positions illustrate an interesting multiple error. The uppermost photograph shows the overprint on a corner fold. The two partial photographs illustrate the front and back with the fold undone; the plate numbers that should have been trimmed from the sheet are visible.

New

200.00

This note, from the lower right hand corner of the sheet, received a fold after the back printing operation was completed. It remained folded for all face printings, as you can see by the blank unfolded portion.

New

375.00

Paper Fold on Torn Sheet

Following normal face and back printing, the sheet from which this $20 1950E note came developed a tear. You will notice that the tear continued through the *W* in "TWENTY" on the face. The torn sheet became folded and received the overprinting of seal and serial numbers. Following the overprinting, the sheet straightened out and was properly cut. It entered circulation in two pieces. This note was found taped together. (Courtesy Lee Worthley and *Paper Money,* No. 3, 1972.)

Very Fine	Extra Fine	New
125.00	200.00	400.00

Overprint Only

The $1 Federal Reserve note illustrated, completely lacks the initial intaglio face printing. Two sheets probably adhered to one another but became separated upon being fed into the COPE machinery where they received final seal and serial number impressions. This error has been observed from other Federal Reserve Districts.

New
900.00

Blank Back, Almost

Notes with blank backs are quite unusual but this error is much more interesting. The face of the above note received normal printings however the back is almost blank except for the "10 TEN DOLLARS 10" at the bottom border. The pressure from the face printing is clearly visible at the top. This error occured during a first or last run when ink had not yet reached the entire plate or when the ink supply ran out before the presses were stopped.

	New	
	400.00	

Accordian Gouge

Sometime after the face and back printing something gouged a small portion of the sheet. The damaged portion was forced accordian fashion toward the face of the note and remained, escaping the trimming process.

	New	
	25.00	

Inverted Notes

The faces of these notes were inverted (the backs are always printed first). The sheet was accidentally rotated 180 degrees before it was fed into the press.

Very Fine	Extra Fine	New
100.00	150.00	200.00

After the initial back printing but before the face printing, the note received a gouge, pushing the paper together in the center, accordion fashion. The tear on the right through the Treasury Seal could have and probably did take place before the final overprint. It was a clean tear which did not interefere with the seal impression.

New
100.00

This replacement note has an inverted face. This is a case of an error note replacing an error note.

Very Fine	Extra Fine	New
150.00	200.00	300.00

Double Denomination
Following the back printing, notes of one denomination were inadvertently placed with those of another for the face printing. Errors of this type are most unusual.

The two notes above came from the same sheet. The note with serial number G1302448A graded EF brought $262.50 at the Grinnell sale in 1946.

Very Fine	Extra Fine	New
2,400.00	3,000.00	4,000.00

Double Denomination

These two large-size notes not only bear two different denominations, but they also were inverted when placed in the press for the face impression.

Very Fine	Extra Fine	New
2,700.00	3,200.00	4,500.00

Overprint on Corner Fold

The sheet from which this note was taken was flat during face and back printings. Before it received the overprint of the serial numbers, it took on a double fold. The outermost fold straightened out before the impression of the Treasury Seal was made.

Very Fine	Extra Fine	New
200.00	300.00	450.00

This note bears the same type of error, but only one fold occurred.

Very Fine	Extra Fine	New
100.00	125.00	200.00

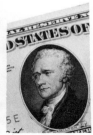

Adhering Loose Paper
Prior to 1957, when issues were wet printed, paper dividers and tickets were inserted in counted stacks of paper destined for the Bureau of Engraving and Printing. Occasionally these tear-out tickets or another loose piece of paper would go unnoticed and adhere to the paper, sometimes throughout the entire printing and cutting operations. (The bottom note was intended as a replacement note.)

New
500.00

Portion of Serial Numbers Missing

Four notes on this sheet lack a seal and complete serial numbers. A loose piece of paper must have been lying on the sheet along the line suggested by the broken line.

New
450.00

Mismatched Charter Numbers

National bank notes of the second and third charter period had the charter numbers printed in the border of each note. There are two similar charter numbers on the two notes above; the 3406 in the border indicates which number is correct. The second note belonged to the late William A. Philpott, Jr., and he thought it was unique. About seven years ago I surprised Mr. Philpott by showing him a similar error from the same bank.

The two charter numbers on the face of the note above agree, but the correct number, 1250, is in the border. Charter number 3557 is that of the Fourth Street National Bank in Philadelphia. Someone withdrew the wrong plate from the shelf when preparing notes for the New York Bank.

Very Fine	Extra Fine	New
600.00	1,200.00	1,650.00

Band-Aid Bill
Immediately after this note received the serial number imprint and just before the overprint of the Federal Reserve Seal was made, a tear-off section of a Band-Aid fell on the sheet. This note entered circulation and most certainly is unique.

$1½ Origami Note

This unique error was discovered in a pack of new notes as it appears in the first photograph; there are three distinct folds.

When the first fold is undone, a partial face and parts of two backs are revealed.

Face
As the note is
unfolded further you
can see three-fourths
of one face and
one-half of a second
face. The illustration
of the back view
shows similar error
proportions

Back

When all the folds are undone we
see one note plus one-half of
another. The partial note bears a
serial number with the fourth digit
differing by two. Both initial face
and back printings were normal. As
the sheet was being ejected, it
became folded in an origami
fashion and remained sandwiched
between other sheets.

New
_____

750.00

Sometime after the face printing but before the overprinting of seal and serial numbers a piece of paper, possibly a tear-out ticket, found its way into the position seen above. It's amazing that this error with a protruding tab escaped the eyes of the examiners.

New

750.00

COUNTERFEIT NOTES

Someone has said that the second coin struck in history was a counterfeit of the first. Counterfeiting therefore may rank as the second oldest profession.

Counterfeiters of coins generally tried to give short weight on the amount of precious metal in the coins. With the advent of paper money the counterfeiter's main concern has been the engraving since the cost of the paper is negligible. The United States printed its paper money on easily obtained commercial paper until 1879. Thereafter, as one more precaution against counterfeiting, a distinctive and unique paper was developed for the nation's currency. From 1879 until 1964, Crane and Company of Dalton, Massachusetts, was the sole supplier of paper to the Bureau of Engraving and Printing. In 1964 the Gilbert Paper Company of Menasha, Wisconsin, was contracted to produce 75 tons of paper annually for the Bureau. The paper manufactured for the Bureau continues to be of the finest quality, with distinctive red and green threads.

One fortunate result of the war against counterfeiting has been the enrichment of the currency to deter the poorer counterfeiters. Governments have employed the best artists to create paper money. The best designers and engravers and the finest inks are used, along with attractive features such as beautiful watermarks and watermarked portraits. All these factors combine to make some notes major works of art.

Following are some excerpts from *Heath's Infallible Counterfeit Detector at Sight,* first printed in 1867. The style is quaint, but I hope the advice will still be useful and interesting.

Art of Detecting Counterfeits, with Rules for General Guidance.

The art of detecting counterfeits consists *in becoming thoroughly familiar with genuine work, and in bringing any new or untested bond or note to a critical comparison with a plate known to be genuine.* It will be seen that this method is precisely the opposite of the old system, which made the counterfeit the basis of investigation, and which was consequently always at the mercy of any new or unfamiliar deception; for, under that system, the counterfeit must be learned before it could be detected, while by this method, as illustrated by this work, an accurate knowledge of the genuine, once obtained, renders any subsequent imposition impossible, except through indifference and neglect.

The following description of the various styles of Bank Note engraving, noting the variations therefrom as observed in counterfeits, and indicating the proper method of discriminating between counterfeit and genuine work, is commended to the careful study of all who desire to become familiar with the art of detecting counterfeits. And the student is advised that a casual or superficial reading of these pages is not sufficient to make him at once a master of this art. He must, by close analysis of, and careful and repeated reference to, these explanations and directions, familiarize his mind with the facts and principles here stated, and, by frequent examinations and comparison of these plates, and of the various devices and sections of Bank Notes, educate his eye to an exact knowledge of the constituent elements of genuine work. In the examination of plates, Bank Notes and Bonds, the microscope should be invariably used until the eye has become sufficiently experienced to dispense with this important aid.

The devices upon Bank Notes consist of vignettes, scrolls, borders, counters, corners, marine views, war scenes, etc. On genuine plates these devices are perfectly formed and symmetrically grouped. Such, however, is not the case in counterfeits; and no matter how near counterfeit work may approximate to the genuine, a close observer, with an ordinary microscope, and with the illustrations in this work from the genuine plates before him, may at once detect the imperfections and irregularities which distinguish the counterfeit from the genuine.

VIGNETTES

The figures and likenesses, which form the principal characteristics in vignettes, are drawn in accordance with a certain ideal standard of perfection. Female figures are generally represented with the arms, neck and feet bare, and their accuracy of proportion, and the delicacy of the work, are important guides in determining the genuineness of the plates. The texture of the skin is represented by fine dots and lines, an admixture of styles of engraving which is to be found in all vignettes, and the fineness and regularity of these dots and lines indicate the quality and reliability of the work. In the human figure, upon genuine plates, the eye, mouth, hair and attitude are perfectly natural, and the features are always sharp and striking. In counterfeits the features are usually blurred and expressionless, the eye is dull, the arms, feet and hair imperfect, and the dots and lines which form the face and the exposed portions of the person are large, coarse and uneven. A careful study of vignettes is recommended to all who desire to become experts in the art of detecting counterfeits.

THE ROUND HAND

This form of lettering is observed in the legend on the Bank Notes (which is the same in all), and in the words "Will pay the bearer." The curves and hair lines are drawn with positive accuracy. There may be a difference in the style of letter, but this will not change the precision of the work, as may be seen by comparing the curves and lines of one with those of another. This precision is never attained in counterfeits, as the microscope will disclose. For genuine specimens see any issue of Bank Notes in the illustrations which accompany this work.

PARALLEL RULING

The shading of letters and all parallel ruling upon Bank Notes is executed by the Parallel Ruling Machine. This machine is governed by an index which regulates the width of the lines. On all genuine notes the work is fine and clear, and the lines are strictly parallel. It is executed with such mathematical accuracy that, by the aid of the microscope, the lines are seen to be perfect, and, however, minute, can be easily counted. Clear skies are also usually formed of fine parallel lines. When cloudy or heavy skies are required, these lines are made to cross each other. Sometimes sky is formed of several broken etched lines. Great care should be taken to learn, by an examination of the plates, which portion of such work upon the genuine notes is done by etching, and which by parallel ruling. Parallel ruling is a very important branch of engraving, and one which cannot be too attentively studied. For specimen of genuine work, see parallel ruling on the lower side of the $1, $10, $50 and $500 United States Greenback. See also the shading of letters on all other plates. In counterfeits this work is usually coarse and imperfect, and the lines are seldom parallel. In endeavoring to count them they will be found broken, of irregular thickness, and lacking uniformity. Observe closely, in the genuine plates, the shading of letters and all other parallel lines.

GEOMETRICAL LATHE WORK

The lathe work upon Bank Notes is executed by the Geometrical Lathe, a machine which no counterfeiter can have opportunity, if he have the means, to properly construct or perfectly operate. By the simple turning of a screw, patterns are arbitrarily formed upon the die, comprising many variegated and beautiful combinations of geometrical figures, mathematically true to each other. This engraving can be made intricate at will, by certain peculiar manipulations, creating at every movement of the machine an intermingling of elaborate figures of design and finish which can never be exactly reproduced by the operator a second time. Lathe work is, therefore, the chief feature in note-engraving. It is found in all the government issues of notes, from the three-cent scrip up to the highest denomination of Bank Notes or Bonds issued by the government.

The borders, corners, denomination counters, and all oval and circular forms upon the Bank Notes are formed by the Geometrical Lathe. Notwithstanding the difficulties attending a successful counterfeiting of lathe work, there has been such work executed; and so well and elaborately was this work performed that additional precautions against deception have been felt to be necessary. Not only must the general clearness, exactness and finish of the genuine work be studied, but it is also essentially requisite that the peculiar formations of the lathe engraving upon any particular genuine note be thoroughly learned, as each plate and figure has its own special and characteristic features.

In examining lathe work for proof of genuineness, begin at the centre of the curvilinear figures, and then gradually follow the lines around the circles, one within the other, for the discovery of special defects which would otherwise be overlooked; also be careful and minute in comparing general designs.

Genuine Bank Notes

It is incorrect to suppose that it is necessary to become familiar with the work on counterfeit Bank Notes to enable the student to determine what is genuine or counterfeit. This method of detecting (which was the old one) would make it necessary to see every denomination of counterfeits issued, from the fact that no two counterfeits of different denominations are alike. This is not so with genuine Bank Notes, they being alike in all the principal parts that go to determine the genuine from the counter-feit. Therefore, if the student becomes *thoroughly* familiar with what constitutes a genuine Bank Note, he will readily detect at sight a counterfeit of any denomination.

PAPER.

The paper used by the government for Bonds and Bank Notes is possessed of a substantial body, has a fine finish, and presents to the eye a fibrous surface. When examined with a microscope these fibres have the appearance of coarse black hairs, of all conceivable lengths and shapes, scattered promiscuously, regardless of regularity, over the entire surface of the bond or note. A narrow strip of bluish color, termed "localized tint," extends across the entire note, and is the result of a second process. This paper is known as the Wilcox fibre, and presents a serious obstacle for counterfeiters to overcome.

INK.

The ink used by the United States Treasury Printing Bureau, and all Bank Note Companies, is manufactured expressly for printing Bonds and Bank Notes. It is jet black, and at first has a glossy appearance; the gloss, however, in time evaporates, yet the ink always retains its original and rich jet-black appearance, never assuming that rusty brown generally observed on counterfeits. The same may be said of the red ink in which the figures, letters and seal are printed on the face of the note. It always retains the original color, in no case turning to a wood-red color, as is the case with the red ink used on counterfeits.

VIGNETTES.

The vignettes on all Bonds and Bank Notes are engraved by the best artists in the country, and no pains are spared in bringing them to the highest state of perfection the mind can imagine. They are always noticeable for their superior workmanship, exquisite beauty and finish. In the vignettes the counterfeiter finds an obstacle not easily overcome, and seldom, if ever, succeeds in producing one that will not betray its base origin.

THE HUMAN FIGURE.

Portraits, male or female, are executed in the most artistic manner; the features being admirably engraved. The texture of the skin is composed of stipple work and lines intermingled. The stipple work, or dots, generally denote the parts on which the light falls, as may be seen by referring to the female portrait on the fifty-dollar Greenback. The lines represent the parts that are slightly shaded, as may also be seen on the same portrait.

The hair is tastefully and naturally arranged, and plainly denotes it is the work of an artist. When examined with a microscope, it will be observed that it is not a mere daub, as if made with a brush, but has a light and wavy appearance, looking perfectly natural.

The eyes are the most important feature of the portrait, and must necessarily be filled with animation, in order to give to the portrait an expression of naturalness. The pupil is, invariably, distinctly visible, showing the white clearly, thereby giving to the countenance a life-like appearance.

The nose, mouth, chin and neck are also engraved with a degree of perfection that is never found in counterfeits. The shape of the neck is displayed by the delicate shading. The arms possess a graceful sphericity. The fingers are natural, and display a life-like sense of touch. The drapery is gracefully arranged, and is composed of heavy and fine lines —the heavy lines denoting the coarser drapery, and the fine lines, that which has a gossamer-like appearance.

Counterfeit Bank Notes.

Herewith we present a few of the principal points which determine counterfeit Bank Notes.

PAPER.

The paper on which counterfeit Bank Notes are printed is generally of a pale-gray color, soft and flimsy to the touch, and wanting the beautiful finish of that used by the government for genuine notes.

Counterfeiters succeeded, however, in producing an article so nearly like the genuine that the government deemed it expedient to have a paper manufactured expressly on which to print Bonds, Bank Notes and Scrip, the result of which was the invention and manufacture of the paper known as the Wilcox fibre, now used exclusively by the government.

It was thought this would baffle the ingenuity of the counterfeiters —and it did for a time; but these brilliant geniuses have overcome *this* difficulty to a great extent in the production of a paper in good imitation of the Wilcox fibre, so that it becomes necessary even for connoisseurs in the art of detecting counterfeits to be on the alert.

INK.

The ink used is generally of an inferior quality, lacking both the body and the rich brilliancy of the genuine, and in a short time assumes a grayish appearance. The letters, figures and characters printed in red soon change to a pale wood-red, instead of retaining the brilliant carmine color like that used by the treasury department.

PRINTING.

It will be observed that the printing, when compared with the genuine, is poorly executed, having a coarse and blurred appearance, and especially when examined with a microscope.

PARALLEL RULING.

The parallel ruling used for shading the letters and backs is invariably imperfect; the lines are coarse and broken, and when subjected to a microscopical examination present a ragged and blurred appearance, and are seldom parallel.

GEOMETRICAL LATHE WORK.

Counterfeit lathe work can be detected by the blurred and dotted appearance of the lines where they intersect each other. These defects, which might be overlooked, can easily be detected by beginning in the centre of the curvilinear figures, and gradually following around the circles. On many counterfeits actual work of the lathe is to be found, the figures being made up of small circles, which would readily be detected by an educated eye.

PRINCIPAL FIGURE.

The object of the counterfeiter is to make the principal figure in the vignette the most attractive, and therefore he gives it the best finish, and brings it nearer to a state of perfection, knowing, if he accomplishes this point, the surrounding imperfections will not so readily be observed, which is true. With this idea deeply impressed upon his mind, he becomes so absorbed in what he considers the principal feature of the note, that he neglects those minor points that invariably add grace and beauty, and give to the note an exquisite finish.

THE HUMAN FIGURE.

In a counterfeit the hair is coarse, and not artistically arranged. The eyes are always imperfect, having a blurred and expressionless appearance. The arms, hands and feet (on earlier issues) are invariably poorly drawn. The dotted lines or stipple work denoting the flesh are coarser and darker. The shaded sides of the arms and legs are generally very dark. The fingers and toes are coarse and clumsy, seldom fully developed, and oftentimes drawn to a point, in both cases lacking the animation of the genuine. The drapery is solvenly arranged, and has an untidy appearance, whilst on the genuine it is artistically and gracefully arranged on the figure.

In conclusion, however, we must add, that counterfeiters have made such rapid strides in the art of counterfeiting on all these points, even experts are oftentimes deceived, unless they subject the counterfeit Bank Note to a microscopical examination.

Today, the unlucky receiver of a counterfeit bill must take the loss and turn the note over to the Secret Service. This wasn't so before the Act of Congress of March 4, 1909, which made the surrender of a counterfeit bill compulsory. Until then life was one big game of "passing the buck." Many a church collection plate in the nineteenth century was filled with dubious dollars, which parishioners had been stuck with the previous week. After all, who could pass on the phoney money for a better cause than the elders of the Church?

COUNTERFEIT OR GENUINE?

Compare any bill about which you are in doubt with a genuine note and observe the following details.

GENUINE

The background of a genuine note resembles a fine screen.

The portrait on a genuine note is lifelike, especially around the eyes.

The saw-tooth points around the rim of the seal are sharp and even.

COUNTERFEIT

The background of a counterfeit note is darker, with irregular, broken lines.

The counterfeit portrait lacks the lifelike quality. Many of the lines in the face merge together.

The same points on the seal of a bad note are uneven and appear to be broken.

The line inside the *1* is precise and un-broken.

Firm, evenly spaced serial numbers characterize genuine notes.

The lacelike engraving serving as a background for the *1* is precise.

Genuine bills are printed on a distinctive paper that has small red and blue threads embedded in it.

Here the line is usually weak and disappears at the lower right.

Serial numbers unevenly spaced and poorly printed suggest a counterfeit note.

On the counterfeit note these lines blend into one another, forming white spots in places.

Red and blue ink lines on paper of poor quality sometimes imitate the threads of a genuine note.

For years many people have believed that one could detect a counterfeit note by rubbing it on white paper. This is not so; ink can be rubbed from both genuine and counterfeit notes.

EXAMPLES FROM COUNTERFEIT DETECTORS

During the late nineteenth and early twentieth centuries, numerous counterfeit detectors were printed so bankers and businessmen would have a tool to aid them in detecting the flood of counterfeit notes which plagued the country. I have selected descriptions of bogus bills from *The National Counterfeit Detector* by Grant & Bushnell, published in 1916. The notes listed below, if authentic, would command a considerable premium today. In the event that one of these bills should turn up between the pages of an old bible, you might compare it with the description below. (The numbers refer to those in this catalog.)

Nos. 926–927 One of the most dangerous counterfeits ever issued. Engraving excellent, numbering good, lathe work fair. On genuine, back of note, small 50's in border are surrounded by octagons; on counterfeit they are circles. Two of these circles on lower left end are run together, omitting cipher, which makes figures read 550. Description of New Series 1, preceding, applies to this note. Portrait of Hamilton.

Note: (It is doubtful if any authentic notes of this issue have survived, including the illustration in this catalog.—the author.)

No. 939 Dangerous. Portrait of Franklin very clear, except line of mouth and opening of ear, more pronounced. Small scalloped carmine-red seal closely resembles genuine Words "Act of March 3, 1863," over portrait of Franklin, also name "Benjamin Franklin," under portrait, the words "Engraved and Printed Bureau Engraving and Printing," to left of portrait of Franklin, and word "Series" over letter "N" in "United States," are omitted on face. Penalty for "Counterfeiting" in panel left end back, words "Series of 1880" in panel in right end back and imprint "Bureau Engraving and Printing, Washington, D. C.," in centre lower border back, are omitted. Paper of good quality, and distributed red and blue silk fibre is cleverly imitated by red and blue ink lines. Other counterfeits are likely to appear differing in number, seal and check letter, and bearing other signatures.

No. 1122 One of most dangerous counterfeits in existence. Engraving and workmanship nearly equal to genuine. Lathe work excellent. Treasury numbers fair and color of ink good. Star on right of Treasury number blurred. Portrait of J. Q. Adams excellent, but lobe of ear is indistinct. In counterfeit, button upon coat, nearest lapel, almost square; in genuine it is round. Vignette of figure Justice finely engraved, except following: As scale is held aloft in left hand, upright holding beam is crooked, and is larger than in genuine; in genuine, upright shows only to lower part of hand, while in counterfeit it shows to second finger from base; white curve in arm is a perfect oval in genuine; in counterfeit it is not. Left foot of vignette, as it extends from garment, presents a clubbed appearance in counterfeit, while toes are short and not one-half length of genuine. Parallel ruling is excellent. Note is printed on fibre paper, signed "John Allison, Register," and "F. E. Spinner, Treasurer," Bankers and others should receive these notes with great care, as it is only by comparison with genuine that majority of experts can positively decide as to genuineness of a note of this class. Nearly all of this issue have been retired by Treasury, very few genuine notes now being in circulation. These notes should be received for collection only.

No. 1221 A very dangerous counterfeit. Most noticeable defect is in portrait. In genuine, Monroe represented as having pronounced cheek bones, one on left side of face being particularly prominent, while in counterfeit left cheek bone is missing, making face appear narrower than in genuine, and giving counterfeit different expression. In genuine right ear plainly parts hair, which is brushed upward in front and back of ear, while in counterfeit hair hides top of ear, and is not brushed upward. In name "James" under portrait letters "J" and "A" are not uniform with rest of letters, and bottom of "J" has more of upward loop than in genuine. Geometric lathe work, lettering, numbering and parallel ruling in panel in which Treasury numbers appear are almost equal to genuine, but a critical examination will show parallel lines to be somewhat broken, particularly in lower left border. Treasury numbers are almost perfect, both in color and formation, but the figure 5 in the Treasury number is different, the space within lower loop being oblong, up and down, instead of being round, and space below top line of 5 is too narrow. One of the best points is the top button of waistcoat; this counterfeit top button has lines on it up and down only, and they show well and distinct, while genuine top button alone is cross lined (lines up and down and crosswise also), but these lines are delicate, and by wear, bad printing, dirt, etc., they may thus be wanting or overlooked. Geometrical lathe work and lettering on back of note to the naked eye appears as good as genuine. Back plate No. 2.

No. 1234 Dangerous lithographic production printed on genuine paper evidently obtained by bleaching a bill of smaller denomination. Some of the work is excellent, notably the signatures of the Register and Treasurer, seal, numbering and portions of border design. The flat appearance of portrait of Benton in medallion is characteristic of lithographic work. The lines "there have been deposited in" and "repayable to the bearer on demand" in script lettering on face of note are too heavy and have the appearance of pen work, no doubt caused by retouching plate. *While we speak of the color of the yellow (gold) ink on the gold certificates being off color, etc., it is a fact that the Government so far has been unable to procure an ink that will stand climatic changes, etc.*

No. 1242 Dangerous photographic pen and ink counterfeit. In portrait of Farragut, nose appears longer and upper lip extends outward, while in genuine latter appears drawn in, giving determined expression. Imprint "Bureau Engraving and Printing," in border, right end, missing. Lathe word surrounding large 100 poor; color of large spiked chocolate real good. Imprint "Bureau Engraving and Printing," bottom centre of note, missing.

Nos. 1376–1378 Very Dangerous. Engraving nearly equal to genuine. A mistake was made in genuine issue under this act, which counterfeiters copied, that of dating notes March 10, 1862, instead of 1863. This error was corrected in a subsequent issue of the genuine. On face of counterfeit lathe work in the border and on corner is much inferior to genuine. On left end of face, in border, words "Act of March 3, 1863," much coarser. Circles of 1,000 surrounding portrait of Morris much more irregular than in genuine. On counterfeit face of Morris is more front view. On genuine eyes cast more to left. Imprint "American Bank Note Co.," on right end of border is much narrower than on genuine. On back of note the four points at each end of note are much more pointed than on genuine. These differences were all noted by comparison with a genuine note of same date and check letter. Very few genuine notes of this denomination and issue are in circulation. Bankers and others are warned to handle these notes with great care.

SOUVENIR CARDS FROM THE BUREAU OF ENGRAVING AND PRINTING

Until a few years ago the Bureau issued souvenir cards for philatelists only. Now we syngraphists have our own handsome souvenir cards to collect. In 1969 the Bureau of Engraving and Printing issued a souvenir card in honor of the 78th annual convention of the American Numismatic Association. This card was beautifully engraved and printed with all the skill and artistry that the Bureau employs on its bills and stamps, with the same inks and techniques. The 1969 souvenir card featured Henry Gugler's American eagle as it appears on the $10 United States notes (No. 466 in this catalog), sometimes irreverently referred to as the "Jackass Note." The first card was issued at $1, and subsequent cards have been issued at the same price.

	Cards Printed
ANA 78th Anniversary Card (1969)	12,362

In 1970 the Bureau of Engraving and Printing honored the American Numismatic Association with the issue of a second souvenir card. The ANA 79th Anniversary card featured eight notes arranged in an attractive collage, "which will exemplify the many facets of the engraver's art and the printer's skill for quality rendition."

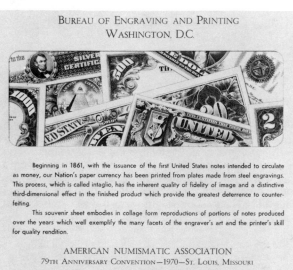

	Cards Printed
ANA 79th Anniversary Card (1970)	12,017

The issuance of a souvenir card to mark the annual convention of the American Numismatic Association seems to have become established as something to look forward to each year. In 1971 the Bureau presented the collecting world with still another handsome example of the engraving art. The card for the 80th Anniversary of the ANA featured the vignette of *History Instructing Youth* as seen on the $1 Educational note of 1896 (No. 359 in this catalog).

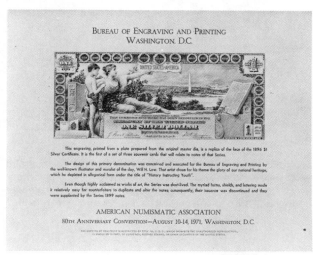

	Cards Printed
ANA 80th Anniversary Card (1971)	54,721

A natural companion of the souvenir card of the previous year would be the engraving of another Educational note, and so the $2 note was chosen. This beautiful vignette of *Science Presenting Steam and Electricity to Commerce and Manufacture* was originally intended for a higher denomination. (No. 186 in this catalog.)

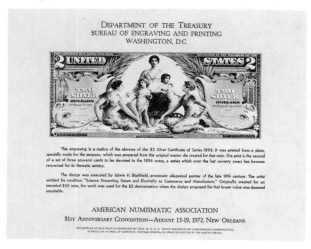

	Cards Printed
ANA 81st Anniversary Card (1972)	74,172

To complete the Educational series reproduced as souvenir cards in 1971 and 1972, the Bureau has given us the $5 note design. See No. 359 for design and engraving information.

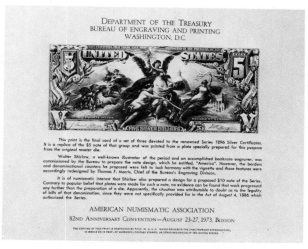

	Cards Printed
ANA 82nd Anniversary Card (1973)	49,544

As a bonus to accompany the three previous souvenir cards, the Bureau of Engraving and Printing produced a card in 1974 which gave us the proposed design for a $10 silver certificate intended to be part of the Educational Series.

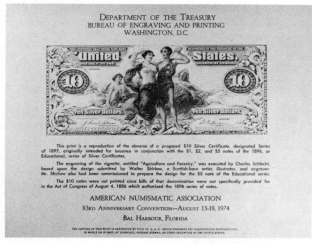

	Cards Printed
ANA 83rd Anniversary Card (1974)	41,591

The back design of the 1896 $1 silver certificate compliments the souvenir card of 1971. 1975 was designated as International Women's Year and the Bureau selected this design which bears the portrait of Martha Washington, the only woman who has appeared on United States currency. See no. 36 in this catalog for designer and engraver information.

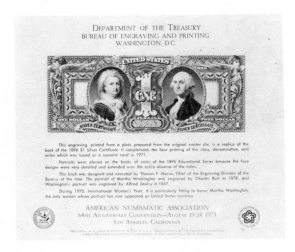

	Cards Printed
ANA 84th Anniversary Card (1975)	45,593

On the occasion of IWY, the Bureau produced a brochure with a removable souvenir card which will satisfy syngraphists and philatelists alike. The card consists of the $1 silver certificate face design of 1886 which bears the image of Martha Washington and three stamp designs with the following portraits: Frances E. Willard, Elizabeth Stanton, Carrie C. Catt, Lucretia Mott, and Jane Addams. See no. 45 in this catalog for designer and engraver information pertaining to the $1 design.

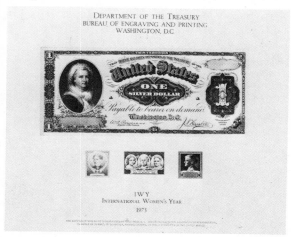

	Cards Printed
IWY, International Women's Year 1975	28,022

The back design of the 1896 $2 silver certificate complements the souvenir card of 1972. The choice for the 1976 card was most appropriate since it was during our bicentennial year that the $2 bill was reintroduced. See No. 186 in this catalog for design and engraver information.

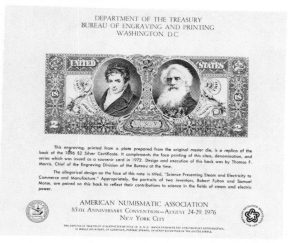

	Cards Printed
ANA 85th Anniversary Card (1976)	38,636

PAPER MONEY CIRCULATED OUTSIDE THE CONTINENTAL U.S.

Alaska

"Seward's Folly" was the purchase of Alaska from the Imperial Russian Government in 1867 for the sum of $7.2 million. William H. Seward, who negotiated the purchase as Secretary of State, took much abuse because of his "Ice Box," but he has been vindicated a thousand times over since then. Alaska is now our largest state, becoming the 49th state of the Union in 1958.

Alaska and its outlying islands were surveyed by the great explorers James Cook, George Vancouver, Alexander MacKenzie, and Vitus Bering under the auspices of the Russian government. The Czar took control of Alaska. In 1790 a joint venture was formed by royal charter, called The Russian-American Company, to exploit the natural resources of Alaska. Trading for furs, skins, and ivory was brisk, and the company issued unusual currency printed on seal skin between 1818 and 1825. The notes were in denominations of 10, 25, and 50 kopecks, and 1 ruble.

Before 1938 privately issued tokens and scrip circulated in Alaska. No special federal currency other than national bank notes was printed for the District of Alaska. The large- and small-size Alaskan national bank notes are of the highest rarity.

Face and back of 1 ruble sealskin note.

No. 311 in this catalog.

No. 793 in this catalog.

No. 390 in this catalog.

No. 627 in this catalog.

The $20 Juneau note is illustrated through the courtesy of Amon Carter, Jr. The two small-size notes were made available by M.O. Warns.

Hawaii

Today, the tourist who comes to Hawaii is welcomed with a lei, a wreath of friendship. Captain James Cook, who sailed to the Hawaiian Islands in 1778, received a shower of spears as a welcome, and his death site is marked by a monument today.

Christian missionaries arrived in Hawaii in large enough numbers to discourage such a hostile reception. In 1840 the missionaries persuaded King Kamehameha III to declare his kingdom a constitutional monarchy. In 1893, with the deposition of Queen Liliuokalani, a provisional government was formed under American control. In 1898 Hawaii was annexed to the United States. It became a territory in 1900 and a state in 1959.

The first paper money to be issued by American authority in Hawaii was the second charter national currency note series. A few of the large- and small-size national currency notes are scarce, but most fall in the extremely rare category. Notes bearing a "Hawaii" overprint were used during World War II, presumably to foil use by the Japanese in the event of a successful invasion. These notes are listed in this catalog with the $1 silver certificates and the $5, $10, and $20 Federal Reserve notes.

The First National Bank of Hawaii at Honolulu became the Bishop First National Bank on July 6, 1929.

All denominations except $20 notes were issued by the National Bank in Hawaii as small-size notes.

The Philippines

As a result of the Spanish-American War of 1898, the United States took control of most of the Spanish Empire in the Caribbean and the Pacific. The war ended with Admiral Dewey's blowing up the Spanish battleships in Manila harbor. By 1901 the American government had successfully replaced Spanish rule. On July 4, 1946, the Philippine Islands gained their independence when they became the Republic of the Philippines.

Spanish-Philippine currency is dated as early as 1852. In 1903 the first notes under American rule were issued. Four issues circulated from 1903 until the end of American authority. They are silver certificates, treasury certificates, Philippine National Bank circulating notes, and the Bank of the Philippine Islands notes. All four issues were printed by the United States Bureau of Engraving and Printing.

Sheet Size

Silver certificates . . . . 5 subjects
Treasury certificates . . . . .10 subjects
Philippine National Bank circulating notes:
   (1916-1920) . . . . 5 subjects
   (1921-1937) . . . . .10 subjects
Bank of the Philippine Islands notes . . . . 5 subjects

For a more comprehensive account of all the Philippine paper money, I refer you to Neil Shafer's authoritative *Guide Book of Philippine Paper Money.*

Silver Certificates (1903-1918)

The convenient, small size of these notes prompted the United States to think of a similar size for all its own currency. The change to this smaller size took place in 1929 for all United States paper money.

The Philippine silver certificates were accepted at the rate of two Philippine pesos for one U.S. dollar. In 1906 the redemption clause was changed, whereby silver certificates were redeemable "in silver pesos or in gold coin of the United States of equivalent value." Originally these notes were redeemable only in silver pesos.

Series	Denominations (Pesos)
1903	2, 5, and 10
1905	20, 50, 100, and 500
1906	2 and 500
1908	20-
1910	5
1912	10
1016	50 and 100

Face: Series 1903; portrait of William McKinley.

Back

Face: Series 1905; the note illustrated is a specimen and bears the portrait of General Henry W. Lawton.

Back

Face: Series 1906;
the note illustrated is
a specimen and
bears the portrait of
the first Spanish
Colonial Governor,
Miguel Lopez de
Legazpi.

Back

Treasury Certificates (1918-1949)

On August 1, 1918, silver certificates were replaced by treasury certificates. New notes in 1936 reflected the Philippines' Commonwealth status, which had come about in 1935. "Philippines" replaced the former legend "Philippine Islands" on the earlier treasury and silver certificates, and a new seal was introduced. Treasury certificates were issued after independence in 1946, and they continued to circulate until 1964.

Series	Denominations (Pesos)
1918	1, 2, 5, 10, 20, 50, 100, and 500
1924	1, 2, 5, 10, 20, and 500
1929	1, 2, 5, 10, 20, 50, 100, and 500
1936	1, 2, 5, 10, 20, 50, 100, and 500
1941	1, 2, 5, 10, and 20
1944 (victory)	1, 2, 5, 10, 20, 50, 100, and 500

The last issue, with "VICTORY" overprinted on the back, was issued to accompany General MacArthur's return.

Face: Series 1929.

Back

Face: Series 1936.

Face: Series 66
(1944).

Back

Philippine National Bank Circulating Notes (1916-1937)

The Philippine National Bank came into existence through the efforts of William A. Jones, whose portrait appears on the 20 peso note. Charles A. Conant, the man who was instrumental in setting up the Philippine currency system, is represented on the 1 peso note. These National Bank circulating notes were used until June 1, 1948, when they were withdrawn. They were redeemable for one year after they left circulation.

Series	Denominations (Pesos)
1916	2, 5, and 10
1917*	10, 20, 50 centavos and 1
1918	1
1919	20
1920	50 and 100
1921	1, 2, 5, 10, and 20
1924	1
1937	5, 10, and 20

*These were emergency notes printed in the Philippines.

Face: Series 1918.

Back

Face: Series 1920.

Back

Face: Series 1921.

Back

Face: Series 1937.

Back

Bank of the Philippine Islands (1908-1933)

In 1852 the Banco Español-Filipino was established; in 1908 the Spanish title was changed to the Bank of the Philippine Islands. With the beginning of World War II all notes issued by this bank were withdrawn.

Series	Denominations (Pesos)
1908*	5, 10, 20, 50, 100, and 200
1912	5, 10, 20, 50, 100, and 200
1920	5, 10, and 20
1928	5, 10, 20, 50, 100, and 200
1933	5, 10, and 20

*This issue retained the original name of Banco Español-Filipino.

Face: 1908 issue:

Back

Face: Series 1933.

Puerto Rico

Puerto Rico, the "rich port" of the West Indies, was taken by the United States as a territory after the Spanish-American War of 1898. The tropical island had been made into a province of the Spanish Empire after Columbus landed there in 1493. Puerto Rico's first governor in 1509 was the famous Juan Ponce de Leon.

Paper money was issued by the Spanish authorities in Puerto Rico as early as 1813. In 1900, when Puerto Rico had become an American possession by the terms of the Treaty of Paris, notes of that date were overprinted as *Moneda Americana* to show the change of authority. These overprinted notes are sometimes collected along with the special notes issued by the United States for the territory. National bank notes were printed for use in Puerto Rico, but these large-size notes are extremely rare.

On December 28, 1898, President McKinley proclaimed that beginning January 1, 1899, the currency of Puerto Rico would consist of United States coins and notes. The Spanish 25 peseta gold piece and the French 20 franc gold piece became the only money acceptable for customs, taxes, and postage. The native Puerto Rican coinage, which closely resembled that of Spain, was gradually withdrawn from circulation and melted. Today, the Territory of Puerto Rico uses current U.S. coins and bills.

Face: 1900 issue. Overprinted *Moneda Americana.*

Back

(Courtesy David Tang)

Face: 1904 issue. Moneta, goddess of money, is in the center.

Back

(Illustrations above through the courtesy of the Western Publishing Co.)

Face: 1909 issue; portrait of Columbus.

Face: No. 316 in this catalog.

See No. 1,196 for $100 notes.

The United States Virgin Islands

On his second voyage to the New World in 1493, Christopher Columbus sailed to a group of islands that he named in honor of the Virgin Mary. The Virgin Island group consists of three large islands, named Saint Thomas, Saint John, and Saint Croix, with a number of smaller islands and cays.

In 1671 the Danish West India Company claimed the islands in the midst of the Spanish Empire. In 1867, after the Civil War, the United States wanted a strategic base in the West Indies, especially after the experience of the French invasion of Mexico under Maximilian. Negotiations for the purchase of the islands were begun in 1867 and were consummated in 1917, when World War I and the advent of German submarines and raiders made the need for a naval base even more urgent.

The National Bank of the Danish West Indies had been in existence since 1905. Under the new American rule, the bank was granted permission to issue gold certificates. All gold certificates were withdrawn in 1934. These notes are especially desirable to the collector since they are unique. They are the only notes in our history to be printed in two languages (Danish and English), to bear the portrait of a foreign monarch (King Christian IX of Denmark), and to be legal tender in the United States.

Three additional notes issued by territories are Nos. 171, 282, and 956 in this catalog.

Face: 1905 issue.

Back

Face: 1905 issue.

Back

ALLIED MILITARY CURRENCY

Allied Military Currency (AMC) was issued during the 1940s for the occupation of Austria, France, Germany, Italy, Japan, and Okinawa. It gave syngraphists another type of paper money to collect. This currency was issued under the authority of the Allied powers, but it is rightfully listed in a catalog of U.S. paper money because of the major role played by the United States (on the part of the Allies) in its issuance and use. The majority of the printing was accomplished in the United States and, most importantly, it was used by millions of U.S. service personnel around the world in daily financial transactions.

The Bureau of Engraving and Printing was unable to print all issues of AMC and consequently authorized private printers to produce some of the notes. These printers were The Forbes Lithograph Co. of Boston and The Stecher-Traung Lithograph Co. of San Francisco. These printing companies were allowed to place an identifying mark on the pieces they printed.

Allied Military Currency was a joint venture of the major Allied powers. Each issue of AMC was intended to fulfill one or more of the following goals:

1. It would meet the need for a currency for immediate use in civil commerce;
2. It would be a convenient way to impose the cost of occupation upon the occupied land by having the Allied Military Government issue the currency but requiring the local government to redeem it at a later date;
3. The use of a common currency by the Allied powers would signify their unity to the occupied lands as well as to the as yet unconquered enemies.

To best fulfill these goals, the notes had to be in local currency units; five distinct issues were used, within which many varieties exist. The units of issue were schillings (Austria), francs (France), marks (Germany), lire (Italy), and yen (Korea, Japan, and Okinawa).

As with Military Payment Certificates, the popularity of collecting AMC in the United States has increased tremendously in the past few years. Its further acceptance as a legitimate addition to a U.S. currency collection should expand this interest.

Even after thirty years there are many details concerning AMC use which remain unknown or obscured. Such obvious facts as the issue and redemption dates are not known for all issues. Information continues to be uncovered and it is hoped that the increasing interest in this field will yield additional data.

The numbering system used here was adapted from *World War II Allied Military Currency* (1974) with permission from the publisher. All of the subvarieties are not listed here, and the numbering of supplemental yen has been modified to reflect changes which will occur in a future edition of the above reference.

AUSTRIA/Series of 1944

The notes printed for use in Austria bear two different water marks. The first, "Allied Military Authority", indicates the U.S. printing; the second, horizontal or wavy lines, will identify notes printed in Great Britain. A portion of the 50 groschen, 1, and 2 schilling notes were printed by Forbes Lithograph Company, but no identifying mark was placed on these bills. An "X" on the face indicates a replacement note.

Sizes: 50 groschen, 1, 2 schilling   114 x 58 mm
       5, 10 schilling   ·   114 x 72 mm
       20, 25, 50 schilling   138 x 77 mm
       100, 1000 schilling   150 x 84 mm

Face Design

No.	Denomination	Printer	Notes Issued	Good	Very Fine	New
1	50 groschen	US	100,000,000	3.00	6.50	14.00
2	50 groschen	GB	Unknown	.50	1.00	2.00
3	1 schilling	US	200,000,000	2.00	4.50	10.00
4	1 schilling	GB	Unknown	.50	1.00	1.75
5	2 schilling	US	100,000,000	2.00	4.50	10.00
6	2 schilling	GB	Unknown	.50	1.00	2.00
7	5 schilling	GB	Unknown	.50	1.25	2.50
8	10 schilling	GB	Unknown	.50	1.25	3.00
9	20 schilling	GB	Unknown	.75	1.75	3.50
10	25 schilling	US	129,000,000	—	35.00	80.00
11	50 schilling	GB	Unknown	.75	1.75	3.50
12	100 schilling	GB	Unknown	1.25	2.50	4.50
13	1000 schilling	GB	Unknown	25.00	60.00	125.00

FRANCE/Series of 1944

Two types of notes were printed entirely by the Forbes Lithograph Co. of Boston, Massachusetts for use in France. An "f", their identifying printer's mark, was placed at the lower left on the 2, 5, and 10 franc notes. Both types of 50, 100, 500, and 1000 franc notes had the "f" placed at the right of the shield at top center. The numbering cylinders at Forbes were limited to eight digits, therefore an "X" was added to 99,999,999 to make the 100,000,000th note. The "X" was also used on replacement notes. A number in bold face type printed twice on the face indicates a note subsequent to the first 100,000,000.

Sizes: 2, 5, 10 francs   77 x 66 mm
       50, 100, 500, 1000 francs   155 x 66 mm

Face Design:
100 franc
replacement note.

Back Design:
Supplemental franc
notes.

Back Design:
Committee franc
notes.

Supplemental Francs

No.	Denomination	Notes Issued	Good	Very Fine	New
14	2 francs	200,000,000	.15	.25	.50
15	5 francs	160,000,000	.15	.25	.50
16	10 francs	80,000,000	.25	.35	.75
17	50 francs	40,000,000	.75	2.00	4.50
18	100 francs	144,000,000	1.00	2.75	7.00
19	500 francs	20,000,000	40.00	90.00	200.00
20	1000 francs	40,000,000	90.00	320.00	500.00
20 a	5000 francs	Not Issued	Specimens Were Made		

Committee Francs

No.	Denomination	Notes Issued	Good	Very Fine	New
21	50 francs	290,000,000	1.00	2.00	3.50
22	100 francs	950,000,000	1.00	3.00	4.50
23	500 francs	Not Issued	Specimens Were Made		
24	1000 francs	250,000,000	50.00	100.00	200.00
25	5000 francs	Officially Unissued			500.00

GERMANY/Series of 1944

All the notes used in the four zones of occupied Germany were printed in the United States or the Soviet Union from plates provided by the Bureau of Engraving and Printing. Once again the identifying "f" is found in the lower right hand corner of the ½, 1, and 5 mark notes and in the upper right hand corner of the 10, 20, 50, 100, and 1000 mark notes. A hyphen was placed before the serial number of all Soviet-printed notes. A hyphen was also used for a U.S. replacement note, however the "f" will differentiate the Soviet and the U.S. notes with hyphens. When the Soviet numbering system reached 100,000,000 the hypen was replaced with a number.

Sizes: ½, 1, 5 marks   78 x 66 mm
   10 marks   112 x 65 mm
   20, 50, 100, 1000 marks 155 x 65 mm

Face Design:
The printer's identification mark on this 1 mark note can be seen in the accompanying enlargement of the lower right-hand portion of the note.

Back Design

Face Design:
This 1000 mark specimen note bears the printer's mark in the upper right-hand portion of the note. See the accompanying enlargement for exact position.

No.	Denomination	Printer	Notes Issued	Good	Very Fine	New
26	½ mark	U.S.	75,448,000	.10	.25	.50
27	½ mark	USSR	Unknown	1.00	2.50	5.00
28	1 mark	U.S.	114,396,000	.10	.25	.50
29	1 mark	USSR	Unknown	.25	.60	1.00
30	5 marks	U.S.	75,896,000	.40	.60	1.00
31	5 marks	USSR	Unknown	.40	.60	1.00
32	10 marks	U.S.	77,800,000	.50	.75	1.50
33	10 marks	USSR	Unknown	.50	.75	1.50
34	20 marks	U.S.	75,544,000	1.00	2.00	4.00
35	20 marks	USSR	Unknown	.50	1.50	3.00
36	50 marks	U.S.	61,120,000	1.00	2.00	4.00
37	50 marks	USSR	Unknown	.75	1.50	3.00
38	100 marks	U.S.	48,084,000	1.00	3.25	6.50
39	100 marks	USSR	Unknown	1.00	2.00	4.00
40	1000 marks	U.S.	4,532,000	(Officially Unissued)		275.00
41	1000 marks	USSR	Unknown	15.00	50.00	100.00

ITALY/Series of 1943

The printing of the notes for use in Italy was shared by the Bureau of Engraving and Printing and the Forbes Lithograph Co. The latter placed an "f" at the lower right hand corner of the face. For the first time a star was used on Allied Military Currency to indicate a replacement note.

Sizes: 1, 2, 5, 10 lire   76 x 66 mm
       50, 100, 1000 lire   155 x 66 mm

Face Design

No.	Denomination	Printer	Notes Issued	Good	Very Fine	New
42	1 lira	BEP	37,600,000	.20	.40	.75
43	1 lira	Forbes	57,000,000	.20	.40	.75
44	2 lire	BEP	36,600,000	.20	.40	.75
45	2 lire	Forbes	37,200,000	.20	.40	.75
46	5 lire	BEP	24,700,000	.25	.50	1.00
47	5 lire	Forbes	42,900,000	.25	.50	1.00
48	10 lire	BEP	10,100,000	.30	.60	1.25
49	10 lire	Forbes	12,100,000	.30	.60	1.25
50	50 lire	BEP	15,600,000	1.00	2.00	4.00
51	50 lire	Forbes	33,700,000	.75	1.75	3.75
52	100 lire	BEP	14,800,000	1.00	2.50	5.00
53	100 lire	Forbes	23,700,000	.75	2.00	4.00
54	500 lire	BEP	6,000,000	7.50	14.00	30.00
55	500 lire	Forbes	1,800,000	9.00	20.00	50.00
56	1000 lire	BEP	3,000,000	12.50	30.00	75.00
57	1000 lire	Forbes	1,200,000	15.00	35.00	100.00

ITALY/Series of 1943A

The Forbes Lithograph Co. printed this entire issue and continued their serial numbering where the 1943 series had ended. The prefix and suffix letters on all 1943 notes were A-A, however when 100,000,000 was reached on the 1943A series, numbering began again with suffix B.

For the first time there was a devious attempt, with some success, at raising the 50 and 100 lire notes to 500 and 1000 by adroitly adding another zero.

Sizes are the same as series of 1943.

Face Design

No.	Denomination	Notes Issued	Good	Very Fine	New
58	5 lire	65,336,000	.20	.50	1.00
59	10 lire	113,696,000	.25	.60	1.25
60	50 lire	94,383,000	.75	2.00	3.75
61	100 lire	161,492,000	1.00	2.75	5.00
62	500 lire	59,108,000	3.50	9.00	22.50
63	1000 lire	69,108,000	7.50	16.50	32.50

JAPAN & OKINAWA/Series 100

These notes, first issued in Korea on September 7, 1945, all have a uniform appearance except for a large "A" or "B" doubly outlined on the face. All notes except the 1000 yen with prefix and suffix A were printed by Stecher-Traung of San Francisco under contract to the Bureau of Engraving and Printing. The prefix A was dropped and an H added for replacement notes. In 1955 the Bureau delivered 2,624,000, 1 yen notes with B-B serial numbers; for replacement notes, the B suffix was deleted. In 1950, the U.S. Civil Service Administration replaced the U.S. Military Government and notes were then ordered from Japan's Ministry of Finance Printing Bureau. Both printing sources used identification marks. Stecher-Traung used an "S" and those notes printed in Japan bear a "J."

Sizes: 10, 50 sen, 1 yen   77 x 65 mm
        5 yen   113 x 65 mm
        20, 100, 1000 yen   156 x 66 mm

Face Design:
The printer's mark on this 1 yen note can be seen in the accompanying enlargement of the lower left side of the note.

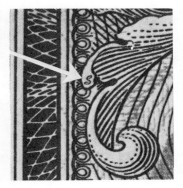

Back Design

Supplemental yen, large A

No.	Denomination	Notes Issued	Good	Very Fine	New
64	10 sen	93,456,000	1.50	3.75	9.50
65	50 sen	76,688,000	1.75	3.50	8.50
66	1 yen	66,176,000	1.00	2.00	5.00
67	5 yen	29,840,000	3.75	8.25	22.00
68	10 yen	51,880,000	4.50	10.00	26.00
69	20 yen	4,506,000	30.00	62.50	200.00
70	100 yen	9,144,000	87.50	260.00	550.00

Supplemental yen, large B

No.	Denomination	Printer	Notes Issued	Good	Very Fine	New
71	10 sen	S-T	51,856,000	.10	.25	.50
72	50 sen	S-T	43,344,000	.10	.25	.50
73	1 yen (A...A)	S-T	53,984,000	.25	.50	.75
73a	1 yen (B...B)	BEP	2,624,000	2.00	5.00	9.50
73b	1 yen (C...C, D...D)	Japan	15,360,000	.15	.35	.75
74	5 yen (A...A)	S-T	27,000,000	.25	.65	1.00
74a	5 yen (B...B)	Japan	2,000,000	2.00	5.00	10.00
75	10 yen	S-T	60,000,000	.75	1.00	1.65
76	20 yen	S-T	35,408,000	1.00	3.00	4.75
77	100 yen	S-T	39,042,000	1.00	3.25	7.50
78	1000 yen	Japan	5,500,000	87.50	300.00	600.00

MILITARY PAYMENT CERTIFICATES

A whole new world of collecting was opened to the syngraphist after World War II. The victorious United States found itself occupying large areas of countries whose economies were in a state of collapse. At this time United States military personnel overseas were being paid in local currencies, which could later be changed into dollars. This system resulted in the conversion to dollars of vast amounts of francs and marks. U.S. servicemen added to their supply of convertible currency by doing a brisk business in cigarettes, silk stockings, and candy bars.

The need for new currency was supplied by the issuance of United States military payment certificates, valid only in certain areas and under the complete control of the occupying military authority. These certificates were issued to American military and civilian personnel. The first issue came out on September 16, 1946, as Series 461.

These new notes differed from the regular United States bills in that they were not printed by engraved plates at the Bureau of Engraving and Printing. Instead, they were lithographed by private printing firms on a paper different from that used for the regular currency. The paper was embedded with planchettes of minute, colored discs rather than with colored threads. Thus there is a similarity to the first printing of the federal greenbacks in that both the military payment certificates and the greenbacks were manufactured by private firms rather than by the government itself.

The printing firms and series issued are as follows:

Series 461 ⎤
Series 471 ⎟
Series 472 ⎟ Tudor Press Corporation, Inc., Boston
Series 541 ⎦
Series 481 ⎤
Series 521 ⎟ Forbes Lithographic Company, Boston
Series 591 ⎦

Series 611, issued on January 6, 1964, and those that have followed were all printed by the Bureau of Engraving and Printing.

As with the regular United States paper money, certain notes are prepared to replace defective ones. Military payment certificate replacement notes have a separate numbering sequence; replacement notes are easily identified, since the suffix letter is deleted.

Periodically, it was necessary to recall all circulating military payment certificates and issue a new series. Change-over, or C-Day, is quietly put into operation and is completed within a 24-hour period. Counterfeiters, black market operators, and unauthorized holders of these certificates are thereby caught off guard.

U.S. military payment certificates no longer circulate anywhere in the world.

Size of Military Payment Certificates

5¢ through 50¢: 110 X 55 mm.
$1: 112 X 66 mm.
$5; Series 461 through 481: 156 X 66 mm.
$5; Series 521 and subsequent issues: 136 X 66 mm.
$10 and $20: 156 X 66 mm.

Series 461/Issued September 16, 1946

Face: Grey and aqua with black print.

Back: Reddish tan, brown print.

Denomination	Notes Issued	Fine	Very Fine	Extra Fine	New
5¢	7,616,000	.75	2.00	5.00	10.00
10¢	8,064,000	.75	2.00	5.00	10.00
25¢	4,704,000	1.75	5.00	9.00	25.00
50¢	4,032,000	2.75	5.00	10.00	25.00
$1	14,560,000	2.00	4.00	10.00	25.00
$5	5,400,000	8.00	12.00	27.50	60.00
$10	40,800,000	12.50	16.00	25.00	55.00

Series 471/Issued March 10, 1947

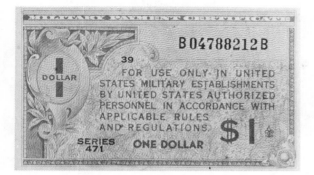

Face: Aqua and red, red print.

Back: Blue, red print.

Denomination	Notes Issued	Fine	Very Fine	Extra Fine	New
5¢	8,288,000	3.00	4.00	7.50	15.00
10¢	7,616,000	3.00	4.00	7.50	15.00
25¢	4,480,000	5.00	7.50	13.00	25.00
50¢	4,032,000	5.00	7.50	13.00	27.50
$1	14,560,000	4.00	7.50	13.00	30.00
$5	5,400,000	350.00	625.00	900.00	1,500.00
$10	13,600,000	100.00	175.00	275.00	450.00

Series 472/Issued March 22, 1948

Face: Aqua, black print.

Back: Violet, brown print.

Denomination	Notes Delivered	Fine	Very Fine	Extra Fine	New
5¢	7,960,000	25.00	.50	.75	1.50
10¢	7,960,000	25.00	.50	.75	2.00
25¢	4,824,000	2.00	3.50	6.00	12.50
50¢	4,232,000	3.50	5.00	8.00	15.00
$1	11,760,000	3.50	5.00	8.00	20.00
$5	4,200,000	85.00	137.50	265.00	625.00
$10	11,600,000	20.00	40.00	65.00	300.00

Series 481/Issued June 20, 1951

Face: Aqua, black print.

Back: Purple, blue print ($5 note is blue with violet print).

Denomination	Notes Delivered	Fine	Very Fine	Extra Fine	New
5¢	23,968,000	.45	.75	1.00	3.00
10¢	23,064,000	.45	.75	1.00	3.00
25¢	14,776,000	2.00	2.75	4.00	7.50
50¢	10,032,000	3.00	4.00	5.00	12.50
$1	25,480,000	3.00	4.00	7.50	12.50
$5*	8,600,000	35.00	50.00	165.00	475.00
$10	24,800,000	17.50	37.50	70.00	275.00

*The same reclining male figure was used on a $50 note. See No. 987 in this catalog.

Series 521/Issued May 25, 1954

5¢
Face: Yellow and green, blue print.
Back: Yellow, blue print.

10¢
Face: Blue and green, violet print.
Back: Pale blue, violet print.

25¢
Face: Green, tan print.
Back: Same as face.

50¢
Face: Violet, pale
green print.
Back: Same as face.

$1
Face: Orange and
pale blue, brown
print. The female
profile was engraved
by J. Eissler.
Back: Pale blue,
brown print.

$5
Face: Violet and
green, blue print.
Back: Violet, blue
print.

$10
Face: Gold and pale blue, reddish tan print.
Back: Reddish tan and blue.

Denomination	Notes Delivered	Fine	Very Fine	Extra Fine	New
5¢	27,216,000	.50	.75	1.75	3.50
10¢	26,880,000	.50	.75	2.50	5.75
25¢	14,448,000	2.50	3.75	5.00	10.00
50¢	11,088,000	3.00	4.00	7.00	12.50
$1	28,000,000	3.50	5.00	11.00	20.00
$5	6,400,000	75.00	150.00	300.00	650.00
$10	24,400,000	90.00	185.00	265.00	465.00

Series 541/Issued May 27, 1958

5¢
Face: Green, violet print.
Back: Pale Green, violet print.

10¢
Face: Orange, green print.
Back: Same as face.

25¢
Face: Green and
pink, blue print.
Back: Pink, blue print.

50¢
Face: Green and
yellow, red print.
Back: Yellow, red
print.

$1
Face: Gold and
green, blue print.
Back: Gold, blue
print.

$5
Face: Yellow and
green, red print.

Back: Pale green, red print. The portrait was engraved by J. C. Benzing.

$10
Face: Aqua, brown print.
Back: Same as face.

Denomination	Notes Delivered	Fine	Very Fine	Extra Fine	New
5¢	18,816,000	.65	1.00	1.50	2.00
10¢	18,816,000	.65	1.00	1.50	3.00
25¢	12,096,000	1.50	2.00	3.00	5.75
50¢	8,064,000	1.75	3.00	4.00	10.00
$1	20,160,000	3.75	5.00	10.00	25.00
$5	6,000,000	200.00	300.00	450.00	750.00
$10*	21,200,000	125.00	215.00	350.00	500.00

*The *10* as seen on the back was originally used on a $10 U.S. note. See No. 492 in this catalog.

Series 591/Issued May 26, 1961

5¢
Face: Yellow and green, red print.
Back: Yellow, red print.

10¢
Face: Pink and green, blue print.
Back: Pink, blue print.

25¢
Face: Blue and purple, green print.
Back: Purple, green print.

50¢
Face: Blue and green, brown print.
Liberty as seen on U.S. 17¢ postage stamp of 1971, was engraved by M. Fenton.
Back: Pale blue, brown print.

$1
Face: Purple and blue, reddish orange print. The female profile was engraved by R. Bower.
Back: Purple, reddish orange print.

$5
Face: Violet and green, blue print. The female face was engraved by C. Brooks.
Back: Violet, blue print.

$10
Face: Red and green, green print.
Back: Same as face.

Denomination	Notes Delivered	Fine	Very Fine	Extra Fine	New
5¢	7,392,000	2.00	2.75	4.50	6.00
10¢	8,400,000	2.00	2.75	4.00	6.00
25¢	4,704,000	3.50	5.00	10.00	17.50
50¢	3,696,000	4.50	6.00	12.50	22.50
$1	10,080,000	4.50	6.00	12.50	25.00
$5	2,400,000	185.00	300.00	375.00	600.00
$10*	6,800,000	75.00	100.00	175.00	315.00

*The borders of the face originally were used on the back of a $10 U.S. note. See No. 483 of this catalog.

Series 611/Issued January 6, 1964

5¢
Face: Violet and green, blue print.
Back: same as face

10¢
Face: Aqua, green print. The image of *Liberty* was engraved by Arthur Dintaman.
Back: Aqua and violet, green print.

25¢
Face: Aqua, pale brown print.
Back: Pale blue, pale brown print.

50¢
Face: Yellow and green, red print.
Back: Yellow, red print.

$1
Face: Vivid orange, aqua print. The Queenly portrait was engraved by M. Fenton.

Back: Same as face.

$5
Face: Pale blue and violet, vivid orange print. The female face was engraved by C. Brooks.

Back: Violet, blue print.

$10
Face: Pale blue and violet, blue print. The female profile was engraved by R. Bower.

Back: Violet, blue print.

Denomination	Notes Delivered	Fine	Very Fine	Extra Fine	New
5¢	9,408,000	.75	1.25	2.00	3.50
10¢	10,080,000	.75	1.25	2.50	4.25
25¢	5,376,000	1.25	2.00	3.50	7.50
50¢	4,704,000	1.50	2.50	4.00	10.00
$1	10,640,000	2.00	3.00	4.50	12.50
$5.	2,800,000	20.00	40.00	75.00	135.00
$10	8,400,000	20.00	32.00	60.00	100.00

Series 641/Issued August 31, 1965

5¢
Face: Pale blue, dark blue numerals, purple print. The female portrait was engraved by R. Bower.
Back: Same as face.

10¢
Face: Aqua and red, red numerals, green print.
Back: Same as face.

25¢
Face: Aqua, deep green numerals, red print.
Back: Same as face.

50¢
Face: Aqua, brown numerals, orange print.
Back: Same as face.

$1
Face: Yellow and green, red print. The female profile was originally engraved by E. J. Hein.

Back: Yellow, red print.

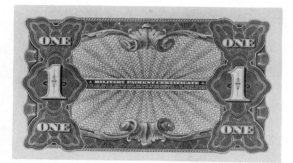

$5
Face: Red and aqua, aqua print. The female face was engraved by R. Bower.

Back: Same as face, the female profile was engraved by A. Dintaman.

$10
Face: Aqua and
orange, brown print.
The female profile
was originally
engraved by M. W.
Baldwin.

Back: Orange, brown
print. The face of
Liberty was engraved
by R. Bower.

Denomination	Notes Delivered	Fine	Very Fine	Extra Fine	New
5¢	22,848,000	.10	.25	.50	1.00
10¢	23,520,000	.20	.25	.50	1.00
25¢	12,096,000	.35	.50	.75	1.25
50¢	11,424,000	.75	1.00	1.25	2.25
$1 *	33,040,000	1.25	1.75	2.50	5.00
$5 **	6,800,000	5.00	7.00	15.00	25.00
$10	20,400,000	10.00	15.00	22.50	45.00

*The same design used at the top center of the back originally was used on No. 28 in this catalog.
**The engraved borders on both face and back originally were used on a $5 silver certificate. See
No. 363 in this catalog.

Series 651/Issued April 28, 1969

$1
Face: Aqua and deep
red, green print.
Back: Deep red,
green print.

$5
Face: Aqua and red,
brown print.
Back: Same as face.

$10
Face: Aqua and
brown, purple print.
Back: Brown, purple
print.

An adaptation of the Minute Man statue by Daniel Chester French was used on the $1, $2, and $5
certificate, and on the U.S. Defense Postal Savings Stamps issued in 1941.

Although different in color, Series 651 bears the same design as Series 641 with the addition of the Minute Man on the left.

Denomination	Notes Delivered	Fine	Very Fine	Extra Fine	New
5¢ 10¢ 25¢ 50¢	Printed, release uncertain				
$1	6,720,000	1.00	1.50	2.50	4.50
$5	1,600,000	5.00	7.00	10.00	25.00
$10	3,600,000	10.00	12.50	17.50	30.00

5, 10, 25 and 50¢ notes were printed but not issued; U.S. coins were used in lieu of these notes. Series 651 was the last to be withdrawn on March 18, 1973. A total of 182,597 notes remain unredeemed.

Series 661/Issued October 21, 1968

5¢
Face: Red, aqua, and green, green numerals.
Back: Green, red print.

10¢
Face: Violet, aqua, and blue, blue numerals. The female profile was engraved by J. Eissler.
Back: Blue, violet print.

25¢
Face: Orange, aqua, and brown, brown numerals.
Back: Orange, brown print.

50¢
Face: Aqua and pale reddish orange, orange-red numerals.
Back: Orange-red, aqua print.

$1
Face: Purple and aqua, blue print. The portrait was engraved by A. L. Wasserback.

$1
Back: Blue and purple, pale blue print, Mt. Rainier in center. Washington State's Mt. Ranier and Mirror Lake are also seen on a U.S. 3¢ postage stamp of 1934.

$5
Face: Red and aqua, brown print.

Back: Red, brown print.

$10
Face: Aqua and orange, red print.

Back: Orange, red print.

$20
Face: Aqua and tan, grey print. The portrait was engraved by F. T. Howe, Jr.

Back: Grey and tan. A similar female figure engraved by E. Felver was used on the 50 peso notes of the Banco Espanol Filipino and the Bank of the Philippine Islands.

Denomination	Notes Delivered	Fine	Very Fine	Extra Fine	New
5¢	23,520,000	.10	.15	.25	.50
10¢	23,520,000	.10	.15	.25	.50
25¢	13,440,000	.25	.35	.50	1.00
50¢	10,080,000	.50	.75	.75	1.50
$1	33,040,000	1.00	1.25	2.00	3.00
$5 *	7,200,000	2.00	3.25	4.50	7.50
$10	4,800,000	12.50	25.00	45.00	100.00
$20	8,000,000	12.50	25.00	50.00	100.00

*The back of this note is a modified version of the design seen on No. 372 in this catalog.

Series 681/Issued August 11, 1969

$20
Face: Aqua, blue,
brown, and pink.

Back: Brown and red.
The bomber was
engraved by E.
Felver.

5¢
Face: Aqua, blue,
and green
Back: Blue and green

10¢
Face: Aqua, blue,
and purple
Back: Blue and
purple

25¢
Face: Aqua, blue,
green, and red
Back: Blue and red

50¢
Face: Aqua, blue,
and brown
Back: Blue and brown

$1
Face: Aqua and red,
purple print
Back: Violet and
orange

$5
Face: Aqua, pale
green, and purple
Back: Yellow and
purple

$10
Face: Aqua, pale red,
and blue.
Back: Blue and
brown.

Denomination	Notes Delivered	Fine	Very Fine	Extra Fine	New
5¢	14,112,000	—	.10	.25	.50
10¢	14,112,000	—	.10	.25	.50
25¢	8,736,000	.20	.35	.65	1.00
50¢	6,720,000	.35	.50	1.00	2.00
$1	22,400,000	.75	1.25	1.75	2.50
$5	4,800,000	2.00	3.00	5.00	7.00
$10	3,200,000	7.00	10.00	14.00	25.00
$20	6,400,000	15.00	20.00	25.00	40.00

Series 692/Issued October 7, 1970

5¢
Face: Tan, pink, and reddish-brown. The sculpture *Guardianship* by James Earld Fraser guards the entrance to the National Archives.
Back: Same as face.

10¢
Face: Aqua, orange, blue, and green.
Back: Aqua, blue, and green.

25¢
Face: Yellow, blue, and grey.
Back: Grey and blue.

50¢
Face: Gold, pink, and purple.
Back: Brown and purple.

$1
Face: Violet, grey-blue, green, and reddish brown.

Back: Grey-blue. The bison vignette was also used on U.S. 30¢ postage stamps of 1923 and 1931, and on No. 483 in this catalog.

$5
Face: Blue, brown, and orange. The female portrait was engraved by E. Felver.

Back: Brown and tan.

$10
Face: Blue, purple pink, and red. Chief Hollow Horn Bear of the Brule Sioux is also seen on U.S. 14¢ postage stamps of 1923 and 1931. The chief was engraved by L. S. Schofield.

Back: Blue and purple.

$20
Face: Purple, deep orange, and pale red. The portrait of Chief Ouray was originally engraved by F. H. Noyes.

Back: Purple and blue.

Denomination	Notes Delivered	Fine	Very Fine	Extra Fine	New
5¢	14,112,000	—	.25	.35	1.00
10¢	14,112,000	—	.25	.35	1.00
25¢	8,736,000	—	.50	.75	1.75
50¢	6,720,000	—	.75	1.50	3.00
$1*	22,400,000	—	2.00	2.50	3.50
$5	4,800,000	1.00	8.00	10.00	15.00
$10	3,200,000	2.00	15.00	17.50	25.00
$20	6,400,000	4.50	25.00	32.50	50.00

*The buffalo on the reverse originally was used on a $10 U.S. note. See No. 483 in this catalog.

FOOD STAMPS AND COUPONS

If you are fortunate enough to be able to collect bank notes, or if you simply have enough money to purchase this catalog, you are probably unfamiliar with food stamps and coupons.

In 1939 a Food Stamp Plan was initiated to allow low-income families to purchase food at a discount; this plan came to an end in 1943. In 1961 President John F. Kennedy instituted a similar program which was expanded in 1962. All issues now bear the words "Food Coupon," and are issued under the jurisdiction of the United States Department of Agriculture. The series of 1967, 50-cent coupons, and all coupons to follow bear serial numbers. The United States Banknote Corporation and the American Bank Note Company have assisted The Bureau of Engraving and Printing in producing some issues.

Change cannot be given for food coupons so each participating store has change substitutes prepared which are redeemable at the same store. These substitutes are sometimes issued in the form of metal or plastic tokens which would interest the numismatist and the exonumist.

Here then, is another form of paper money to collect, providing allowances are granted by the USDA. Food Coupons are now issued to authorized recipients only, however we hope a decision will be made very soon which will allow syngraphists to collect yet another form of paper money—one that will probably prove extremely interesting.

A food stamp used during the early days of the program.

A 50-cent coupon, series of 1967.

A recent coupon, series of 1975A.

493

One of the most recent coupons, series of 1975B.

Typical change substitutes issued by participating stores.

The following list is adapted from one compiled and copyrighted by Jerry Bates who granted permission for usage in this catalog.

F.S.C.C.-U.S.D.A. Food Orders and Surplus Orders
(F.S.C.C. is the Federal Surplus Commodities Corporation)

Issue Date	Series	Denomination	Color
May 1939	None Shown	.25	Orange-Red
May 1939	None Shown	.25	Blue
1939	None Shown	.25	Orange-Red

Issue Date	Series	Denomination	Color
1939	None Shown	.25	Blue
1940	None Shown	.25	Orange-Red
1940	None Shown	.25	Blue
1941	None Shown	.25	Orange-Red
1941	None Shown	.25	Blue
U.S.D.A. Food Stamp Plan Coupons			
3-7-61	None Shown	.25	Pink
3-7-61	None Shown	1.00	Gray
1964	None Shown	.50	Orange
1964	None Shown	2.00	Blue
1967	1967	.50	Orange
1967	1967	2.00	Blue
1967*	None Shown	.25	Green
1969	1967	.50	Orange
1969	1967	2.00	Blue
1970	1970	5.00	Maroon
1971	1971	.50	Orange
1971	1971	2.00	Blue
1971	1971	5.00	Maroon
1972	1971A	.50	Orange
1972	1971A	2.00	Blue
1972	1971A	5.00	Maroon
1973	1973	.50	Orange
1973	1973	2.00	Blue
1973	1973	5.00	Maroon
1975	1975	1.00	Brown
1975	1975	5.00	Blue
1975	1975	10.00	Green
1975	1975A**	1.00	Brown
1975	1975A**	5.00	Blue
1975	1975A**	10.00	Green
1975	1975B***	1.00	Brown
1975	1975B***	5.00	Blue
1975	1975B***	10.00	Green

*This is a food certificate, not a coupon, printed on yellow instead of white paper.
**Printed by The American Bank Note Company
***Printed by The United States Banknote Corporation

CHAPTER FOUR

Cleaning, Housing, and Care of Paper Money

When a desirable note, soiled and dirty, is found in circulation, why not clean it? I do not recommend this procedure since one could easily become a victim of the practice.

BEWARE OF "RESTORED" PAPER MONEY

Along with the numismatist and the philatelist, the syngraphist has the constant problem of the collector's item that has been "upgraded" by a little bit of washing and ironing, a bit of cutting and snipping, and a bit of retouching here and there. These restorations are just plain fraud when they are used to palm off a Fine bill as a Very Fine.

The best counterattack against these practices is to educate the collector to accept a note in its original condition. We can't have all gems. Learn to detect the evidences of upgrading and avoid bills that have been tampered with. Of course, minor care is needed with some notes, but the rule with paper money as with coins or stamps is to enjoy them but don't attempt to *improve* them.

The most prevalent attempt to upgrade paper notes is washing and drying. On a worn note, be sure to look for mottled paper or for streaks of white or yellow where the cleaning agent overdid its work. Faded inks and colors may be due to washing, especially in the seals and serial numbers. Overprinted black ink signatures are especially prone to paling, running, and smearing.

Drying a note after washing can result in scorching if a hot iron is used. A steam iron can leave obvious blisters. Beware of notes that seem sticky or too thick. This is usually the result of starching the paper in an effort to restore body. Toning may have been done by applying coffee to cover bleached areas. Be especially careful with the 1929 series, which has numbers, names, and signatures overprinted in black ink on dry paper, all easily damaged or removed by washing and drying. Know that the wet-printed notes issued prior to the 1957 silver certificate series in Uncirculated condition *should* have minor ripples and creases because they were allowed to dry in the pack and should have these features to be virginal.

After the bath and the drier, beware of the eraser and the scissors. Soft erasers may sometimes be used ethically to remove a minor pencil mark. However, extensive erasures can be detected by the loss of surface sheen and the mottled scarring. The use of scissors to trim the edge of a bill is the worst offense. Check the edges and the size of the bill if there is any doubt. To protect the hobby, learn to detect the signs of fraud.

For an in-depth treatment of this subject, I suggest you see Peter Huntoon's four-part series in *Coin World*, March 7, March 14, April 4, and April 11, 1973.

HOUSING PAPER MONEY

In the *Canadian Paper Money Journal*, Vol. VIII, Nos. 1 and 2 (1972), editor William H. McDonald made a report to Canadian syngraphists concerning tests made by two chemical laboratories. Without going into great detail, Mr. McDonald simply stated that products made of cellulose acetate (Kodacel and Forticel) and polyester or polyethylene (Celmar and Mylar) are safe for the housing of paper money. We should never even consider using holders made of polyvinyl chloride (which in time might produce hydrochloric acid) or polypropylene. These flimsy materials contain plasticizers that in time could seriously affect both paper and ink.

I fervently agree with Mr. McDonald when he says, "Only the purest forms of acetate and polyester should be used, whatever the cost."

CARE OF YOUR COLLECTION

Captain Kidd was primarily a coin collector, but the James Boys were more interested in paper money. Things haven't changed much, and the syngraphist should give some thought to the security of his collection before rather than afterward.

Fortunately, the paper money collector can store even a large collection of notes in a relatively small container or a bank safe deposit box. In the home the collection can be hidden under the rug or in the traditional place, the mattress. According to the numerous stories in the hobby newspapers, though, the present-day Jesse James is astute enough to discover the latter two hiding places.

Insurance can be obtained in most areas for collections, even with the new emphasis in burglar circles on works of art. Regions usually differ in premiums and requirements for insurance, but the American Numismatic Association now has a group plan for syngraphists holding membership in the Association. For those of you who are members and who do not already know about this plan, I suggest you write to the American Numismatic Association, Box 2366, Colorado Springs, Colorado, 80901.

A record of identification is of prime importance. No recovery is possible without complete proof of ownership. Syngraphists have an advantage over the coin or stamp collector since most notes are very individual, with serial numbers proper to one bill only. An accurate record of all the notes in your collection can be made with little effort.

A record of ownership, as well as a complete record of the price paid for each item, is necessary for resale or auction. We all have to go some day, and when we do we should leave enough of a record so that our heirs need pay only the taxes on the capital gains. This means that if you can prove you paid $10 above the face value for a note, and it goes for $20 in an auction, you need pay tax only on the difference. Check with your lawyer. Otherwise, you or your heirs may be taxed on the entire resale of your collection.

It is advisable to designate at least one person in your family to be familiar with your collection, where you keep it and the records of purchase. It would also be a good idea to suggest the names of a few dealers or friends who could assist in disposing of your collection if necessary.

Bibliography

Annual Reports of the Director of the Bureau of Engraving and Printing, 1871-1973. Government Printing Office, Washington, D.C.

Appleton's Cyclopaedia of American History. D. Appleton & Co., New York, 1887.

Blake, George H. *United States Paper Money*. Published by the author, 1908.

Bowen, Harold L. *State Bank Notes of Michigan*. Havelt Advertising Service Inc., 1956.

Columbia Viking Desk Encyclopedia. Viking Press, New York, 1968.

Dillistin, William H. *A Descriptive History of National Bank Notes*. Private printing, 1956.

Donlon, William P. *United States Large Size Paper Money 1861-1923*. Published by the author. 1973–1974.

Fielding, Mantle. *Dictionary of American Painters, Sculptors, and Engravers*. James F. Carr, New York, 1965.

Friedberg, Robert. *Paper Money of the United States*. Coin and Currency Institute, Inc., New York, 1972.

Gould, Maurice. *Hawaiian Coins, Tokens and Paper Money*. Whitman Publishing Company, Racine, Wisconsin, 1960.

Gould, Maurice and Higgie, L.W. *The Money of Puerto Rico*. Whitman Publishing Company, Racine, Wisconsin, 1962.

Griffiths, William H. *Story of the American Bank Note Company*. American Bank Note Company, New York, 1959.

Groce, George C. and Wallace, David H. *New York Historical Society Dictionary of Artists in America, 1564-1860*. Yale University Press, New Haven, 1957.

Hepburn, A. Barton. *A History of Currency in the United States*. MacMillan Co., New York, 1924.

Hessler, Gene. *Buy and Sell Price Guide to U.S. Currency*. Dafran House, New York, 1972.

Hewitt-Donlon. *Catalog of United States Small Size Paper Money.* Hewitt Bros., Chicago, Illinois, 1973.

History of the Bureau of Engraving and Printing 1862-1962. Treasury Department, Washington, D.C., 1964.

Huntoon, P., and L. Van Belkum. *The National Bank Note Issues of 1929-1935.* Ed. by M.O. Warns, The Society of Paper Money Collectors, Hewitt Bros., Chicago, Illinois, 1970.

Knox, John Jay. *United States Notes.* T. Fisher Unwin, London, 1885.

Limpert, Frank Alvin. *United States Paper Money, Old Series 1861-1923 Inclusive.* Published by the author, 1948.

Morris, Thomas F., II. *The Life and Works of Thomas F. Morris, 1852-1898.* Published by the author, 1968.

Muscalus, John A. *Famous Paintings Reproduced on Paper Money of State Banks 1800-1866.* Published by the author, 1939.

O'Donnell, Chuck. *The Standard Handbook of Modern United States Paper Money.* Published by the author, Williamstown, New Jersey, 1975.

Price Guide for United States Paper Money Errors. Amos Press, Sidney, Ohio, 1973.

Shafer, Neil. *A Guide Book of Modern United States Currency.* Western Publishing Co., Inc., Racine, Wisconsin, 1975.

Shafer, Neil. *A Guide Book of Philippine Paper Money.* Whitman Publishing Co., Racine, Wisconsin, 1964.

Springs, Agnes Wright. *The First National Bank of Denver: The Formative Years 1860-1865.* Bradford-Robinson Printing Co., Denver, Colorado.

Toy, Raymond S. and Schwan, Carlton F. *World War II Allied Military Currency.* Published by Carlton F. Schwan, Portage, Ohio, 1974.

Van Belkum, Louis. *National Banks of the Note Issuing Period 1863-1935.* Hewitt Bros., Chicago, Illinois, 1968.

Wade, James M. *Collection of U.S. Paper Money.* Cataloged by Aubrey E. Bebee, 1956.

The Bank Note Reporter   *The Numismatist*
Coins Magazine   *Numismatic News*
Coin World   *Paper Money*
The Essay-Proof Journal

Auction catalogs and/or price lists:

A.M. & Don Kagin

William P. Donlon

Albert A. Grinnell (reprinted by William T. Anton, Jr., and Morey Perlmutter, 1971)

Mayflower Coin Auctions

Lester Merkin

Dean Oakes

Pine Tree Auction Co.

Robert A. Siegal

Superior Stamp & Coin Co.

L.S. Werner